HEYWOOD BROUN

HEYWOOD BROUN
A Biography

by Richard O'Connor

G. P. Putnam's Sons, New York

SBN: 399-11503-X

Library of Congress Catalog
Card Number: 74-30572

PRINTED IN THE UNITED STATES OF AMERICA

To Morris L. Ernst
in gratitude and admiration

Contents

Illustrations appear after page 128.

Foreword

HEYWOOD BROUN was a public man. All his adult life he thrust himself, in rusty and ill-fitting armor, into the front lines of controversy. Though his bellicose instincts were minimal, he saw so many wrongs that needed righting, so many injustices that needed to be redressed that he was inclined to "launch a crusade every hour," as one of his oldest friends recalls. During the period in which the newspaper column flowered into the status of a leading opinion molder it was his opinion and those of a very few other contemporaries which American liberals sought for guidance on the good and decent way to think and act. For a readership that steadily mounted into the millions, from his journalistic podiums during the turbulent twenties and thirties, he offered his prescriptions for a nation confronted by the anarchic radicalism of the early twenties, the violent reaction to that violence, the problem of growing up to the newly acquired status of a world power, the surfeit of materialism before the Depression and the inequities revealed after the crash of 1929, and finally, just before his life ended, the necessity to intervene once again in Europe.

Mild though his disposition, "timid" though his character, as he kept insisting as he waded into another ideological free-for-all, he involved himself in everything that stirred the passions of his time, for two decades, from the question of whether Christy Mathewson was the greatest pitcher in baseball history to the guilt/innocence of Sacco and Vanzetti. And he could become almost as impassioned in defending Mathewson against the counterclaims of Walter Johnson's partisans as in denouncing the reactionaries thronging the corridors of the Harding, Coolidge, and Hoover administrations.

He was one of the first columnists, at a time when the newspaper by-liner began to assume an oracular importance, to offer himself as an identifiable personality to his readers. By no mischance was his column headed "It Seems to Me"—and by no coincidence his publishers often felt compelled to point out that his views weren't necessarily those of the newspaper which published them. There was nothing impersonal about the public Heywood Broun; he revealed himself, exposed his frailties, and vented his enthusiasms in what he called "my old shop window," his column.

He was unique, an original. He was not a stylist in the literary sense, but there was an inimitable stamp on his writings. The Broun benchmark, its seeming artlessness, was not transferable, as would-be imitators have discovered. Morris L. Ernst, the man who knew him longest and perhaps better than anyone outside his family was discussing Broun's originality on a recent day in his New York law firm's offices, to which at the age of eighty-seven he repairs daily. As an experiment, he had just detailed three young women to tape the networks' news broadcasts' commentary: the nightly Eric-David-Howard encapsulations. Trying them out on his friends, Ernst found that no one could tell one commentator from the other, in transcript form, divorced from the personality of their delivery. Heywood Broun, as he observed, was immediately identifiable. "And who is the Heywood Broun of today?" His place has never been filled; his "old shop window" can only display a MOVED TO NEW LOCATION sign.

There was also a private Heywood Broun, though many of his contemporaries would have found it hard to believe. Few, if any, knew him. His existence may have been fragmentary, in moments stolen from the public man, but it was indicated by the fact that the Heywood Broun Papers, if there were such a collection in being, would have consisted of old speakeasy cards, laundry bills, and invitations to the White House during the Roosevelt tenancy. No diaries, no journals, no correspondence. Obviously he conducted his affairs without a future biographer in mind. He wrote only a few personal notes and letters, and they have not survived. Writing was so easy for him that he tossed off a column in thirty or forty minutes, but he did not lavish his productive powers on the sort of correspondence dear to soul-searching writers of an earlier generation. What he was, thought, felt is contained in the thousands of columns he wrote, and there it must be sought.

The author is grateful to those contemporaries who, in their memoirs or in what they confided to their own biographers, provided the footnotes to Broun's serial account of his life in newsprint. That indebtedness is recorded in the bibliography. More specifically and personally, my thanks also to Heywood Hale Broun, Patricia Broun, Morris L. Ernst, E. B. White, Jack Wiggins, Frank Sullivan, Robert Woodward, the late Gene Fowler and his son Will, the late Joseph Jefferson O'Neill, and others who remembered Broun with unvarying affection.

R. O'C.

HEYWOOD BROUN

1. The Atypical Harvard Man

DURING the years 1906–1910 the Harvard Yard was both the citadel of social conformity and upper-class manners and the seedbed of social and political dissent. The sleek lords of the campus were the "college aristocrats" who had proceeded, by birthright, from Fifth Avenue homes to prep schools to Harvard. They held carnival in the openly arrogant style of pre-World War I gilded youth in the "gold coast" dormitories along Mount Vernon Street and in their exclusive clubs, attended by personal servants, with chauffeur-driven automobiles at their disposal, even while their less privileged classmates and some of the faculty were earnestly considering how to pull down the social and economic structures which provided those privileges.

The more or less typical Harvard man was an arrogant specimen with a ten-thousand-a-year allowance from home and the assurance of a cushy berth in the society which sponsored him. He was predestined for a Wall Street brokerage or a corporate boardroom no matter if he maintained a "gentlemanly C" standard of scholarship and spent most of his time on Sabine raids against the Radcliffe and Wellesley maidenhood.

What distinguished the class of 1910, however, was a sunburst of talent, which would dazzle the World War I generation and which still casts a remarkable afterglow. Never, probably, has one college class been so laden with literary and theatrical talent; its closest rival is that Princeton class which produced Scott Fitzgerald and Edmund Wilson.

In the years between 1906 and 1910 the Harvard Yard was effulgent with the differing personalities and aspirations of the poets T. S. Eliot and Alan Seeger and Conrad Aiken . . . the journalist-pundits Walter Lippmann and H. V. Kaltenborn . . . the noted economist Stuart Chase . . . the theatrical personages Lee Simonson, Kenneth MacGowan, and Robert Edmond Jones

. . . the editor John Hall Wheelock and the biographer Hermann Hagedorn . . . the crusading liberal Senator from New Mexico Bronson Cutting . . . the writer-revolutionary John Reed . . . the Brahmin critic Willard Huntington Wright, who under the pseudonym S. S. Van Dine wrote the strikingly successful Philo Vance detective novels. . . .

And then there was Heywood Broun, a large, untidy, indolent youth of seventeen, the subject of this biographical essay. In some ways he was the most remarkable of the lot, not that he would be garlanded with laurel like T. S. Eliot, or be ennobled by the tragic fate of Alan Seeger in the trenches of the western front, or be buried in the Kremlin Wall like John Reed. Broun's chief claim to sharing in the shining collective accomplishment of his class was his career as a newspaper columnist, like but also unlike Walter Lippmann. A journalist's grip on renown is usually as tenuous as the pulp on which his last bit of writing was printed. Broun, however, survives as a legend, not for the perishable quality of the things he wrote so much as for the purity of the example he set for American liberalism. He was an unkempt Galahad, though without that knightly fellow's singleness of purpose. If the American liberal is an endangered species, under fire from the left and the right, scorned for his temperance, reviled for his good intentions, and denigrated for his innocent faith in the perfectibility of the human species—if he is dodging the fallout from the doomed expectations of the Kennedy/Johnson years—he can still look back with satisfaction on the career of Heywood Broun and his generation of liberals, who could afford to be optimistic and were surrounded by certainties (as they saw them).

From the beginning there was a loose-jointed amiability, an almost visible emanation of goodwill and easy humor about Heywood Broun. He was not a firebrand like Lippmann or a "grind" like some of the scholarship boys; he was more of an unmoneyed playboy. With a handsomer allowance, he would have joined in the revels of the Mount Vernon Street nabobs. Unlike John Reed, he was not affronted by what Reed called the "cold cruel stupidity" of the gold-coast dormitories, and class-consciousness did not come easily to him, perhaps because he lacked the envy which fosters such awareness.

Broun came to Harvard from a solid middle-class family in comfortable circumstances. He was born December 7, 1888, the third son of Heywood Cox Broun, who had migrated to the United States with his parents from Scotland and who had prospered as the partner in a printing and stationery business lucrative enough to allow him to establish his household on Pineapple Street in Brooklyn Heights across the East River from Manhattan. The senior Broun was a member of the fashionable Seventh Regiment and put down his son's name for membership in the Racquet and Tennis Club at birth. His mother was the former Henrietta Brose, the daughter of a German-American broker, a well-educated, gracious, and firm-willed woman with strong opinions on practically everything. Thus Heywood Broun was Scottish-German by ancestry, a mixture of two volatile and possibly antipathetic elements, Teuton and Celt. Yet—and so much for race memory, inherited characteristics, blood lines, and the mystique of certain nationalistic philosophers—he possessed neither the flintiness of the traditional Scot, much less the stinginess celebrated by vaudeville comedians, nor the harsh determination and dogged ambition of the traditional German. He was everything he should not have been, a biological sport, a crossbreed of Bobbie Burns and one of those Heidelberg student princes who refused to go in for saber scars.

When Heywood junior was two years old, the family uprooted itself from Brooklyn Heights and moved to a brownstone at 140 West Eighty-seventh Street. An Irishwoman named Delia Feddis served as nurse for Heywood and his siblings until she eloped with the French butler. There were also a cook and several maids. For Heywood and his surviving brother, Irving, and sister, Virginia, it was the usual childhood of the upper-middle-class West Side, west of Broadway and east of Riverside Drive, with its streets sedately lined by brownstone houses with all their solidity, their air of permanence so important to the bourgeoisie, with their immaculate stoops fronting on well-cleaned streets and their polished brass fittings, each occupied by one family with its live-in servants.

The quality of life in those quiet streets off Riverside Drive was nostalgically recalled by Broun in more turbulent times. "The street of my childhood," he recollected, "was one of closely packed families. We were brownstone folk except at the corners where apartments stood. Indeed it was customary to ask a boy with whom you played, 'Do you live in a house or a flat?' "

The boys brought up in those streets were not dead-end kids

playing stickball or raising pigeons in a coop on the roof or diving off stringpieces into the Hudson, but were raised to be proper little gentlemen who would take their places in the commercial establishments downtown as a birthright.

To the older Broun, however, there was at least one serious flaw in that generally idyllic boyhood. That was the racial prejudice directed against the Jews who lived on the avenues bisecting the crosstown streets, the source of which (whether it was a reflection of parental prejudice, or religious, or whatever) he didn't specify. But it was based, he said, largely on economic circumstances. "Irving Cohen was a sheeny and Monte Jacobs was a Jew"—because Irving's parents were poor and Monte's were well off. "It is my recollection, then, that my earliest lessons in prejudice were based for the most part on an economic issue and one more subtle. Since the gangs of the avenue were more numerous than our own and decidedly to be feared, it became necessary to invent some insulting epithet to hurl at them behind their backs. We could not lick them in fair fight and so we atoned for our lack of power by calling names."

Irving Cohen, he explained, would be permitted to join their games only if they needed another player. The more privileged Monte Jacobs, however, was always welcome to join in the fun. "I can't remember that Monte was ever barred from anything. He was just about the most popular boy on the block because he was the best at the games and had taken boxing lessons in a gymnasium. But I do remember hearing some parent say that it was too bad Monte was a Jew because he was such a nice boy and had such good manners." Even Monte, he recalled, referred to Irving as a "sheeny." Broun could attribute his boyhood prejudice only to the "mean and savage instincts" of children and their tendency to "band together against some minority in the group."

By the time Heywood was seven, the Broun children had already toured Europe with their mother. Naturally it was the family expectation that Heywood and his brother, like their father and maternal grandfather, would stolidly progress into substantial careers. The course of their future, in their elders' opinion, was predetermined by the advantages of their class.

Even in his early childhood, though, there were indications that Heywood might not settle willingly into the routine dictated by parental hopes. The child was lovable—a quality that never vanished—and had winsome brown eyes and was tractable enough. He was also a daydreamer and prone to easy solutions: the classic predisposition, a conservative might say, of the embryonic liberal. When he and his brother, Irving, played with their toy soldiers, Irving would deploy his troops with the care and sagacity of a general staff officer working out a tactical problem on a War Department sand table. Heywood's strategy was to hurl a handful of his soldiers at Irving's carefully aligned ranks and bowl them over with shouts of glee.

He attended an excellent private school, Horace Mann, to which he rode on the horsecars every morning, for both his elementary and secondary education. By the time he reached the high school years he was taller and heavier than most of his classmates, over six feet tall and weighing about 190 pounds, but he was ill coordinated, like many boys who grow too fast. His style of dress, then and later, was haphazard. He had a mischievous sense of humor and was popular with his contemporaries, qualities which proved enduring.

A native gift for self-expression was early noted by his preceptors and by one of his classmates, Morris Ernst, who became a celebrated advocate in the civil-liberties field and was Broun's lifelong friend. Their English teacher was Miss Helen Baker, who was Heywood's second cousin but whom he called "aunt." Miss Baker, as Ernst recalls, was an inspiring teacher and encouraged Heywood's literary inclinations to the extent that he became editor of the school paper. And at fourteen, as he later testified, he had already made up his mind that he would make a career in journalism.

In the field of languages, however, young Heywood showed no similar promise; his struggles with German so infuriated the instructor in that language that the teacher hurled an inkpot at Heywood. Nevertheless, his graduating class voted him "best all-around student."

His general excellence, his parents believed, recommended him for a Harvard education. Academically he was well qualified. Socially it was a different matter. Graduating from Horace Mann was a lot better than possessing a public high school diploma, but it didn't impress most of those entering Harvard with him—they had known each other since childhood and had passed through the more exclusive prep schools together. A Groton boy looked down on a Horace Mann boy from a towering eminence. Heywood Broun, however, was blithely unaware of being looked down on, condescended to, or socially downgraded. He went his own way; he had come to Harvard to get a superior education and if possible enjoy himself in the process and could not be concerned by the possibilities of social advancement. That built-in egalitarianism insulated him against the humiliations felt by other classmates when they ran up against the Groton-Exeter-St. Mark's barriers, the snobbism prevalent in the Mount Vernon Street dormitories. He would not agonize as did John Reed, who had attended a lesser prep school and would become a flaming advocate of Soviet Communism and who (as he would recall) "used to *pray* to be liked, to have friends, to be popular with the crowd."

Heywood's carelessness in dress alone would have disqualified him with the college aristocrats. It was later said that his sartorial style—a new suit immediately developed elephantine wrinkles the moment Heywood put it on—resembled that of an unmade bed. During his sophomore year he roomed with Theodore Kenyon, a Horace Mann classmate, in Weld Hall. Mrs. Broun came up to Boston to see the boys settled in their rooms, and she asked his roommate if he was sure he wanted to share accommodations with Heywood, adding, "Don't you realize that Heywood will wear your clothes? You're big, but he's bigger, and your shirts and suits will be ruined." Heywood's sloppiness, she said, was a Broun household legend; his method of packing was to hurl all his possessions into a trunk, climb in, and trample them to get the lid closed. His older brother, Irving, also attending Harvard, had taken care to avoid having Heywood as a roommate on a permanent basis.

Much of Heywood's Harvard life was extracurricular. He went out for the freshman basketball team, for which sheer size recommended him, but distressed the coach by his frivolous attitude. The freshman team often played against teams from the New England mill towns, and Heywood offered a satirical impression of the typical Harvard man for the edification of his opponents. "I say," he would call to a teammate across the court, "would you mind hurling the spheroid in my direction?" A knee injury cut short his athletic career just in time, it was felt, to spare the Harvard freshman basketball team from the possibility of being tarred and feathered in Holyoke or Brockton or Chicopee Falls.

Heywood ambled through collegiate life. He would drop in on Irving to borrow a silk shirt (and rip it up the back to make it fit, causing his dapper brother much anguish) before going over to one of the neighboring girls'-school campuses to try his luck at romance. His pursuits were hearty and masculine rather than effete or intellectual. He became an expert poker player and learned how to ingest a certain amount of alcohol without falling out of a dormitory window.

The more hectic forms of intellectualism then engaging a number of his classmates did not appeal to him, nor was he enraptured by the campaigning for social and political reform undertaken by others. That owlishly solemn youth Walter Lippmann had organized the Socialist Club, but Heywood was not among his first recruits. H. V. Kaltenborn, later the editor of the Brooklyn *Eagle* and a radio commentator with a national audience around the time of World War II, had organized the Dramatic Club along with John Reed, future playwright Owen Davis, and future set designer Lee Simonson, but Heywood Broun, future drama critic, was not attracted to its activities. He preferred to slip across the river to the Boston theaters, particularly when the tiny, licorice-eyed Marie Doro was appearing in a pre-Broadway tryout.

He had experienced for several years those twitchings and yearnings which signified an interest in journalism or literature, but he was rejected for membership on the *Crimson* staff. Not once, but three times.

And while John Reed doused his social frustrations by turning himself into the noisiest and most energetic cheerleader Harvard had seen for years, Heywood consoled himself for the *Crimson*'s snubs, largely social in nature, with beer-drinking exploits, skirt chasing, and a growing interest in baseball. By Harvard standards, of course, baseball was a plebeian pursuit reserved for the peanut-munching proletariat. But Heywood found it had an esthetic appeal, especially when watching the great Boston Red Sox outfield—Tris Speaker, Duffy Lewis, and Harry Hooper—in action. It seemed to him that the trio of outfielders performed with a grace equal to any Russian ballet company, that a tie score in the last of the ninth with the visiting New York Yankees had as much dramatic tension as the final act of a Greek tragedy.

The demonstrated brilliance of the class of 1910 was almost matched by the excellence of the Harvard faculty, from which

Heywood profited in varying degrees. Some of his preceptors were men of legendary stature, not least among them the celebrated "Copey," whose tutorials nurtured a number of great careers. Professor Charles Townsend Copeland was a small, waspish, and bitterly witty man who taught English 12, advanced composition, one of whose flintier epigrams dealt with the subject of fornication: "The sensation is momentary, and the position is ridiculous." Copeland vigorously advocated in youthful writers the search for that lean, sinewy quality which distinguished American prose from its English ancestry, and the impact he made on a generation of Harvard students was tremendous.

Copeland's star protégé in the class of 1910 was John Reed, who credited Copeland with stimulating him to "find color and strength and beauty in books and the world, and to express it again." Copeland was almost violently antipathetic to radical causes and could not have foreseen that he was encouraging the talent of the man who would glorify Lenin's conspiratorial triumph over the nascent Russian democracy (as detailed in Reed's *Ten Days That Shook the World*) and would be one of the first leaders of American Communism. Yet, as Broun would later point out, Professor Copeland was the prime shaper of Reed's talents as a journalist and propagandist. "Copeland," Broun wrote, "had a great deal to do with the making of John Reed. Copey did not know, and no one of us knew, that this humorous, light-hearted youngster would burn himself up in a fever of revolution. We believe only a few things which Reed believed. As a political economist he did not inspire admiration, but he stuck closely to the creed which an artist ought to have as any man we have ever known. He wrote what he felt. Copey did not groan in vain for this pupil."

But Heywood's literary proclivities did wring an occasional groan of protest, of outraged sensibility from Professor Copeland, to whom bad (or youthfully excessive) writing was almost as intolerable as oafish behavior. Copey did not perceive in Heywood the same intimations of genius that young John Reed displayed. Nor did Heywood take to heart, as Reed did, one of Copey's wiser encomiums, this one on the subject of a career in journalism: "Get in, get wise, get out."

In the Socratic tradition, Professor Copeland gathered his more promising students around him in an adoring circle. Every

Saturday night, in his chambers in Hollis Hall, he held get-togethers with himself seated in an armchair in front of the fire and his students sitting on the floor around him. He pleaded the cause of literary art, read approvingly or contemptuously from a wide range of literature, and listened to his students read from manuscripts of their own composition. Abhorring purplish prose and melodramatic contrivances, he found many of the faults of youthful writers in Heywood Broun. One night Heywood read him a story he had written in which the protagonist succumbed to insanity, and that was only the beginning of his troubles. As usual, when confronted by a tyro's excesses, Copeland squirmed in his chair, rolled his eyes ceilingward at the gorier passages, and did not quite manage to suppress an occasional groan.

"Broun," he said wearily, "try to solve your problems without recourse to death or madness."

Another man on the Harvard faculty whom Heywood found impressive was Professor George Lyman Kittredge, who taught English 2 and was a renowned Shakespearean scholar. Years after he sat in Kittredge's class, on the occasion of the professor's retirement, he noted that under the crusty New Englander "the high and florid tradition of Shakespeare was revised into the swaggering underemphasis of New England."

Heywood also attended Professor George Pierce Baker's famous English 47 Workshop for budding dramatists, which nurtured the careers of Edward Sheldon and Eugene O'Neill, among many others. He succumbed to an urge to write plays as naturally, he felt, as children contract measles. It wasn't Professor Baker's fault, as he made clear in writing of his experiences in the workshop. Baker produced a number of excellent dramatists, he wrote, but "the course also had a splendid record of cures." Like most persons, he explained, he felt that he had a play gestating in his subconscious until the hard realities were revealed in Baker's workshop. "Freudians know the complaint as the Euripidean complex. The sufferer is ailing because his play lies suppressed in his subconscious mind. Professor Baker digs these plays out. People who come to English 47 may talk about their plays as much as they choose, but they must write them, too. Often a cure follows within forty-eight hours after the completion of the play." The script, he explained, would be read aloud by Professor Baker and subjected to the criticism of his peers. Only a dedicated playwright could survive that experience with his dramaturgic ambitions intact. During his period as a student of the drama, Broun wrote, everyone was obsessed with Life in the manner of world-weary dilettantes and wrote windy dramas expressing their disillusionment. "There were times, naturally, when we regretted our lost illusions and longed to be freshmen again and to believe everything the Sunday newspapers said about Lillian Russell. But usually there was no time for regrets; we were too busy telling Life what we thought about it."

Much less of an academic impression was left on Heywood's mind by Professor Thomas Carver and his economics course. Carver was one of the resident conservatives on the faculty, and his course, it seemed to Heywood in writing of it later, might have been subtitled "radical panaceas and their underlying fallacies."

With tongue in cheek, Heywood blamed Professor Carver—and indirectly the Boston Red Sox—for his tendencies toward liberalism. During the autumn and winter sessions of his class, as Heywood explained, Professor Carver would outline the radical doctrines as they pertained to the economic system, then in the spring sessions would demolish them. Broun took the course in 1908. "Faithful to the Harvard tradition of fair play, the Professor gave the revolutionaries an ample amount of rope. Indeed, he did not undertake to state the case himself for the various aberrant philosophies, but invited a leader of each school of thought to tell all from his particular point of view. . . . We had an anarchist, a socialist, a syndicalist, a single-taxer and a few other theorists whose special lines escape me now. . . . It may be that I was more susceptible than my fellow students, for I must report that I hit the sawdust trail at each and every lecture in the creation of a united front against the capitalist system."

Heywood absorbed all those panaceas during the first semester and nodded in agreement, but by the time Professor Carver got around to explaining how they were all nonsense and that human affairs were regulated, as Adam Smith laid down the rule in 1790, by the demands of the marketplace, Heywood was cutting classes in favor of going out to Fenway Park and watching the Red Sox demolish their opponents. If Professor Carver's economics class had met in the morning, instead of salubrious spring afternoons, Heywood might have been converted to conservatism.

It wasn't until his last year at Harvard that Walter Lippmann got around to enlisting Broun as a member of the Socialist Club and "as I had failed to make either Gas House or Fly [social clubs] I yielded to his blandishments." It would be many more years before Heywood was actually converted to Socialism for a time, and by then Lippmann had decided (as Professor Carver could have told him) that Marxism didn't have all the answers.

In the glimpses of his undergraduate career he later afforded newspaper and magazine readers, he pictured himself, no doubt accurately, as a young man in search of himself, but not in any dead-serious way. He did not feel it necessary to scrabble for a footing. He was inclined to depend on intuition, rather than any rigid doctrines offered by his preceptors, as a way of determining the direction of his adult life; he was born to drift, to let opportunity seek him out; and agonizing over Life was reserved for the manuscripts he submitted as samples of creative writing—something to be inflicted on the Goethean heroes of his imagination, not the living, breathing, enjoying Heywood Broun.

Thus his Harvard years, essentially, provided him with a series of negatives rather than opening up vistas or showing him fields of future conquest. Some of his classmates were set firmly on courses charted toward success or tragic fame; Alan Seeger to write "I Have a Rendezvous with Death" before dying in a French army uniform, John Reed to embark on a blazingly revolutionary career, others to develop their talents in literature and the theater.

To Heywood Broun, Harvard merely demonstrated that it would be better if he didn't waste his time writing plays, or take economic problems of larger scope than his laundry bill too seriously, or try to approach too precipitously the high table of American literature. Doors closed quietly in his face, thus sparing him years of frustrated effort.

Journalism then provided a sanctuary for young men in Broun's condition. It was a low-paid vocation, and its practitioners, to an alarming degree, succumbed to alcoholism, insanity, or careers in public relations if they weren't nimble enough to "get in, get wise, get out," as Professor Copeland prescribed. Each city had its morning and evening papers in vigorous competition, but there were few places for a Richard Harding Davis or a Frank Ward O'Malley, the New York *Sun*'s brilliant feature writer. A man who made a hundred a week in the newspaper business was highly unusual and probably related to the publisher. Nevertheless, even as an undergraduate Heywood had started sideslipping toward a career in journalism. During his summer vacations, his father being a friend of the managing editor, he worked on the New York *Morning Telegraph*'s staff as an apprentice reporter.

Naturally his family hoped that a Harvard degree would inspire him to something more lucrative and dignified than newspaper work. The fact that he failed to make the *Crimson* staff, which was largely a social function, didn't mean Heywood as a Harvard man wouldn't be eligible for a magazine job. Unfortunately his tangle-tongued approach to foreign languages posed a threat to matriculation. At Horace Mann his exasperated German teacher had hurled an inkpot at him; at Harvard the complexities of French were overpowering. And in the last lap of his senior year Heywood flunked French, and there was no diploma with his name on it when the class of 1910 was graduated.

He always meant to go back and make up that missing credit but never got around to it. Failing that, he hoped that Harvard, in view of his journalistic celebrity, would one day telegraph him, "Oh, all right, Heywood, come and get your degree." He waited in vain for that summons. In the summer of 1910 he went out into the world, or at least downtown to a newspaper office.

2. The Car-Barn School of Journalism

BEING almost a Harvard graduate, it might have seemed that Heywood Broun would gracefully condescend to join the staff of one of New York's more eminent journals. During the pre-World War I years New York journalism reached its most resplendent period, and among its dozen dailies were Joseph Pulitzer's *Morning* and *Evening World*, James Gordon Bennett's *Herald* and *Telegram*, the morning and evening *Sun*, Adolph Ochs' *Times*, Whitelaw Reid's *Tribune*, as the statelier organs of news and opinion, and William Randolph Hearst's morning *American* and evening *Journal*, the *Mail*, the *Globe*, the *Commercial Advertiser*, the *Evening Post*, and the pretabloid *Daily News*, as those of lesser circulation or distinction.

At the very bottom of the journalistic scale was the *Morning Telegraph*, which wasn't even on Park Row and never on the more respectable breakfast tables. It was published in a building at West Fiftieth and Eighth Avenue which had once served as the stables for the horsecar lines. The stable odor persisted, fittingly enough, because the paper's largest concern was horse racing, with only slightly less emphasis on other sports, the Broadway theater, and any sort of scandal. Its tone was determinedly flippant. The headline over a story telling how the English poet laureate had refused to be interviewed on his arrival in New York: KING'S CANARY REFUSES TO CHIRP.

Heywood Broun joined its staff on a permanent basis after working as a reporter on space rates the previous two summers because his father was a friend of the publisher. His starting salary was $20 a week. From the beginning he felt comfortable in the raffish atmosphere of the *Morning Telegraph*'s editorial rooms. "It was like a tough *Emporia Gazette*," he wrote many years later. "The city room was always cluttered up with all sorts of people who didn't seem to have any business there. Very often you couldn't get to your desk because there would be a couple of chorus girls sitting there waiting for a friend who was finishing an editorial. I used to write editorials myself and it made me feel very lonely. Everybody wrote editorials. Generally at the last moment somebody would remember that we didn't have any editorials. . . . The editorials were not regarded as very important because the *Telegraph* had no policy about anything except that it was against reformers. Vaudeville reviews were very important because the actors advertised."

Even after the passage of a quarter century, he added, he couldn't say that he was sorry "I went to a car barn instead of a school of journalism." Heywood found immediate acceptance; with his bonhomous style, his haphazard dress, his black slouch hat, his keen interest in sports and the theater rather than any more recondite subjects, he succeeded entirely in disguising the fact that he had spent four years at Harvard. He was one of the boys—a warm feeling that had never enveloped him in the Harvard Yard.

The informal, unbuttoned atmosphere of the *Morning Telegraph* delighted him, while he would have been frightened stiff at the *Times* or *Herald*, whose reporters were expected to dress and comport themselves like a second secretary in the British embassy. The editor and general manager, William E. Lewis, was an easy-mannered fellow who had bounced around on papers from coast to coast and had commanded one of Hearst's dispatch boats off Cuba during the Spanish-American War. The managing editor was his brother Irving. One of the star contributors was another brother, Alfred Henry Lewis, who also turned out Western fiction.

The big gun in the *Telegraph*'s battery, however, was one William B. Masterson, a short, bald, middle-aged man who wore a brown derby and, occasionally, when one of his enemies was in town, a .45-caliber revolver. Mr. Masterson was the sports editor and boxing expert whose views on prizefighting and horse racing were generally regarded as magisterial. Out West he had been more familiarly known as Bat Masterson, gunfighter, army scout, gambler, sheriff at Dodge City when it was the most dangerous town in the country. Naturally young Heywood looked on Mr. Masterson with awe. One night a Texas editor named Dinklesheets roared into town boasting he was going to even an old score with Masterson. The latter confronted Dinklesheets in the bar at the Waldorf Astoria, someone screamed, "Bat's going to flash his cannon," there was a stampede for the exits, and Dinklesheets led all the rest. Masterson later commented, in the imperturbable style that had carried him through so many fracases out on the old frontier, that the concealed weapon he was reaching for was a package of cigarettes.

Heywood, who continued to make his home with his parents in their Upper West Side brownstone, though he rarely beat the sunrise home, knew he had found the right profession when he was given one of his first assignments by the *Telegraph* city editor. Most young reporters had to chase fire engines, cover ax murders, or write obituaries, but Heywood was assigned to interview the glamorous Valeska Suratt at Hammerstein's Victoria on Forty-second Street.

Managing editor Irving Lewis overheard the assignment, and while Heywood was straightening his tie, for once, and shining his shoes on the backs of his trousers, Lewis sauntered over and announced he'd walk down to Forty-second with Heywood. On the way Lewis expanded on the technique of the interview, how to deal with actresses, etc. When they reached the stage door of the Victoria, Lewis told him, "I think I'll do this interview myself. You better wait outside. You know she always kisses me."

After that initial frustration Heywood spent much of his time in Broadway dressing rooms interviewing actresses and, less pleasurably, actors. He wrote pieces for the "Beau Broadway" column, which ran on page one, covered some baseball games, and inside of two years found his salary increased to $28 a week.

At twenty-three he was not inclined to brood over the fact that he was wandering into a dead end. The life suited him fine. He was learning his trade at an easy pace, he liked the atmosphere of the saloons on Eighth Avenue, he found lighthearted adventure in the dance halls where the girls were a lot friendlier and less intellectual than those he had met on the Radcliffe and Wellesley campuses, and his continuing scientific interest in the laws of chance as they could be observed over a game of poker was satisfied. A poker game had been going on in the *Telegraph* city room practically since Teddy Roosevelt charged up San Juan Hill. The game took place on the copydesk and really warmed up around midnight, after most of the copy had been sent to the composing room. "A story had to be very hot to get any attention after midnight," Heywood recalled. "Even when I wanted to go home early I couldn't because Shep Friedman, the night editor, used to say, 'I'm assigning you to the game, Broun.' The reasons for this developed early. . . . Shep was a good newspaperman but a terrible poker player. Most of the players in the game were printers, and when he tried to borrow money from them they would laugh at him. But I was a cub reporter. We played with money, and Shep would reach over to my pile and say, 'I'll raise you fifty cents.' If I raised him he'd take another of my dollars and say, 'I'll raise you again.' Pretty soon I realized that even if I won I'd only get my money back."

When the night's work and poker playing were done, he and the assistant foreman of the composing room would repair to the Eldorado dance hall, where both were smitten by a girl named Elaine who did an exhibition dance with a male partner. Elaine would sit with Broun and his friend until it was time for her to perform, then hand one of them a silver dollar. Just when Elaine finished performing, the silver dollar was thrown out on the floor to encourage other donors. Heywood prided himself on his split-second timing when it was his turn to start the silver shower; a little too early or late, and it would be followed by only a patter of coins. Heywood acquired the knack of tossing out the dollar just at the moment Elaine stopped whirling around and bringing down a rain of quarters and dimes.

Broun and his friend eventually gave up on Elaine, who apparently valued them only as shills, and began hanging out at the less respectable Sweeney's music hall. Heywood had never distinguished himself in hand-to-hand combat, but gave a good account of himself, by his own telling of the incident, when proprietor Sweeney came to his table one night and tried to make off with the girl sitting with Heywood. Heywood got up from his chair and punched Mr. Sweeney in the nose. The two men grappled, fell to the floor, and rolled around trying to clobber each other with little dignity and less expertise. A waiter grabbed a bottle and tried to hit Heywood over the head with it, but "couldn't tell which was which," and the combatants were separated before further damage could be done to the manly tradition of fisticuffs.

Heywood felt so encouraged by the fact that he had received several by-lines that he approached the management of the *Morning Telegraph* with a demand that his salary be raised to $30 a week. The management countered with the suggestion that Heywood pursue his career elsewhere.

It was no serious matter being discharged from a New York newspaper in those days. You simply got on a streetcar and sauntered into another city room; the newspaperman who hadn't worked on a dozen papers before he was thirty was regarded as a stick-in-the-mud.

Heywood's quest took him downtown to Park Row, where all the city's newspapers except the *Times* (near Times Square) and the *Herald* (on Herald Square) and of course the *Telegraph* in its old stables were published. The *Tribune* was the scene of his next employment. The nine-story red-stone Tribune Building facing Printing House Square, with its needlelike 285-foot clock tower, had once been the tallest building on Manhattan Island. It had once resounded to the organ tones of Horace Greeley, but now, as the property of Whitelaw Reid, the ambassador to Great Britain, it was the mouthpiece of the conservative, Republican, property-owning burghers of Manhattan. Heywood didn't mind; his years of enlightenment were far in the future, and the *Tribune*'s editorial policy was of less concern to him than the possibility that manager John J. McGraw would send in Christy Mathewson to pitch for the Giants the next day.

The *Tribune* hired him as a copyreader on the lobster trick, a lowly position, at $25 a week. As a subeditor he was required to correct syntax, cut stories to measure, and write headlines, all this during the slack period (or lobster trick) before the city room began filling up and the daily gallop toward the first deadline began. He might have reflected that in his first years as a newspaperman he had worked himself down from $28 to $25 a week.

After a few months among the pastepots of the copydesk he took a leave of absence from the *Tribune* to accept an offer from the theatrical firm of Liebling and Company, whose chief creative mind had decided that a play with a Chinese background might be just what Broadway needed. Broun was hired to go over to Shanghai on an expense account, but without salary, to research the background for such a play.

Heywood was eager for the experience because the newspaper business then was enthralled by the legendary, blindingly magnificent career of Richard Harding Davis, war correspondent and sun-helmeted traveler extraordinary. Every young reporter aspired to take on Davis' luster and find Davis-like adventure abroad. Nobody had ever considered the tall, stout Heywood, as clumsy and appealing as a baby elephant, a dashing fellow likely to knock Davis off his carefully constructed pedestal, but Heywood saw himself in a rather more romantic light.

There was no reason that he could perceive why, in a few years, he wouldn't be scurrying off to some colorful but not too bloody Balkan war and offering advice on strategy to a Bulgarian field marshal. The trip to Shanghai was the first step on that glory road. It wasn't until more than twenty years later that he realized he lacked the dispassionate objectivity necessary to shape the career of a journalistic magnifico, that ability to "cast a cold eye on life, on death," as Yeats prescribed on his tombstone. "It has been said that the perfect reporter ought to be patterned more or less along the physical and chemical lines of a plate glass window. It is not his function to take the light from the sun and shade it into blue, green, yellow or even red. He is an associate member of the light brigade, and when cannon roar from the right or left his mission is to keep precisely in the middle of the road in the hope that he will find the truth, which is always said to lie between the two." Broun confessed he could never be "neutral" in any situation, which makes him a spiritual antecedent of those hot-eyed young men of contemporary journalism who not only confess to but boast of being partisan and belabor those whom they consider the wrong guys.

He arrived in China at the time Sun Yat-sen's republican revolutionaries were toppling the Manchu dynasty from the throne it had occupied for centuries. China, as editorial writers solemnly pointed out, usually appending Napoleon's famous dictum, was awakening.

Heywood, dutifully visiting Peking and Shanghai in quest of material that might be converted into dramatic form by another and more practiced hand, noted that there were soldiers and machine guns everywhere and that the legation quarter of Peking, which the rebellious Boxers had besieged less than a dozen years before, was barricaded behind sandbags.

It was a historic moment, a turning point, the beginning of a gigantic upheaval in the world's largest nation. But Heywood

Broun, whose social conscience and political awareness were to make him a totem figure among American liberals, simply wasn't interested. Quite forgotten, too, were his dreams of stepping into Richard Harding Davis' polished riding boots.

His main interest was in searching out some of that picturesque Oriental sin he had long heard about. Every American was steeped in tales of Oriental vice, lurid nights on the Shanghai bund, singsong girls, female-slave auctions, and opium parlors. As he candidly admitted in later and rueful recollection, he journeyed to China as naïvely sensation-seeking as any tourist from Grand Rapids. In more ways than one, he was the burdensome white man, as he learned when rickshaw boys made him pay double for a ride. " 'Chop, chop,' I'd cry, since somebody told me that meant to run fast, and we would go roaring down the Bubbling Well Road into the night life of Shanghai." A 100-pound half-starved Chinese hauling a 220-pound American at a chop-chop pace was not a memory the latter-day liberal would recall with joy.

One thing Heywood found that he had in common with the residents of Shanghai was a feverish love of gambling. "A couple of United States marines introduced me to a poker game which we played with a group of Chinese merchants. Only one of them could speak English, but they all thought they knew the value of the hands. It turned out that I had made a good bargain for myself by agreeing to go to China without salary and simply on an expense account.

"Although I looked, I never was able to find that place later celebrated in *The Shanghai Gesture*. If you remember the play, young women were put on the auction block. Perhaps it's just as well I didn't run it down. Auctions excite me and I'm always bidding for things I don't particularly want. If I had come away with a blonde I really wouldn't know what to do with her now. . . ."

Heywood returned stateside with a sheaf of notes dutifully compiled in his role as a researcher and illustrated by photographs he took himself and dumped them on the desk of producer Liebling. Whatever their scholarly merit, they didn't inspire the production of a play. Heywood returned to his chair on the horseshoe-shaped rim of the copydesk at the *Tribune* until he persuaded the city editor, George Burdick, that he was too young to be consigned to the desk work and was appointed a general assignments reporter.*

After several years of amiably drifting around city rooms, Heywood finally began to attract the attention of his seniors in the newspaper business. They recognized that he had a deft touch with humorous stories, human-interest stuff, the little happenings that leavened the day's budget of tragedy, horror, and corruption. In recognition of that talent, he was promoted to the rewrite desk and given most of the stories requiring a light touch. Among his fellow rewrite men was Ogden Reid, the son of the publisher, who in several years would become the publisher of the *Tribune* himself.

Heywood's craftsmanship caught the eye of the sports editor, George Daley, who had been loudly complaining that his department was leaning too heavily on wire-service copy and publicity handouts and demanding that a couple of bright young men with some knowledge of sports be transferred to his pages. One of those he chose from the city staff was Heywood Broun, who would be assigned to cover the New York Giants baseball team and begin making a name for himself outside the *Tribune* city room.

Shortly after Broun became the *Tribune*'s minnesinger of John J. McGraw's Giants, a photograph was taken of the men from the various New York papers assigned to that beat. It perfectly captures the essence of Heywood Broun in his carefree early years as a journalist and suggests quite strongly that a catalytic agent of some potent kind was required to inspire the future crusader. Most of the seven men pictured wore cloth caps and looked like a group frozen into still life outside a Gashouse district poolroom. The only men wearing hats were Heywood Broun, under the battered black slouch hat that had traveled from Park Row to China and back with him, and the New York *American*'s Damon Runyon, already a fashion plate and a conscious fabricator of the laconic style that would make him famous. Heywood faced the camera with a moonfaced amiabil-

---

* Burdick was reputed to be the least loquacious editor on a New York newspaper. Once a reporter returned from an assignment, agonized endlessly over getting the lead paragraph of his story just right. Finally Burdick tapped him on the shoulder and told him, "Just one word after another will do."

ity, his shirt collar furled as though it had never been starched or ironed, his badly knotted tie askew.

Park Row was never a scene of sartorial splendor. Most of its labor force on the editorial side were notable for dressing more in the style of the nearby Bowery than Fifth Avenue; a well-tailored journalist, Runyon excepted, was suspected of being on the take if he owned more than two suits, dared to sport a cane or spats, or wore a tie any more resplendent than a Chinese coolie's garter. Most of them, it was observed, looked like old archery targets.

It would take some doing to win and hold the title of Park Row's worst-dressed man, but Heywood achieved the distinction with an easy grace. Occasionally he made attempts to spruce himself up, but clothing of any fabric, style, or cut perversely turned into a rumpled and wrinkled mass on his long but pudgy frame. For years he would be an easy target for phrasemakers attempting to convey the exact quality of his disarray, the favorite simile being his resemblance to an unmade bed somehow made ambulatory.

Gene Fowler, then one of Hearst's bright young men but later a celebrated biographer, remembered Heywood as "Park Row's all-time example of how to scare a scarecrow. Those of us who seldom looked presentable were grateful to Broun. I can best explain this by an incident taken from my own experience. When the faultlessly groomed Edwin C. Hill of the *Sun* one day asked how I had the nerve to show up in golf knickers, and with no necktie, to meet President Woodrow Wilson upon his return from the Paris Peace Conference, I replied, 'Oh, no one noticed me. You see, I took the precaution to stand next to Heywood Broun.' "

Being paid to go out to the Polo Grounds and watch a baseball game was Heywood's dream of the sweet life and had been ever since he wrecked his academic career by cutting Harvard classes and choosing the peerless Red Sox outfield over French verbs and the theories of Proudhon. He loved the sport and writing about it so much that he soon ranked with Damon Runyon, Bozeman Bulger of the *Sun*, and Grantland Rice of the *Mail* as a fabricator of prose glorifying the accomplishments of Christy Mathewson and Rube Marquard and their teammates.

It was typical of Broun that he found it difficult—then and

evermore—to achieve the objectivity which was the hallmark of the Old Journalism. He was a partisan, emotionally involved, even in something so inconsequential as a game played between professional athletes.

There was a proper attitude for a representative of a New York newspaper in the press box. Cigarette drooping from one corner of a cynical mouth, clipped phrases issuing from the other corner as he dictated a running account to the telegrapher at his side, he maintained the demeanor of a dispassionate observer. Even if he had a sawbuck riding on the home team.

"Unfortunately," Broun recalled twenty-odd years later, "I was wholly unable to attain objectivity, and veterans such as Sid Mercer and Damon Runyon were shocked each afternoon as I broke all traditions of the craft by rooting violently in the press box."

Along with the players on the field, Heywood conceived an unqualified admiration for manager McGraw, a white-haired, red-faced man with a choleric temper when confronted by his players' occasional ineptitude but amiably disposed toward sportswriters. After every game Heywood and the other writers would gather over a bottle of bourbon in McGraw's cubicle, then go downtown to write their stories. Late that night Heywood would return to his parents' home; he was in no hurry to leave the nest, which was now an apartment on Claremont Avenue, since his brother, Irving, had gone to Mexico as the employee of an oil company and his sister, Virginia, had married, and thoughts of marriage rarely crossed his mind. His ambitions were limited to newspaper work; neither then nor later could he imagine a finer occupation. He was happy with a raise in salary to $35 a week at a time when other classmates at Harvard were already beginning to make their way up in a wider world—John Reed as a magazine writer, Alan Seeger as a poet, Robert Edmond Jones in the theater. While they were starting the trudge up the slopes of Parnassus, he was content to observe and report on a world no larger than a baseball diamond and the dressing rooms under the grandstand. While John Reed was analyzing the techniques of the Mexican revolutionaries, Heywood Broun was studying the showmanship of John J. McGraw, who knew that you had to win at the ticket windows as well as on the field. "McGraw, when on the road, would make all members of his club dress in the hotel where the team was resident. He would escort them to the top of a bus and they would proceed slowly through the main street like circus elephants on exhibition. The ballplayers would leer from the top of their lofty perch at the hostile fans and the rooters would leer back, throw eggs and tomatoes and grow maniacal. If a crucial series were in progress it was frequently necessary to call out the reserves in order to limit the number of killed and injured. Those were the happy days of baseball. . . ."

And he celebrated the feats of Christy Mathewson, who seemed to be carrying the Giants on his back during the 1913–1914 season when the team was riddled by injuries, in slightly overheated prose: "Robbed of his catcher, a wrecked machine tottering to ruin at his back, and the greatest sluggers in baseball poised for the onslaught, old Chris Mathewson, master, king, emperor and ruler of all baseball pitchers at home and in the dominions beyond the seas, annihilated the attack of the Philadelphia Athletics by the might of his wizardry. . . ."

The Homeric quality of his prose when expended on something so relatively footling as a baseball game apparently convinced the editors of the *Tribune* that his talents were being wasted in the press box at the Polo Grounds.

In midsummer, 1915, Heywood was appointed the *Tribune's* dramatic critic, thus giving a license to the failed playwright of Professor Baker's 47 Workshop to frown on the works of his betters. The reasoning by which a baseball writer became a dramatic critic was not clear to anyone unacquainted with the Byzantine workings of the executive minds under the clock tower on Nassau Street. The main qualification Heywood had, it seems, was an ability to write amusingly and without missing deadlines; it was also true that he loved the theater and presumably would be able to achieve a critical viewpoint.

Heywood lost no time in demonstrating that, unlike the heroes of the baseball diamond, he was able to find flaws in the actors and dramatists who presented themselves behind the proscenium arch. The man who found it difficult to come down hard on a Giant shortstop who booted an easy roller hit right at him, could be hard-nosed about failings behind the footlights.

One of the first performances he reviewed at the beginning of the 1915 theatrical season featured the presence of an actor named Steyne, to which Heywood took violent exception. Mr. Steyne's performance, he wrote, was the "worst to be seen in the contemporary theater." Mr. Steyne sued for damages to his professional reputation. While the suit was still pending, Steyne appeared in another production and bristled accordingly when Broun reviewed the new play. "He is not up to his usual standard," Broun noted. Worse yet for Mr. Steyne, his suit against Broun was dismissed.

Heywood came to his theatrical duties without any great burden of prejudices. He did think that actresses were prettier than actors and was subject to infatuation with the comelier of the female of the species. He regarded George Bernard Shaw as the greatest living playwright, and he was interested in and willing to grant indulgences to the experimental theaters then springing up around Washington Square and other off-Broadway locations. He admired professionalism in a playmaker as in a center fielder, as witnessed by his comments on a new George M. Cohan production: "Somebody should create a foundation which will endow all stage aspirants with tickets for the new Cohan play. They will not find a more likely master. And I would particularly request the aspirants to note the way in which Cohan listens. He is all attention when the other person in the scene is speaking. You forget that he not only wrote the play, but produced it. He seems eager not to miss a line of the dialogue, and it is all surprising to him, as if this were the first time the lines had ever been said."

On the other hand, he did not hesitate to crack down on professionals who, he felt, let the audience down. His candor on that subject soon made him one of Park Row's more controversial critics. He slapped down Ethel Barrymore for a slipshod performance, which brought on a caustic exchange between actress and critic. Miss Barrymore wondered aloud whether a baseball writer was qualified to comment authoritatively on the drama. Heywood's old comrades in the Baseball Writers Association immediately announced that they had been insulted en masse.

Regarding Jules Eckert Goodman's new play, *Just Outside the Door*, he remarked that "whenever the long arm of coincidence intrudes, the author seizes it and shakes hands." Another melodrama, he observed, solved its dramaturgic problems by having a child "fall sick of some dramatic ailment."

He even found fault with the high-spirited Eva Tanguay, the "I Don't Care Girl," whose style was borrowed from the whirling dervishes. Finding her performance more energetic than skillful, he addressed a review to her titled "Something About Which Eva Tanguay Should Be Made to Care."

Miss Tanguay was unaccustomed to a blunt-edged and objective discussion of her performing style and responded with a full-page ad in the show-business weekly *Variety*, one of its rhymed paragraphs reading: "Have you ever noticed when a woman succeeds how they attack her until her character bleeds? They snap at her heels like mongrels unfed, just because she has escaped being dropped in FAILURE's big web. They don't give her credit for talent or art. They don't discount a very hard start. They don't give her credit for heartaches or pains; how grimly she held tight to the reins when the road was rocky and drear; how smiling she met every discouraging sneer. . . ."

It was plain that the neophyte critic was more interested in playwrights who were extending themselves, bringing realism to the stage, and warring on the puritanical view that life had to be well laundered before it was converted to dramatic form than in Broadway commercialism. The pre-World War I theater was plastered with taboos; moral tone was given priority over faithfulness to the truth about human relations. Thus Heywood would heartily praise a taboo-breaking play like Louis K. Anspacher's *The Unchastened Woman* for its grasp on reality. "Persons who like to see vice triumph or virtue prevail will not like it. Dr. Anspacher is one of those delightful neutrals who sets his folks on the stage and then lets them fight it out. We like it that way. It is our experience—bitter, too—that the rewards of virtue are by no means certain. Life, we find, does not deal in exact judgments. . . ."

With that outlook on the theatrical arts, Heywood was naturally in a receptive mood one autumn night in 1915 when a new and experimental group called the Washington Square Players opened at the Bandbox Theater on West Fifty-seventh Street in Percy MacKaye's *The Antick*. The company included a number of future luminaries, Katharine Cornell, Helen Westley, Frank Conroy, and Roland Young. MacKaye had been a student in Professor Baker's 47 Workshop. So Broun approached his professional duties that night in an anticipatory mood, even though he could not have foreseen that the youthful company would form the nucleus of the prestigious Theater Guild.

Katharine Cornell was just beginning her long and honorable career as a dramatic star, and the incandescence of her talent was already visible, but it wasn't the raven-haired and lissome Miss Cornell who caught the eye of the *Tribune*'s critic.

Heywood was transfixed by the person and performance of another member of the company, Lydia Lopokova, whom another smitten critic had mooned over as "a winged fairy, dainty as a white violet, light as thistledown." Miss Lopokova was a tiny creature, barely five feet tall, with a porcelain complexion, huge blue eyes, and a mane of dark brown hair. Then twenty-three years old, she was the daughter of a czarist bureaucrat who had entered the imperial ballet school in St. Petersburg at the age of eight, had danced with the Diaghilev Ballet in Paris, and later was the leading ballerina of the Russian Ballet at the Winter Garden in New York. She had joined the Washington Square Players to obtain experience as an actress.

For Heywood Broun, indubitably, Lydia Lopokova was alone on stage the moment she made her entrance in *The Antick*. He thereupon committed the cardinal sin of the dramatic critic: He fell in love with an actress. His review the next morning accordingly went overboard in assessing Lydia's performance:

"We regret now wasted adjectives and we pine for every superlative with which we have lightly parted. All words denoting, connoting or appertaining in any way to charm we would bestow upon Lydia Lopokova. As Julie Bonhear, a Canuck girl, Lydia is a mite mighty in enticement. Never have we. . . . But no; we'll set no time limit on our opinion for Julie herself complains: 'These Yankees, they say only that: I love you always, forever! Why not they say: I love you—all this week?'

"And so until Tuesday, October 12, we will continue to maintain that Lydia Lopokova is the most charming young person who has trod the stage in New York this season. But she did not tread. She did not even walk. She skipped, she danced, she pranced, and, like as not, she never touched the stage. Or so it seemed."

Heywood followed that up by arranging an introduction to Miss Lopokova through the company press agent and took her to supper to Mouquin's, which he and most New Yorkers regarded as the epitome of old-world elegance. Thereafter Heywood pursued a headlong courtship, took her walking afternoons in Central Park, to supper after the nightly performance. They were the original odd couple: the tiny sophisticated Russian ballerina and the hulking Broun in his raccoon coat and black hat. Other admirers of the Russian girl couldn't understand what she saw in the ungainly Broun in eternal dishabille, but women had and would always find him attractive in a teddy-bear sort of way. He appealed to their maternal instincts. The first thought any woman had on glimpsing Broun was that he needed taking care of—and reforming. His tousled hair and his off-center necktie, his slightly forlorn air, his generally unkempt condition (despite his mother's continuing efforts) recommended even to a Russian dancer-actress intent on her own career the need for someone to take Heywood in hand.

Heywood was determined to marry her, though his friends found it hard to believe Mlle. Lopokova would abandon her career to take up the hopeless task of keeping Heywood's pants creased. She was ambitious and seemingly had a great career ahead of her, one that would hardly be enhanced by marriage to a journalist.

Yet, in her lighthearted way, she agreed to Heywood's proposal that they be married at some hazy time in the future when the urgencies of her career permitted. Heywood couldn't help babbling the good news to his owlish friend, Franklin P. Adams, whose column in the Samuel Pepys style was appearing in the New York *Mail*. As Adams wrote, "H. Broun, the critick, I hear hath become engaged to Mistress Lydia Lopokova, the pretty play-actress and dancer. He did introduce her to me last night and she seemed a merry elf and a modest."

Elfin, undoubtedly, was a good description of the Lopokova personality. She did like Heywood, but she was easily distracted.

Diaghilev's ballet company was coming to New York for an American tour and she was invited to rejoin it, which she did. The Diaghilev troupe was a hotbed of sexual intrigue, hetero and otherwise; and aside from that the ballet was an intensely self-involved little world which rigorously excluded outsiders. Lydia was caught up in the collective passions of the troupe and had less and less time for her fiancé—and more and more time for Randolfo Barocini, who was Diaghilev's secretary-manager.

Heywood knew he was losing out with Lydia but could find no way of reasserting his claim on her affections. The ballet trouped through a number of American cities, then returned to New York for almost immediate departure for its home base in Paris.

During its brief Manhattan stopover, Lydia explained to Heywood that she had fallen in love with Barocini and in any case didn't want to commit herself to marriage at that promising stage of her career.

Heywood took it hard, though he must have realized all along that they had little in common. Lydia many years later recalled that "my professional career involved me in a whirl of excitement. I felt I did not want to be tied up to Heywood—so I broke it off, hurting him very much at the time, I am sorry to say."

(A rather astonishing career lay ahead of the Russian dancer. She married Barocini and continued her career, which made her a brief but blazing star in the European dance theater. Eventually she divorced Barocini and in 1925 married the most renowned of modern economists, John Maynard Keynes. Her life spanned the brilliance of the czarist Russian ballet and the equal effulgence of the Bloomsbury intellectuals, and little Lydia wound up as Lady Keynes.)

That had been Heywood's first serious love affair, and no doubt it left a mark on him. It always does. He had just passed his twenty-eighth birthday and it seemed to him that life was passing him by. Much as he liked play reviewing, too, the *Tribune* management just about the time Mlle. Lopokova slipped out of his life decided that his talents were more urgently needed back in the sports department. The sports editor, George Daley, had turned in his resignation, and the newspaper's executives felt that Broun was just the man to continue Daley's program of building up the paper's sports coverage. He was replaced by George S. Kaufman of the *Mail* in the drama critic's cubicle.

It was a promotion, of course, but Heywood's temperament was not suited to executive tasks. There was nothing of the brass hat in his makeup. When he gave an order it came out more like an apology. Furthermore, the exactions of an editor's role irked him: handing out the assignments, presiding over the makeup of the sports pages daily, dealing with the editorial auditor. It was a lot more fun sitting in a press box than reading the copy of those who did.

One valuable trait he did possess as an editor was an eye for talent. The New York *Journal*'s boxing column for years had been signed by "Right Cross," a pseudonym under which a number of experts had labored. The current holder of that title, Broun learned, was a man named W. O. McGeehan, whose acerb style delighted Broun.

Broun called McGeehan and asked him to come over to the *Tribune* to discuss the possibility of McGeehan's moving over to the *Tribune* sports department.

McGeehan, who would become a rival of Damon Runyon as a sports columnist, would never forget his first interview with sports editor Broun. He found a large, rumpled man with dark twinkling eyes lounging behind the railing of the sports department and using a wastebasket as a footstool.

The interview was brief and businesslike.

"Mr. McGeehan," Broun said, "the management has authorized me to haggle with you over salary."

McGeehan braced himself for a tough bargaining session.

"You may have forty-five or fifty dollars a week," Broun continued. "Whichever you want."

"Fifty's a nice round number," McGeehan replied.

"You're hired. If you'd taken less, I'd have kicked you downstairs."

Little things like that occasionally made the *Tribune*'s management wonder whether Heywood Broun was really of executive caliber.

3. Then and Always, Miss Ruth Hale

SOME months before he had become infatuated with Lydia Lopokova, Heywood met a young Southern-born woman who would become a much more permanent influence on his life—the strongest and most indelible, in fact, the one which infused him with some of the zealotry which would convert him from an easygoing observer of life to an active and controversial participant. It would be easy to exaggerate her influence, or infer too much from her own hectically active nature, but Heywood himself would always give full credit to the sometimes abrasive, often comradely quality of the moral force exerted by Miss Ruth Hale.

She was fiercely independent, a bluestocking, a crusader for women's rights before that cause became fashionable and was taken up by society women and actresses. "Concerning her major contention we were in almost complete disagreement for seventeen years," Heywood wrote many years later. "Out of a thousand debates I lost a thousand. Nobody ever defeated Miss Ruth Hale in an argument. The dispute was about feminism. We both agreed that in law and art and industry and anything else you can think of women should be equal. Ruth Hale felt that this could be brought about only through the organization of women along sex lines. I think that this equality will always be an inevitable and essential part of any thoroughgoing economic upheaval. 'Come on and be radical,' I used to say, but Miss Hale insisted on being a militant feminist—all that and nothing more and nothing less."

Looking back, he considered it a "curious collaboration, because Ruth Hale gave me out of the very best she had to equip me for the understanding of human problems. She gave this under protest, with many reservations, and a vast rancor. But she gave."

Ruth Hale was born a few years before Heywood in Rogers-ville, Tennessee, the daughter of a horse breeder and farmer. She started her rebellion against conventional standards early in life by riding astride her pony instead of sidesaddle like any properly reared Southern (white) female. She also reacted strongly to her mother's beliefs. Mrs. Annie Riley Hale was vigorously opposed to the feminist cause and took to the platform all over eastern Tennessee to inveigh against women's rights and declare that woman's place was in the home with her children. Before she reached puberty, Ruth had taken the opposite side of the debate despite her mother's indignation. At thirteen she was sent to a Virginia boarding school to study music and painting and later to the Academy of Fine Arts in Philadelphia. All the time preaching the feminist doctrine—this, of course, during the pre-World War I years when men could treat with genial contempt or gentle laughter the idea that women should be allowed to vote and have control of their own property—Ruth Hale went into journalism at the age of eighteen and became a reporter for the Washington *Star* and four years later the dramatic critic of the Philadelphia *Ledger*. Subsequently she moved to New York and worked as a critic for *Vogue* and a reporter for the New York *Times*. She was an intelligent and ambitious young woman and furiously resented the patronizing, if not downright scornful, attitude she found among her male editors and colleagues, who considered her something of an oddity because she was doing what had been regarded as a man's work and vociferously argued in any forum she could find against the idea that women were inherently inferior.

She was working as the press agent for Arthur Hopkins, the theatrical producer, when her friend Alice Duer Miller invited her to attend a game at the Polo Grounds. Alice was a feature writer for the Sunday edition of the *Tribune* and, like Ruth, a militant crusader for women's rights; in the future she would attain some renown as a literary figure, particularly for her long poem "The White Cliffs of Dover," which both in itself and as a popular song served as an inspiration for the Allied cause in World War II.

The two young women, militant suffragettes though they may have been, dressed themselves carefully for their trip to the Polo Grounds and made a fetching picture in their wide-brimmed and elegantly veiled picture hats and crisp shirtwaist dresses. Their intention, however, was more political than social. The press box at the Polo Grounds was a male sanctuary with an unwritten law against invasion by females no less stringent than that of the Union League Club. The sportswriters felt that any female influence might destroy the ambience of their roost over home plate, with its tobacco quids and cigar butts, half-empty beer bottles and whiskey flasks, its carpeting of wadded-up copy paper which daily threatened to catch fire from carelessly thrown cigarettes, its cheerful cursing and unbuttoned masculinity.

Ruth Hale and Alice Miller tripped up the steps to the press box, and the latter asked at the door for Heywood Broun, then still covering baseball for the *Tribune.* As one colleague to another, she indicated she and her friend would like to watch the game from the press box. Heywood, of course, was too polite to bid them be gone, and despite the frowns and muttered imprecations of his fellow males, he ushered them to seats beside his own.

From the moment he was introduced to Ruth Hale, he was intrigued by her—perhaps she reminded him of his strong-minded mother. Ruth was not a conventional beauty, but she had a striking face with large gray eyes and dark blond hair and a slender, willowy figure. Her vitality, her candor, her mental vigor and intellectual curiosity—and her combativeness—were apparent the moment you met her. She must have been the least coy, the least subtle female ever to emerge from the ranks of Southern womanhood. She laid it all on the line, take it or leave it. She challenged, questioned, hammered away at every preconception, particularly those affecting the male attitude toward her sex.

Women, it was tolerantly assumed by men, were too feather-brained to understand the complexities of a baseball game. They might admire the uniforms and thrill to the mysterious activity on the diamond below, but the fine points of the game, naturally, were beyond their frivolous little minds.

Heywood was taken aback when Ruth questioned several shots he called as that day's official scorer. She also delivered the opinion that his prose, which was much admired in Park Row circles, was more than a little too cute for its earthy subject; he was only writing about a game also played by small boys on corner lots, not the Trojan wars, she did not hesitate to remind him.

Heywood was intrigued, not affronted by the frontal assault, perhaps feeling it was a corrective he needed to reduce the growing circumference of his hatband. He suggested that he and Ruth meet the next day to discuss his journalistic failings, and she accepted. They went for a walk in Central Park. Ruth was touched by the fact that Heywood showed up wearing one black shoe and one brown. Heywood was fascinated by the range and unconventionality of her opinions, by her high-spirited personality, even by her militant feminism. That evening they went to the Broun apartment in upper Manhattan and Heywood introduced her to his mother and father.

Given the law of the attraction of opposites—endearing Heywood and tough-minded Ruth, easygoing and ineffably amiable Heywood and vociferous, crusading Ruth—they might have proceeded immediately to a deeper emotional attachment. For the time being, however, they valued each other's company; and Ruth was determined to hold his attention, not with feminine wiles and sexual magnetism, but with the quality of her mind. She was too proud to play the Victorian woman's game, all fainting spells and squeals and giggles. Heywood would have to value her as she was and would always be—her own person. It would be dishonest, worse yet, soft-centered, to gaff him by pretending to be something she wasn't.

That forthrightness subsequently was proven to be a tactical error, as viewed from the more conventional feminine viewpoint. Their intellectual comradeship continued, but did not emotionally ripen. And then Heywood was distracted by the utterly and unequivocally feminine Lydia Lopokova. Against Lopokova's professional charms Ruth Hale's intellectuality didn't stand a chance.

She must have been dismayed at the way her rival captivated Heywood by mere physical beauty and a fascinating foreign accent. Certain that he and the ballerina were a classic mismatch, she kept her own counsel and remained Heywood's friend even after he became engaged to Lopokova.

And when Lopokova threw him over, inevitably, she was waiting on the sidelines, not quite a patient Griselda, but wise enough not to rub any salt into his emotional wounds.

She listened approvingly as he talked of plans for his future, his determination to get out of the sports department and into something more intellectually weighty. And she agreed that, despite his disappointment with Lydia Lopokova, it was time that he got married. There was something a little ridiculous about a grown man still living at home with his parents, he averred, and he had always wanted a family of his own.

Naturally, and without any overt maneuvering from Ruth Hale, the discussions of marriage turned to a suitable candidate for the honor. Heywood didn't know any young woman he cared for as much as Ruth. They edged to the brink of matrimony; Heywood more or less proposed and was conditionally accepted. Ruth made it clear that theirs would be a modern marriage. She would retain her identity and independence; she would continue to pursue her own career. They would be coequal heads of the household. Heywood almost desperately wanted to be a father, particularly, to Ruth's disgust, the father of a son, just like any Oriental peasant. She deplored his attitude but admitted it was her duty to produce a child. One child only. If the child turned out to be a boy, fine; if not, he would have to be satisfied with a daughter.

Their plans matured in the spring of 1917 just after the United States went to war with the Central Powers. Both had received assignments that would take them to France. She had arranged a job on the staff of the Paris edition of the Chicago *Tribune*. The New York *Tribune* had decided to send Heywood with the first echelon of the American Expeditionary Force. Heywood Broun, war correspondent. It was the sort of boyish dream he had nurtured, like most other young newspapermen, ever since they had been bedazzled by the glamorous adventures of Richard Harding Davis. Yet the assignment was more of a professional triumph than a confirmation of any patriotic stirrings. Even in a time of war hysteria, he could not feel any urge to wave a metaphorical spear, join in the war dance, and clamor for victory; he was too much the liberal humanitarian and instinctive pacifist to believe there was any glory to be won on a battlefield, and being German on his mother's side, it was difficult for him to believe that all Germans were blood-dripping Huns determined to destroy Western civilization. Broun would tackle his job as a thoroughgoing professional, without offering himself as a propagandist for the United States Army. He had always hated firearms, hunting, inflicting needless pain, the bellicose joys of militarism. The sight of blood appalled him. The regimentation necessary to armed combat deeply offended him.

In all, he was a perfectly terrible choice for the role of war correspondent; whatever the late Richard Harding Davis was, he wasn't. Several years later, dwelling on the subject of the Unknown Soldier and his elaborate commemoration, he wrote, "War may have been well enough in the days when it was a game for heroes, but now it sweeps into combat everything and every man within a nation. The unknown soldier stands for us as a symbol of this blind and far-reaching fury of modern conflict. His death was in vain unless it helps us to see that the whole world is our business."

Somewhat hastily, because they were awaiting their sailing orders, they set the date for their marriage, June 7, 1917.

Right up to the moment they marched toward the altar it was the bride-to-be rather than the bridegroom who suffered qualms about the wisdom of their venture. Ruth kept offering qualifications almost as though she hoped Heywood would find them unacceptable—or perhaps, subconsciously, she was testing the depth of his emotional commitment. After all, she hadn't been his first choice. One thing she wanted to establish was that each was entitled to a private life of his/her own. They weren't to be shackled; each could have separate friends and go out on the town alone. If things didn't work out, if one or the other was attracted to someone else, the marriage would be dissolved for the asking. Heywood agreed.

It was a trying time for Ruth's mother and for her future mother-in-law. Both of the ladies and Heywood himself wanted a church wedding. Ruth declared that the whole idea of marriage was ridiculous and a religious ceremony was a relic of the Middle Ages. She held out for a civil ceremony, but her mother and mother-in-law prevailed.

Then, on the eve of their wedding, Ruth balked again. She was sharing an apartment with her mother and her brother Richard, an aspiring singer, on East Sixty-sixth Street; her other brother, Shelton, an attorney, had come up from Washington to give the bride away, her father having died a dozen years earlier. What aroused all of Ruth's combative instincts was the arrival of a booklet from St. Agnes Episcopal Church on West Ninety-second Street, where they were to be married the following day. It was titled "Form of Solemnization of Matrimony" and was a handbook for those to be united in the richly robed and incense-laden High Church Episcopal ceremony.

Ruth felt like tearing up her bridal gown when she read it. She was infuriated by the news that she would be expected to kneel before the priest, by certain phrases in the ritual such as the fact that the ceremony was performed "in the fear of God" and under the future threat of a "dreadful day of judgment."

But what really infuriated her was the use of the word "obey" in the service. Why, she hadn't obeyed her own mother since puberty; she had never obeyed anyone or anything but her conscience. It seemed to her that, in the Church of England tradition, she was being treated as a chattel, that she was no better than some peasant girl for whom a neighboring farmer had paid her father four cows and a few roods of pasture.

"And what if I don't obey?" she shouted. "Has Broun got the right to beat me with a stick? I'd like to see him try that!"

She thereupon declared the marriage was off. Only the arguments of her two brothers dissuaded her from throwing her bridal array out the window.

And she did show up at the church, gowned and veiled and still fretful. It was rather a tense scene, as some of the witnesses would recall. Heywood looked to be on the verge of nervous collapse. The bride glowered and muttered.

Halfway down the aisle toward the altar she halted and appeared to be about to make a bolt for the doors, but her brother Shelton had an armlock on her, and the entourage arrived safely at the altar, where Heywood and his best man (Franklin P. Adams, the columnist "F.P.A.") were waiting more in trepidation than joy. Ruth, however, made the proper responses and the ceremony was concluded. There was one more tense moment when some careless wedding guest addressed Ruth, with an attempted gallantry, as "Mrs. Broun." Ruth loudly advised him that she was not and would never be known as Mrs. Broun; she was and always would be Ruth Hale.

Ruth would always be a prickly, stubbornly independent, determinedly unsubmissive female, yet in the view of their friends the marriage was a good thing. One friend of the family, George Oppenheimer, the writer, publisher, and drama critic, believed that Ruth was the making of Broun the partisan. "Heywood was a superb man," Oppenheimer wrote in his memoir. "Forgetful, sloppy and neurotic, he had inherent goodness, a crusading courage aginst ills and injustices, and a loyalty rare in mankind. He was a knight in ill-fitting, slightly rusty armor, but a knight nonetheless. . . . It was Ruth Hale who, more often than not, buckled on Heywood's armor and sent him into battle. Not that he had to be pushed, but Ruth was a fellow crusader and thought up new causes and new crusades for him to pursue. . . . I like to think that the ghosts of Heywood and Ruth were in the forefront of the Freedom March from Selma to Montgomery. . . ."

If the marriage was regarded as a dangerous venture for Ruth and Heywood by their more pessimistic friends, their honeymoon was perfectly in key. There was no carefree atmosphere about a honeymoon on a ship sailing through the war zones of the Atlantic with German U-boats likely at any moment to surface and bang away with their deck guns or launch torpedoes. The German navy then was making a determined effort to discourage the United States from sending its divisions to Europe.

Heywood and his bride sailed the day following the wedding on a French passenger liner which was part of an Allied convoy. Also aboard were a number of other American war correspondents including Charles Grasty of the New York *Times*, Floyd Gibbons of the Chicago *Tribune*, Wilbur Forrest of the United Press, and Philip Powers of the Associated Press, all of them being shepherded by Major Frederick Palmer, himself a noted correspondent in earlier wars.

Even a loud bang was distressing to Heywood, and admittedly it was an uneasy crossing for the bridegroom. Ruth Hale, however, was as contemptuous of danger as any of the Confederate cavalrymen among her ancestors; serene in the knowledge that, after all, those German submariners were mere men. Heywood found a certain amount of consolation in the bar and at the poker table with his fellow correspondents. And there were a number of interesting passengers aboard, not the least of them the sportive heir to the railroad fortune, William K. Vanderbilt, who could not be kept away from a Paris springtime by mere wartime exigencies, zeppelin raids, and Big Bertha barrages.

The ship was several days out on its zigzag course for the French port of St.-Nazaire when the convoy in which it was traveling came to the attention of the Germans. A French sailor dashed into the saloon one afternoon shouting in French—which Broun had flunked—and dramatically pointing downward. Broun seized his meaning immediately: A U-boat had been sighted.

He and Ruth climbed into their life jackets and joined a group of American nurses at the rail who pointed to a periscope clearly visible across the water. The U-boat, as Heywood learned, had loosed a torpedo which missed the ship's bow by only ninety feet. The ship's deck guns were now ranging on the submarine and bracketing it with their fire.

A short time later the periscope disappeared. The captain informed the passengers that his ship's fire had sunk the U-boat, but no wreckage could be sighted. The enemy, which traveled in undersea packs, was undoubtedly still lurking under the gray waters around them.

Nevertheless, the ship docked safely at St.-Nazaire, and the press contingent entrained for Paris, where they were greeted by a dozen French journalists eager to interview them. Heywood had not as yet formulated any strategy by which the American forces would break the deadlock on the western front, but was polite to his fellow craftsmen.

For his first story from embattled France Heywood wrote an account of the attempted torpedoing with mostly humorous sidelights. Nobody on shipboard, he noted, cheered for the submarine. His attention also was drawn to the impenetrable poise of William K. Vanderbilt, who apparently regarded the torpedoing as an example of German boorishness. Vanderbilt, he observed, "did not put on a life preserver, nor did he leave his deck chair. He just sat up a bit and watched the whole affair tolerantly. After all, the submarine captain was a complete stranger to him."

The dispatch betrayed no military or naval secrets, yet for unfathomable reasons it was held up by the military censorship for several weeks while Heywood fumed. It was the beginning of his war with the brass hats and also the beginning of his career as a controversialist.

4. At War with the Army

RUTH and Heywood established themselves in a small apartment near the Luxembourg Gardens and plunged into their separate careers, their voyage through submarine-infested waters having to serve as their honeymoon.

Miss Hale reported for work at the Chicago *Tribune*'s Paris edition, and Heywood grappled with the problem of turning himself into a war correspondent and trying to accommodate his disorganized nature with the demands of military discipline.

The American Expeditionary Force and its grim, jut-jawed commander, General John J. Pershing, who didn't care much for newspapermen and their careless attitudes, had made it clear that American correspondents were not only the guests of the U.S. Army but must try to be a credit to that institution. They would dress in military uniform without rank badges, they would behave more or less like officers (and gentlemen), and they would submit their dispatches to army censorship. To guarantee the latter, their newspapers were required to post a $1,000 bond which was to be forfeited if they broke their word and tried to slip their stories past the censorship.

Immediately on being notified at press headquarters that an officer's uniform was required dress, Heywood set out for the Galeries Lafayette, the leading Paris department store, and flung himself on the mercy of the shopgirls. His French was even worse than their English, but with much gesticulation he managed to convey the idea that he wanted to be outfitted in military fashion. Heywood's concept of men's tailoring was notoriously vague, absolutely nonexistent when it came to military fashion. From then on, his appearance and demeanor, not to mention the odd little salutes he threw, were one of the minor scandals of the AEF, a menace to the American program of securing the respect of its allies, and an affront to every brass hat on whom he inflicted his presence. He acquired a billowy sort of tunic in a burnt-orange shade that might have been abandoned in the retreat of a Balkan army, a size 48 Sam Browne belt to girdle his unsoldierly girth, riding boots, and breeches in a shade of pink not seen since the Mamzelle Champagne troupe disbanded. Since an officer's hat of modern design could not be found on the shelves, and he felt that a dragoon's brass helmet of Franco-Prussian War vintage might be a trifle too flamboyant, he topped off his costume with the black slouch hat that made him look like one of the seedier Southern Congressmen. Later in the year, when cold weather came, he wrapped all that in his molting raccoon coat. A walking satire on military modes, many thought. It was rumored that several senior generals turned an apoplectic purple when they caught sight of him. The French military police kept stopping him and demanding to have a look at his papers on suspicion that he had deserted from one of the labor battalions, in which dress was equally haphazard.

From the beginning, Heywood declared his opposition to serving as a mouthpiece or propaganda organ for the AEF. The landing of the advance echelon of American troops in France saw his first brush with the rule-bound censorship.

With the other correspondents he journeyed to St.-Nazaire late in June to await the arrival of the first U.S. troop-bearing convoy, watched the steamer *Invicta* unload the first of two million doughboys and the cruiser *Seattle* ushering the rest of the transports into the port. Then they all rushed to their typewriters and banged out dispatches describing the historic moment—the first time American troops had landed to engage in a European war—in suitably throbbing prose. They might as well have written with quill pens. The army's chief watchdog on the correspondents, Major Frederick Palmer, though formerly a distinguished correspondent himself, sat on their stories for five days on the theory that the convoy's arrival would, somehow, be of crucial interest to the enemy. The Paris daily *Ce Soir* had already bannerlined the news, and more modest accounts had appeared in the London newspapers, but the American correspondents fumed while their offices demanded to know where their copy was. There was a considerable uproar in St.-Nazaire in which Major Palmer offered to resign his commission if any of his critics would take over his thankless job.

Broun's story of the convoy's debarkation, it seemed to the

AEF press officers, lacked a sense of the dignity, the awe-inspiring significance of the moment. In his first paragraph he dutifully described the arrival of the troops, but in his second he sounded a note displeasing to an army command highly conscious of the fact that mothers back in the States were being emotional about the possibility that their sons would be led astray by foreign booze and bad women in notoriously sinful France. It read:

"Since little things are important at moments when history is being made, it may be recorded that the first remark of the first soldier to land was: 'Do they allow enlisted men in the saloons in this town?' "

The covey of censors flapped their wings indignantly over the paragraph. No other correspondent, on being questioned, had heard the doughboy's plaintive query. And Broun admitted it wasn't literally true, but insisted that his conversations with the troopers indicated that a shot of hard liquor was uppermost in their minds when they came down the gangplanks after the long, dry Atlantic crossing. He held his ground with the censors, argued that his account made the doughboys more human and could hardly bring joy to the German General Staff, and defied them to delete it. Grudgingly it was allowed to pass. That was the beginning of Heywood's war with the army.

Heywood did not intend to write dissertations on strategy and tactics or flag-waving propaganda for the Allied cause. He regarded himself as a reporter, not a standard-bearer for patriotism. Initially it was the impact of the first American soldiers on the French people that interested him as a journalist. It was a Franco-American honeymoon period in which the French regarded the doughboys as their saviors after their own armies had been decimated in the fighting around Verdun, and hopes of victory had disappeared until the almost miraculous appearance of the Americans.

Paris was determined to love everything about the American soldiers, he wrote. "Even the taxicab drivers refrained from overcharging Americans very much. Schoolchildren studied the history of America and 'The Star-Spangled Banner.' There were pictures of President Wilson and General Pershing in many shops and some had framed translations of the President's message to Congress. In fact, so eager were the French to take America to their hearts that they even made desperate efforts to acquire a working knowledge of baseball. . . . The theaters gave the Americans almost as much recognition as the press. No musical show was complete without an American finale and each soubrette learned a little English, 'I give you kees,' or something like that, to please the doughboys. . . . The Alhambra was filled with Tommies and doughboys on the night I went. Now and again the comedians had lapses of language and the Americans were forced to let jokes go zipping by without response. It was a pity, too, for they were good jokes even if French. . . . The management was careful to state that all the male performers had fulfilled their military obligations." Thus he noted that under the lobby photograph of Maurice Chevalier it was stated that the song-and-dance man had been wounded in the lung and had been a prisoner of the Germans for twenty-six days before escaping.

American enlisted men were fed mostly in French barracks, he observed, and did not take immediately to French cuisine. He heard one American complaining over the French custom of serving food one dish at a time: "I don't want to be surprised, I want to be fed."

Nor did some of the soldiers from the Bible Belt take to what they regarded as a Parisian slackness in morals. In the bar of a music hall Heywood came across a trooper from Terre Haute, Indiana, who was staring indignantly at two young women not only drinking at the bar—a practice banned in any decent American saloon before Prohibition—but, worse yet, openly puffing on cigarettes. Only whores smoked in public, the Indiana boy believed. "I don't like this Bohemia," he told Heywood. Pointing to one of the girls, he said, "You may believe it or not, but when I first sat down she came right over here and said, 'Hello, American. You nice boy. I nice girl. You buy me a drink.' I told her to go away or I'll call a policeman. . . . I don't think I'll ever get used to this Bohemia business. . . ." The soldier, Heywood wrote, yearned for the drugstore in Terre Haute, in which he had been in charge of the soda fountain and no young lady spoke to strangers or puffed on a cigarette.

Heywood believed that the "high tide in the American conquest of Paris" came one spring day in 1917 when American soldiers played baseball in the Esplanade des Invalides, with Napoleon Bonaparte's tomb in the background. He wondered whether the crack of the baseball bat made the sleeping conqueror imagine "it was the British winning new battles on other cricket fields." A much-decorated French soldier joined the game as one of the outfielders until he was struck on the nose by a well-hit line drive. The *poilu*, jangling with medals won on several battlefields, retreated from the game complaining it was "too dangerous."

His first, rather distant glimpse of the fighting at the front came when he and other American correspondents were invited to the British army headquarters at Amiens. They toured the front well behind the rearmost support trenches, and the only fighting they saw was in the sky when a British and a German plane engaged in a dogfight.

At army headquarters there was a Sandhurst smartness of uniform and an upper-class crispness of manner. Heywood's colleagues naturally were fearful that he would let them down with his curious quasi-military costume and his offhand manner. One of the American correspondents implored him to "try and look like an officer. You don't want to make Americans seem foolish. Your puttees are on the wrong side, too."

Dining in the staff officers' mess, however, Heywood found nothing but cordiality. Nobody seemed to notice his "uniform." The next morning, wandering around the GHQ area, a British soldier gave him one of those elaborate British salutes that looked to Heywood like "three nip-ups and a swan dive," and Heywood felt at a loss to provide a proper response. His own salute looked like a man brushing off flies. "He stood rigidly at attention waiting to see what I would do. We both were petrified. . . . And so I smiled broadly and said, 'Nice morning, sir,' and I went upon my way. It seemed to me that it would be wrong to deceive him. I wasn't really an officer."

He didn't come off quite so well at an AEF headquarters inspection. It was a headquarters without an army—the few American troops in France were training in several villages in the Vosges well behind the French lines—and General Pershing found time to wonder how the U.S. press corps was shaping up. The correspondents had been given simulated officers' rank, courtesy of his headquarters, and he was determined that they would comport themselves with some semblance of military discipline. Therefore he announced that the platoon of journalists would assemble for a review.

The correspondents, most of them handsomely tailored, lined up for Pershing's inspection, nervously recalling that Pershing wasn't called Black Jack for nothing and that as a young cavalry officer he hadn't hesitated to take his fists to recalcitrant troopers behind the stables. At the end of the line stood Heywood Broun, one of his puttees unraveling, his pockets stuffed with rations, and a spoon and can opener—his sidearms—sticking out of a pocket.

When Pershing reached Broun, he stared at the *Tribune* man in bewilderment, suspecting that a drunken hostler had slipped into the lineup. He stepped back for a more careful look and assured himself that Broun was indeed a temporary and conditional officer of the AEF.

"What happened?" General Pershing roared. "Did you fall down?"

For his part Broun found little to admire about Pershing. When the general laid a wreath at the tomb of Lafayette, most of the correspondents attributed the ringing pronouncement—"Lafayette, we are here!"—to Pershing himself. Broun, however, pointed out that the much-headlined proclamation was uttered by an obscure paymaster, Major Charles E. Stanton. He early formed the opinion, not entirely justified, that Pershing was your typical brass hat with just enough imagination to conduct operations against dissidents with Stone Age weapons, as he had on the western frontier and in the southern Philippines. General Pershing managed to restrain himself from using his fists on any of the AEF correspondents, but it soon became apparent that Heywood Broun would be his No. 1 choice if he ever unleashed his temper.

Broun took a dim view of the AEF and all its works, most particularly its hidebound censorship. In the name of military security, the correspondents were forbidden to mention any name in their dispatches but General Pershing's. No units could be identified. Anything reflecting on the morale of the American troops or hinting that they were filled with anything but the highest resolve to get at the Hun was regarded at AEF headquarters as negative thinking and, worse yet, censorable. Broun toured the AEF training quarters in the cold, wet mountains at the eastern end of the western front and found the conditions downright wretched. American soldiers were quartered in stinking barns and cowsheds, surrounded by the mountains of manure so dear to the French peasant. Their food was cooked in unsanitary conditions. Furthermore, their training was supervised by the French, whose failures to break the deadlock in the trenches had convinced them that defensive tactics must prevail, instead of the British, who still believed the war could be won by all-out offensives. Broun ached to tell something of that side of the story, to indicate that the immense resources of the United States were being inefficiently used, but there was little hope of getting anything past the censors. If he evaded the censorship, of course, his credentials would be lifted and he'd be sent home on a slow boat.

He spent as much time as possible when in Paris with Ruth Hale and with the ex-newspapermen who were getting out the *Stars and Stripes*, including his old Park Row friend Sergeant Alexander Woollcott; Harold Ross, a Western journalist with a rugged face and disposition; John T. Winterich, and others. Woollcott's approximation of the military manner was almost as oddly conceived as Broun's. Some years later Broun described the Woollcott style on the western front, quoting William Slavens McNutt, who became a topflight scenarist in Hollywood. Woollcott was proceeding to the battle line during an intense German bombardment. "Aleck had a frying pan strapped around his waist, and an old gray shawl wrapped around his shoulders. Whenever it was necessary to duck from a burst of shellfire, Aleck would place the shawl carefully in the middle of the road and sit on it. In another quarter of a mile we would be in the thick of it. I saw that [Arthur] Ruhl [a war correspondent] and Aleck were having a terrific argument, and so I managed to catch up to find out what they would quarrel about at such a moment. Suddenly we all had to fall flat, but while still reclining on his belly Woollcott turned to Ruhl and said, 'I never heard anything so preposterous. To me Maude Adams as Peter Pan was gay and spirited and altogether charming as the silver star on top of the tree on Christmas morning.' "

In mid-October, 1917, Broun was lingering in Paris just when rumors were circulating that the first arrivals of the American Expeditionary Force, part of the First Division, were going to move up to a sector of the western front. Incredibly, considering the less stringent rules governing American correspondents in subsequent wars, Heywood and his colleagues were regarded as being under military discipline and had to request leave if they planned to wander away from AEF headquarters at Neufchâteau.

On October 19 Major Palmer, as the correspondents' father

superior, sternly wrote Heywood Broun a note directed to his Paris apartment informing him: "Your leave was up on the 18th and though you have not returned we have heard nothing from you. I may say it is important that if you do not return within the limits of your leave a request be made for its extension. Otherwise we shall hardly be running our office systematically. Again, if we did not know where you were, you might miss something worthwhile."

Heywood was reluctant to leave Ruth Hale's side at the moment because she had learned that she was going to have a baby. She had fainted in a restaurant, which only increased her rage at what she considered the injustice of the female condition. Watching her husband and coauthor of the prospective birth lumbering around without a sign of morning sickness, she demanded to know why the female had to bear all the burdens of childbearing. Heywood could find no answer to the ancient question and could provide only his sympathy. The humiliation of her public collapse only strengthened her determination to bear one child and no more.

With Ruth in that mood of despair and anger, Heywood tore himself away from her side on receiving the warning note from Palmer, because he was certain the summons from Neufchâteau was a hint that American troops would be going into action. On his return to AEF headquarters, however, he found the usual muddle of cross purposes. The high command evidently had determined on a closemouthed policy despite the protests of the press officers that it was bad public relations. Heywood and his fellow correspondents questioned the brass around HQ but found them as tight-lipped as usual. Then they began talking to the doughboys and learned that the First Division had received alert orders. They also tapped the journalistic grapevine and learned that the Paris newspapers were about to announce the move— and thereupon they exploded en masse. They'd been scooped on the story of the arrival of the first U.S. troop transports; now it was about to happen again, but they weren't going to allow it to happen.

Heywood and his colleagues were further aroused by a report from Paris that a member of the Chamber of Deputies was going to announce the troop movement on the legislative floor. Major Palmer succeeded in having a gag applied to the French deputy, argued the correspondents' case with Pershing's chief of staff, and finally got permission for them to witness the frontward march of the First Division.

They were hastily briefed on the plans to send one battalion in each regiment of the First Division to be brigaded with veteran French troops in the quiet sector around Arracourt, then packed into a convoy of motorcars and hauled to Einville, just behind the Arracourt sector. All the time they were dogged by French and American "conducting officers," who herded them around like sheep in the evident belief that the Kaiser's agents were hiding behind every hedge.

Heywood, who disliked being drenched and had a hypochondriac fear of catching cold, was chivied along with the rest of his colleagues to a crossroads just behind the sector. When the historic moment came, it was night and rain was falling. All he and the other correspondents could see was the column of U.S. infantrymen marching up to the line. They were forbidden to march along with their countrymen or follow them into the trenches. Their only glimpse of the war was a few white-hot flares arching over the sky of no-man's-land.

Heywood and most of the correspondents made their headquarters in Einville to glean such tidbits as the firing of the first shell at the German lines by an American battery, the first German to be captured (a young Bavarian mail orderly who had wandered into the American lines by mistake), the first wounding of an American soldier. All trivia. The bigger story was concealed behind the fogbanks of AEF censorship: How well was the expeditionary force doing in training, equipping, and supplying the growing number of divisions coming to France? The correspondents, with their movements circumscribed, could catch only rumbles of discontent, rumors of a supply system so botched it became a national scandal, grapevine reports on the arrogance and incompetence of West Pointers given more responsibility than they could handle, scuttlebutt about brass hats living high off the hog in Paris while the troops existed at a subhuman level.

Heywood finally decided that his journalistic conscience could not be bound by army regulations.

He admitted to two of his cronies at *Stars and Stripes,* lieutenants Guy T. Viskniskki and Joseph C. Green, that he was slipping stories through the censorship by mailing them to the *Tribune.* The agreement he had signed on receiving his AEF credentials, he explained, was signed under compulsion, and therefore he did not consider it binding. If he hadn't signed, he wouldn't have been accredited. There was an overriding national interest, he further told his friends at the army newspaper. The reputation of the AEF high command was less important than the construction of a military machine which would do its job properly and efficiently. Military historians accord General Pershing a much higher rating than Broun, who could not know that many of the AEF's difficulties were manufactured in Washington by a blundering War Department, but Broun believed that Pershing and his staff were not only fouling up the supply and training systems but failing, through the application of Old Army discipline, unyielding and inhuman as it was, to inspire the soldiers under their command.

Some of the stories he mailed to the *Tribune* included tangential assaults on Black Jack Pershing's personality, his ramrod attitude toward his troops. (Pershing's view, conditioned by his years in command of hard-bitten regulars, was that his men had to be toughened as much as possible for the misery of trench warfare. He wasn't there to provide them with a father figure; a man commanding almost two million men couldn't waste time being lovable. To a man of Broun's humane instincts, of course, this businesslike attitude was unacceptable.) In one story Heywood pointed out that Marshal Joffre, a fatherly but rather incompetent fellow, had been known to the French armies as "Papa" before he was replaced by less empathetic commanders. But as for Black Jack Pershing: "Nobody will ever call him 'Papa' Pershing. He is a stepfather to the inefficient and even when he is pleased he says little."

A Pershing inspection, he reported in another mailed dispatch to the *Tribune,* was about as pleasant as a mass infliction of the bastinado. After the general inspected one of the new infantry divisions and delivered his usual blistering critiques of the general sloppiness of citizen soldiers, Broun wrote, "The American Army is doing as well as could be expected."

Toward the end of 1917 Ruth Hale went back to the States to bear her child, since she and Heywood didn't want to take a chance on any difficulties over the child's citizenship. Heywood followed a few weeks later and arrived back in New York in January, 1918. The idea was that he would write a series of highly critical articles for the *Tribune* without running any risk of interference from the censorship. Then, perhaps, he would return to France for the bloody campaigns which would close out the war.

The *Tribune* was not inclined to throttle him down. It was a Republican organ generally opposed to President Woodrow Wilson and all his works, never forgetting the federal income tax he had maneuvered through Congress in 1913. Blasting the AEF was a way of getting at Wilson, the commander in chief. Already other newspapers were demanding that the censorship be relaxed so the public could be informed of the truth about the AEF situation, and Congress too was rumbling with complaints about the AEF's logistical failures.

Just about then came the first of Heywood's broadsides under the headline: SUPPLY BLUNDERS HAMPERED FIRST U.S. UNITS IN FRANCE. He wrote of troops in the field lacking guns, boots, warm clothing, decent food. Other articles hit hard at the AEF censorship, which seemed designed to protect the reputations of senior generals rather than foster military security. "A proper and intelligent public opinion," he wrote, "should not tolerate it." The inference he drew was that the army "seemed to doubt the courage of the American people" in facing any adverse reporting on the expeditionary force's problems.

His articles caused a considerable, though short-lived flurry in Congress. No doubt they helped to persuade the AEF to relax its censorship well before the American divisions took part in large-scale operations. They also aided in reforming the supply system, from the Washington end, first of all, then in a shake-up of the logistical command over in France.

In his role as a war correspondent Heywood first tried on the suit of crusader's armor which figuratively he would wear, mostly with distinction, throughout most of his career. He had discovered in himself a fighter's instincts which no one else, and probably not himself, had thought he possessed. They were aroused by the military caste system so offensive to a determined egalitarian, by the demands of military discipline so much an affront to a man almost aggressively undisciplined, by the clanking arrogance of men who wore the stars and braid of a general officer. They constituted the first Establishment which Heywood would bring under attack.

Meanwhile, back in France, Pershing's staff was collecting evidence against Broun, proof of his negative attitude toward the war effort. The G-2-D (press section) file on Heywood was fattened by clippings of his series in the *Tribune*. Pershing's aides considered much of his reporting, aside from the criticism of supply blunders, deliberately derogatory. The *Tribune* correspondent, it seemed to them, had paid too much attention to the standard griping of enlisted men; one could gather from Broun's series that the AEF was an aggregation of malcontents on the verge of mutiny. And every time a senior officer was portrayed, the correspondent made him out a pompous fool.

One of Pershing's staff drew up an indictment of Broun based on his G-2-D file, at the end of which it was announced that Broun's credentials were being revoked. Just then Major Palmer returned to AEF headquarters from a mission to Washington concerning the relaxation of censorship. Palmer had been promoted from chief press officer to confidential adviser to General Pershing. As a veteran newspaperman Palmer knew that revocation of Broun's credentials would be a public relations blunder—it would be seen as Pershing's revenge for Broun's barbed remarks.

"All right," Pershing told Palmer, tossing aside the denunciation of Broun, "to hell with it."

In March, Broun was still lingering in New York with no definite plans to return to France. He wasn't exactly charged up with eagerness to return to the western front; witnessing the predictable mass slaughter in the trenches wasn't something a sensitive man willingly inflicted on himself. In any event, the matter was taken out of his hands. In mid-March he wrote a story about eighteen major generals traveling to France on the same troopship which questioned the War Department's collective sanity in risking a whole batch of senior commanders on one vulnerable transport. As it turned out, Broun's story was based on faulty intelligence; it simply wasn't true, and thus the West Point Protective Association was enabled to swat one of its more persistent gadflies. Broun's correspondent's credentials were revoked and the *Tribune*'s $1,000 bond was seized by the War Department on charges that Broun had broken one rule too many.

It was of little comfort to the brass hats whom he had offended that Heywood Broun, with no further contact with their forces in France, was commissioned to write two books, *The AEF: With General Pershing and the American Forces* and *Our Army at the Front*, which he turned out at top speed in time for both to be published in 1918. They might observe that he produced two full-length books on the basis of six months behind the lines, but both were found acceptable by the public.

5. The Self-Discovery of a Columnist

HIS career as a military expert safely and permanently behind him, Heywood early in 1919 took up the position of presiding magistrate over literature and the drama as viewed from the editorial rooms of the New York *Tribune*. At thirty his stature as a journalist was increasing, and the editors of his paper decided to appoint him to wear two hats as both literary editor and editor of the drama page. In addition to presiding over the Saturday book page, he would turn out a thrice-weekly column, "Books and Things," which would indicate his appeal as a minor essayist, or columnist.

He could consider himself lucky in having a safe berth at the *Tribune*. Park Row was entering a period of violent flux. Frank Munsey, who had made a fortune in publishing magazines of no great distinction, had embarked on his career of cannibalizing the financially weaker New York newspapers. He had bought the New York *Herald* and *Evening Telegram* from James Gordon Bennett's estate, the *Morning* and *Evening Sun* from the Dana family; combined the *Morning Sun* and the *Herald*; bought the *Globe and Commercial Advertiser* and merged it with the *Evening Sun*; bought the *Evening Mail* and combined it with the *Evening Telegram*. He tried to move in on the *Tribune*, but the Reids still had the financial resources to ward him off, and eventually the *Tribune* bought the *Herald* and became the *Herald Tribune* until several decades later it too was merged out of existence.

Heywood was dug in securely at the *Tribune*, and at the moment job security was important to him. Ruth had given birth to their son, Heywood Hale Broun, on March 10, 1918. He and his wife and infant son were established in an old and gloomy but comfortable apartment building at Seventh Avenue and Fifty-fifth Street. If things continued to go well, he hoped to buy a house in Manhattan. The Heywood Broun of the immediate postwar years was almost as settled and bourgeois as his father.

His problem was how to expand from his journalistic base. The careers of all too many newspapermen were short and brutish. You had to lift yourself from the ruck of the city room or risk ending up prematurely on the slag pile, burned out at forty. One form of security could be found in the upper echelon of the editorial department, among the executives, but Heywood had found he had little taste for ordering other men around, that he lacked the executive corpuscles. Aside from the editors and a few highly paid stars like the late Richard Harding Davis, the real luminaries were the columnists like Don Marquis of the *Sun* with his fables about archy the cockroach and mehitabel the cat, Franklin P. Adams with his diary, Finley Peter Dunne and his Mr. Dooley. They pulled in circulation and drew salaries commensurate to that pull.

The trouble with most newspaper work was that it was so anonymous. You could do brilliant work for years and be known only to your peers. What you had to do, Broun figured, was to personalize your work, make yourself stand out as an individual with the newspaper reader. The personal pronoun (singular) had to be worked in to establish an intimacy with the reader, though editors were inclined to slash away at copy which stressed the writer's personal opinions, to become disgruntled with "picket-fence writing," that is, sentences with too many "I's." Editors wanted to keep their staffs blanketed in anonymity as much as possible because big names meant bigger payrolls.

Broun labored to establish himself as a journalistic personality in his "Books and Things" columns. It was supposed to be about current literature, but Heywood often strayed from that territory to write about "things" rather than "books." One of his earliest subjects was his infant son, whom he referred to in print as "H. the 3rd." Heywood dragged in H. the 3rd in discussing a book which presumed to tell mothers how to raise their children and especially inveighed against using baby talk with children. Heywood, on the advice of H. the 3rd, as he claimed, argued that it was parents, not babies, who insisted on baby talk.

In his discussions of the new postwar school of novelists Heywood also attracted attention to himself by forcefully expressing his opinions at a time when book reviewing was still a rather genteel occupation and harsh criticism was regarded as unmannerly. The new stars on the literary horizon were vigorous young men like Sinclair Lewis, Scott Fitzgerald, James Branch Cabell, and others whose candor, Heywood felt, demanded the utmost candor from a reviewer.

His feeling that their honesty called for equal honesty in criticism was, however, a serious misjudgment of the literary personality. The novelist who is grateful for a salutary shriving of his misdeeds is the rarest member of his species. Sinclair Lewis would blossom like an orchid under Broun's praise of *Main Street* as "almost disconcertingly good." So would the romantic novelist Leonard Merrick, now all but forgotten but praised to the skies by Broun for *The Worldlings* and *Conrad in Quest of His Youth.* James Branch Cabell's *Jurgen*, regarded by Broun and other contemporaries as a masterpiece, though its labored style would not recommend it to a later generation, was also defended with vigor in "Books and Things." The successors to Anthony Comstock decried the sexual symbolism in *Jurgen* and demanded its suppression, but Heywood naturally, as an inveterate civil libertarian, rose to its defense.

Oddly enough, the sensational debut of young Scott Fitzgerald with his novel *This Side of Paradise* did not cause Broun to throw his battered hat in the air.

Fitzgerald's picture of flaming Ivy League youth and his glossy hero, Amory Blaine, seemed overwrought and self-infatuated to the conductor of "Books and Things." In his review Broun critized the callowness of Fitzgerald's approach and said he doubted whether the author was really as old as twenty-three, as the dust jacket claimed. The characters were "male flappers." Regarding the protagonist, he wrote, "We are afraid that not a few undergraduates are given to the sin of not kissing and then telling anyway." As for the author, Broun considered him a "rather complacent, somewhat pretentious, and altogether self-conscious young man."

Those gibes brought him scores of letters from readers who had discovered *This Side of Paradise* and felt it spoke for them. Heywood still would not be swayed. He conceded that there were passages of "fine writing," but he could not "catch the glint in it of greatness not yet fully attained but on the way." Fitzgerald invited Broun to lunch and huffily remarked that it was a pity Broun (then only thirty-one, after all) had let life's big parade pass him by and was so bitter with regret over his lack of accomplishment that he couldn't appreciate the fresh genius of

This Side of Paradise. Broun was one of the few critical holdouts against the general acclaim for Fitzgerald's first novel. He did manage to find a few kind words for Fitzgerald's short story collection *Flappers and Philosophers,* and a year or two later, when he had left the *Tribune* for the *World,* he tried to recruit Fitzgerald as a feature writer.

Wearing his theatrical hat, as editor of the drama page and writer of a Sunday feature on the new plays, he also refused to be impressed by another burgeoning talent, that of Eugene O'Neill. The unremitting tragedy of *Beyond the Horizon* depressed Heywood, who believed there was more banality than high drama in real life. It was time that playwrights like young O'Neill, he wrote, realized that "the most moving tragedies are those in which people go on living."

Five and a half decades later those critical judgments appear to have been reversed on appeal to the high court of posterity. Fitzgerald and O'Neill are accorded a deathless quality while Lewis and Cabell have steadily faded from literary consciousness.

Literary tastes were an important matter to any intelligent young man, as he advised a reader who wrote to him asking his help in dealing with a young woman who didn't care much for reading. Broun's faithful reader wanted him to suggest a list of fifty books which he would present to the girl he was in love with. If she showed any signs of appreciation for that feast of literature, he would go ahead with plans to marry her; otherwise he did not want to be trapped in marriage with a woman of uncultivated tastes.

Heywood replied with tongue-in-cheek solicitude for his reader's problem. "Of course," he wrote in his column, "it would be a great deal easier for us to advise the young man if we knew just what sort of wife he wanted. If she likes *Dombey and Son* and *Little Dorrit* it seems to us fair to assume that she will be able to do a little plain mending and some of the cooking. On the other hand, if her favorite author is May Sinclair, we rather think it would be well to be prepared to provide hired help from the beginning. . . .

"Since marriage is at best a gamble, we advise him earnestly not to compromise his ardor with any dreary round of fifty books. Let him chance it all on a single volume. And what shall it be? Personally, we have always been strongly attracted by persons who liked *Joan and Peter,* but we know that there are excellent wives and mothers who find this particular novel of Wells' dreary stuff. There are certain likes and dislikes which might well serve as green signals of caution."

If the girl couldn't find such works as *Conrad in Search of His Youth, Tono-Bungay, Far From the Madding Crowd,* or especially *Huckleberry Finn* suitable for her literary palate, the suitor should "by all means stipulate a long engagement." If she confessed to a dislike for *Alice in Wonderland,* the case was hopeless. "It is then his plain duty to tell her that he has made a mistake and that what he took for love was no more than the passing infatuation of physical passion."

In branching out from purely literary and theatrical concerns, columnist Broun often found himself at odds not only with the conservative readership of the *Tribune,* which was probably the No. 1 breakfast-table choice of Park Avenue and the Westchester suburbs, but in conflict with the paper's editorial policy. The *Tribune* was hard-rock Republican and found it glorious when Warren G. Harding succeeded Woodrow Wilson in the White House. It was also devoted to Christian ideals and an abhorrence of the sinfulness that had always afflicted the metropolis. But its totems and heroes were not Heywood Broun's. He was already finding causes and standard-bearers leftward of the Harding Administration's ideal of "normalcy." And though he was not prominent enough as a columnist to pull in circulation on the strength of his by-line, he defied the prejudices of the executive suite and expressed himself, with increasing boldness, in opposition to the policies stated on the editorial page.

He vigorously panned a book by Dr. Nicholas Murray Butler, the president of Columbia and the guru of Republican intellectuals, who was the idol of the *Tribune*'s editors and readership. The hellfire fundamentalist Reverend John Roach Stratton of the Calvary Baptist Church toured New York's night life and reported, for the edification of his parishioners and a deputation from Park Row, that Manhattan was outdoing Sodom in its pursuit of sinful pleasures, that it was a "gluttonous monster without ideals or restraints." The *Tribune* respectfully reported the Reverend Stratton's jeremiad, though knowledgeable New Yorkers could recall that a publicity-thirsting evangel rose at least once a generation from the Manhattan pulpits to make a name for himself as a sin killer. Heywood was largely unimpressed by Stratton's vocalizing; it was too damn easy to deplore

naughtiness from a pastor's study without offering any alternatives. He slyly observed that if Sodom's fate were visited on New
York, Stratton would glance back and be turned into a pillar of
salt, like Lot's wife, not out of regret for the city's destruction but
to see whether the last banner headlines published on Park Row
credited him with having foretold the retribution.

It must have seemed to the *Tribune*'s executives that Broun had
appointed himself the house nay sayer, had determined to act as
the loyal opposition to everything the paper stood for or against.
Most right-thinking New Yorkers approved when the state
legislature kicked out five Socialists who had been elected legally
enough from Manhattan assembly districts, but Broun sided with
Governor Alfred E. Smith and the minority in demanding that
they be seated. He also deplored the activities of the Attorney
General's office in rounding up foreign-born radicals and
deporting them by the thousands. He expressed sympathy for the
imprisoned Socialist leader Eugene V. Debs as a victim of
wartime hysteria. As he saw it, every newspaper should make
house room for one or more dissidents who, for the sake of
balance, would contest the revealed wisdom on its editorial page.
A great newspaper could afford to provide a platform for the
voices of dissent. Doubtless the "new journalism" born in the
sixties, with its practitioners taking an active partisan stance on
issues rather than striving for objectivity, would have greatly
pleased him.

With his career progressing nicely, Heywood must have been a
happy man in the early twenties. He was a prideful father and an
attentive husband. The world seemed a better place, now that
the League of Nations promised to keep Woodrow Wilson's
pledge that the last of all wars had been fought; Harding had
not, after all, turned the clock back to the Hayes Administration;
the women had been granted the right to vote, and capitalism
was holding out the promise of a car in every garage and a
striped silk shirt for every workingman's back. The gaiety of the
decade had not yet become frenetic, and the postwar prosperity
had not yet attained the flushed and feverish aspect it would
acquire as the stock market rocketed to greater heights than
anyone had imagined possible. Prohibition was, of course,
irksome. Instead of quaffing openly in a well-run saloon on Park
Row, he and millions of his fellow citizens had to slip into

speakeasies and break the law—not that they weren't in good company, neither the President of the United States nor the governor of New York having gone on the wagon when the dry laws took effect—every time they wanted to wet their whistles. In the old-time saloons, he observed, the drinker at least didn't have to fight his way to the bar "through a crowd of schoolgirls." As the dozen-year experiment with enforced abstinence proceeded, Broun would grow increasingly bitter. He became especially critical of President Hoover's messages to Congress on the subject, commenting that he didn't see how it was possible for the man to say he loved the Constitution and also the amendment which, through the government's almost total inability to enforce it, was bringing the Constitution into such disrepute. "One might as well maintain that he is for both the heroine and the villain who threatens her, Red Riding Hood and the wolf, Nancy Sikes and also Bill."

Aside from the perils of drinking bathtub gin in various horrendous mixtures (orange blossoms, gin bucks, and other concoctions designed to disguise the flavor of the prime ingredient), Heywood and Ruth jointly presided over a cheerful and vibrant household. Its keynote of informality was sounded when their son, Woodie, was encouraged to call his parents by their first names, which was then a rather daring innovation. They had established themselves in a three-story brownstone at 333 West Eighty-fifth Street, close to the apartment-house palisades of Riverside Drive, which Heywood bought with the help of three mortgages. Sunday nights they entertained with steak dinners prepared by Edward McNamara, an ex-policeman with a magnificent voice which had recommended him to the concert stage, who would be a family intimate for many years. Mild tippling was the rule at their Sunday-night gatherings, and only occasionally was there an outbreak of unpleasantness at a Broun-Hale party. One such incident occurred when Jules Bledsoe, the original Joe of Jerome Kern's musical *Show Boat*, sang "Under the Bamboo Tree." One line ran, "I'm gonna change your name." When the black singer reached that line, Ruth Hale hissed so loudly Bledsoe had to stop singing in bewilderment.

Neither motherhood nor the federal legislation formally granting women their rights had satisfied Ruth Hale's feminist urges. She was more determined than ever to organize, propagandize, and demonstrate for the further liberation of her sex—most particularly for the right of women to retain their maiden names after marriage. Anyone who forgetfully or out of ignorance of her attitudes called Ruth Hale "Mrs. Broun" was rewarded with a scorching lecture. A more organized campaign for the independence of married women was soon under way.

Because of the housing shortage following the war, the Brouns were sharing their brownstone with Harold Ross and Jane Grant, who were married. Ross was a member of the old *Stars and Stripes* crowd in Paris, Miss Grant, like Miss Hale, a writer and feminist. The unpolished but ambitious Ross, formerly a wandering newspaperman, Western-born, and determinedly anti-metropolitan, was rattling around the magazine world trying to find a footing, which several years later he would with the founding of the phenomenally successful *New Yorker* magazine. Unlike Broun, who had fallen into line almost immediately after Miss Hale expounded her ideas, the tactless and profane Ross was not inclined to be tolerant of Miss Hale's and Miss Grant's flaming activism on the feminist front; he wearied of the constant speechmaking, the denunciation of masculine attitudes, around the household he was sharing.

"Why the hell," he one day roared at Miss Hale and Miss Grant, "don't you women hire a hall?"

They decided that was good, if ill-tempered, advice and on May 18, 1921, called a meeting of all persons interested in furthering the cause of women's rights. The organization, it was decided at the meeting held in the Hotel Pennsylvania, would be called the Lucy Stone League.

Its purpose was to establish a woman's right to be known by her maiden name after marriage, and it is still a going concern. Fittingly enough, it was named for the pioneer in that effort, a doughty little woman who had participated in the feminist struggle before and after the Civil War, when such activists met a lot more opposition and scorn than they did in the tolerant 1920's. As one historian of the movement has written, "Of all the rebels against male dominance none has survived the erosion of years more engagingly than Lucy Stone. None was readier, if need be, to face those blazing faggots of suffrage verse, none was quite half so consistent in the demand for equal rights before the law. When late in life, at thirty-seven, she took a husband, she did not become Mrs. Henry Blackwell but remained Lucy Stone, either Miss or Mrs., it was all the same to her, the first married woman to keep her name. It was one way to give point to the claim that she was an individual human being and dramatically effective to register protest that *this* woman was not to be sold 'like a beast to the highest bidder.' She had been heard to remark that no more legal respect was paid to a woman's marriage 'than a farmer pays to the conjunctions of his swine.' "

After obtaining a college education, Lucy Stone proceeded to turn the power structure of masculinity on its ear, converted Susan B. Anthony and Julia Ward Howe to the cause of women's rights, and made the term "Lucy Stoner" synonymous with any female who stood up for her individual rights. She spent decades campaigning across the country and addressing rallies despite the interference of ruffianly males. As some indication of the following she and her cohorts attracted, they obtained 400,000 signatures on a petition for emancipation which was presented to Congress.

The first membership list of the Lucy Stone League contained only fifty names, two of them men. Along with the literary critic Francis Hackett, Heywood joined the organization. No doubt he believed in the league's principles, but his membership also preserved domestic harmony with the strong-minded Ruth Hale. Harold Ross' name, however, was not to be found on its rolls; he was one of those old-fashioned hypermasculine types the league's activities were aimed at. Doubtless Broun and Hackett suffered at the hands of fellow males who believed that they had already been too generous in giving women their civil rights.

Ruth Hale was elected president of the Lucy Stone League, Jane Grant secretary-treasurer, and Beulah Livingstone vice-president. Its principles were forcefully expressed in a booklet written by Miss Hale: "We are repeatedly asked why we resent taking one man's name instead of another's—why, in other words, we object to taking a husband's name, when all we have anyhow is a father's name. Perhaps the shortest answer to that is that in the time since it was our father's name it has become our own—that between birth and marriage a human being has grown up, with all the emotions, thoughts, activities, etc., of any new person. Sometimes it is helpful to reserve an image we have too long looked on, as a painter might turn his canvas to a mirror to catch, by a new alignment, faults he might have overlooked from growing used to them. . . .

"What would any man answer if told that he should change his name when he married, because his original name was, after all, only his father's? Even aside from the fact that I am more truly described by the name of my father, whose flesh and blood I am, than I would be by that of my husband, who is merely a co-worker with me—however loving—in a certain social enterprise, am I myself not to be counted for anything?"

The Lucy Stone League snowballed, under the efforts of its highly articulate directorate, to a membership of five thousand. It provided Ruth Hale with a cause and a career of her own, frustrated as she had felt herself to be by the failure of her artistic ambitions and later by her inability to achieve stature as a writer. She continued to be the mainstay of Heywood's flourishing career, his most unsparing critic, his personal gadfly. A good share of his success was attributable to Ruth Hale's influence, as he was always the first to admit. Ruth kept him stirred up. She may not have actually booted him into the many controversies which marked his career, but without her he probably would not have joined so many crusades or shaped himself into a top-ranking public enemy of the surviving puritanism in American life and its reluctance to undertake social reforms. It would be easy to imagine that if Heywood had never met Ruth, he would have stayed an amiable, boozy member of the sportswriting fraternity. Easy, but unjust. He simply warmed to combat a lot quicker under Ruth's goading.

If he ever hoped that time would mellow her, that gradually she would submerge her own identity in an atmosphere of domestic tranquillity, he was to be sorely disappointed. Ruth only became more vigorously feminist and independent. She threw herself into the struggle when the City Council attempted to pass an ordinance prohibiting women from smoking in restaurants. She insisted that she and Heywood lead separate lives, to the extent that they made their own friends and lived on separate floors of their three-story brownstone on the West Side.

Heywood accepted all this and made it plain his acceptance was based on principle rather than the conventional wish of a browbeaten husband to appease an aggressive woman. In an essay written during the time of the Lucy Stone League's organization, he wrote that the oldest masculine ploy in history was a man's claim that he had no aptitude for domestic chores or for sharing in the responsibility for rearing children. Men had been getting away for centuries, he noted, with the claim that household chores required some special knack, which only the female was born with. Men claimed they couldn't sew on a button even though they could build railroads across deserts and mountains.

It was especially fallacious to argue that men couldn't share in the delicate business of caring for a child. "Most things that have to be done for children are of the simplest sort. They should tax the intelligence of no one. Men profess a total lack of ability to wash baby's face simply because they believe there's no great fun in the business, at either end of the sponge. Protectively, man must go the whole distance and pretend that there is not one single thing which he can do for baby. He must even maintain that he doesn't know how to hold one. From this pretense has grown the shockingly transparent fallacy that holding a baby correctly is one of the fine arts; or, perhaps even more fearsome than that, a wonderful intuition, which has come down after centuries of effort to women only. . . . There are one hundred and fifty-two distinctly different ways of holding a baby—and all are right!' "

Helping to care for his child from infancy on, he urged, would add immeasurably to rounding out a man's life. "I have no feeling of being a traitor to my sex, when I say that I believe in at least a rough equality of parenthood. In shirking all the business of caring for children we have escaped much hard labor. It has been convenient. Perhaps it has been too convenient. If we have avoided arduous tasks, we have also missed much fun of a very special kind. Like children in a toy shop, we have chosen to live with the most amusing of walking-and-talking dolls, without ever attempting to tear down the sign which says 'Do not touch.' "

It would even be good for the masculine ego, he argued, if men shared in child rearing. In a child's eyes, a man would assume godlike proportions for the first and only time in his life. "He is a veritable Adam and you loom up in his life as more than mortal. Golf is well enough for a Sunday sport, but it is a trifling thing beside the privilege of taking a small son to the zoo and letting him see his first lion, his first tiger and, best of all, his first elephant. Perhaps he will think that they are part of your own handiwork turned out for his pleasure. To a child, at least, even the meanest of us may seem glamorous with magic and wisdom. It seems a pity not to take the fullest advantage of this before the opportunity is lost. There must come a day when even the most nimble-witted father has to reply, 'I don't know.' "

It was just as well that Heywood came to conclusions on what a modern marriage should be, which jigsawed neatly with Ruth's unconventional concepts. If he had been one of those male supremacists who still abounded in the nation, the marriage would hardly have lasted a year. Since he was amenable even to her Lucy Stoner activism, he managed to keep a partner indispensable to him as a frequently controversial crusading journalist.

6. Under the Golden Dome

IF one newspaper could be said to have represented the good and brave and trustworthy in American journalism, to have served most faithfully as the people's surrogate, it was the New York *World*. Its glory as a journalistic institution may be recaptured now only in the brittle, yellowing files of its thousands of issues, but to most objective newspaper historians its eminence has never been equaled.

During its heyday it was the Mecca, the Vatican, the Great Temple of the newspaper industry. In the 1920's the fourteen-story building capped with a golden dome was still the Pharos light of American journalism. When the Hungarian-Jewish immigrant Joseph Pulitzer came to New York and rescued the *World* from the corrupt ownership of Jay Gould, he proclaimed, "There is room in this great and growing city for a journal that is not only cheap but bright, not only bright but large, not only large but truly democratic—dedicated to the cause of the people rather than that of the purse potentates—devoted more to the news of the new than the old world, that will expose all fraud and sham, fight all public evils and abuses—that will serve and battle for the people with earnest sincerity. . . ." And to a large degree that promise had been kept.

By 1921 Joseph Pulitzer had been dead for ten years, his place taken if not completely filled by his son Ralph, but the *World* with its powerhouse of reportorial and editorial talent was still humming along. The *Herald* had fallen into Frank Munsey's hands and also the *Sun*; and the *Times* had not yet attained the dominance it was to acquire largely through default. The *Daily News* had been reborn as a lively and prospering tabloid. Only the *World* could still claim to be a national newspaper, the one even a Republican in the White House, occasionally grimacing, would regard as required reading at the breakfast table. Foreign correspondents based in this country would quote the *World* before any other newspaper. It had that magisterial quality that made it sound as though its editorial board ranked with cabinet ministers. And yet only ten years later it too foundered, and its logotype, but not its animating spirit, was transferred to a more businesslike ownership.

The New York *Times* even then was putting forth the claim that it was *the* paper of record, the indispensable daily guide to current events. Under the senior Pulitzer the *World* would probably have challenged that boast. In the twenties the paper was still making money, but Pulitzer's three sons and heirs drained off the profits rather than modernizing the *World*'s plant or increasing its editorial payroll. The Pulitzers' editors therefore had to maintain the *World*'s position by making it more interesting, lively, and enterprising, without stationing correspondents all over the globe. During the twenties, as one admirer wrote, it was a "bright and glistening candle in the singularly materialistic and conscienceless times."

Much of its spirited quality was credited, not only to the brilliant journalistic talent attracted to the *World* building on Park Row but to the swashbuckling executive editor, Herbert Bayard Swope, a self-propelled rocket from the day he stepped into its city room as a young reporter, and Frank I. Cobb, the editor of the editorial page and a man of the most unassailable integrity. Swope's credo, in the absence of plentiful funds, was, "Pick out the best story of the day and hammer the hell out of it."

Not since the salad days of Richard Harding Davis had any newspaperman possessed the persuasive quality of Herbert Bayard Swope. Red-haired, with a prowlike jaw and a jaunty, well-tailored figure, a man of cyclonic energies, he had battled his way up through the reportorial ranks to the city desk, had imposed a field marshal's presence on World War I as something more than a correspondent and less than a plenipotentiary, and had published the first account of the Versailles Treaty and the League of Nations covenant. "He is as easy to ignore as a cyclone," as the late Stanley Walker, the celebrated city editor of the New York *Herald Tribune*, wrote. "His gift of gab is a torrential and terrifying thing. He is probably the most charming extrovert in the western world. His brain is crammed with a million oddments of information, and only a dolt would make a bet with him on an issue concerning facts. . . . In the days when he was a dynamic practicing journalist in New York, many other newspapermen were distinguished by their gall and brass, but the man who stood out among his fellows, like a snorting Caesar in a company of Caspar Milquetoasts, was Herbert Bayard Swope. . . . He met all the big men of that momentous time, and he met them as an equal. He played golf with Lord Northcliffe. He captivated Queen Marie of Rumania. He put his hand to limericks to please President Wilson. This, then, was history, and Herbert Bayard Swope was in the middle of it, helping make it." Swope was what his English friends would call a thruster, an egocentric if not an egomaniac, but he had a quality few such men possess—he was ambitious for himself but he also joyously pushed along other men to success, got the best out of them, and made them share in his enjoyment of achievement. As one of his star reporters, later a highly successful Hollywood writer, Dudley Nichols said, Swope "always loved nothing better than pushing the strong around and giving a hand to the weak."

It was that vivacity of temperament with which Swope infused the *World*; otherwise it might have been moribund after the senior Pulitzer's death. "What I try to do in my paper," Swope once told Heywood Broun, "is to give the public part of what it wants and part of what it ought to have whether it wants it or not." In the *World*'s news columns its readership got what it wanted; in its editorial page it got what it ought, by Swope's reckoning, to have—a strong dose of liberal humanism as exemplified by the ideals of the Democratic Party.

Swope labored endlessly to make the *World* more exciting, without succumbing to sensationalism, while entrusting the integrity of his editorial page to Frank I. Cobb. Thus he invented the opposite editorial page, more familiarly known as the op ed page. When he became executive editor, the page following the editorials was a mélange of book and play reviews, obituaries and society chitchat. That page, he finally decided, should be made into something more significant—a sort of no-man's-land between the fact in the news columns and the principles enunciated on the editorial page, a place where opinion could be given free play. As he later wrote a colleague on how he had concocted the op ed page, he had long observed both as a reporter and later as city editor that "the opinion stories which had crept in, in spite of our hard and fast principle of having little or no opinion in our news columns, had been dominantly interesting. It occurred to me that nothing is more interesting than opinion when opinion is interesting, so I devised a method of cleaning off the page opposite the editorial, which became the most important in America . . . and thereon I decided to print opinions, ignoring facts."

Not only did Swope preside at the genesis of the sort of columns presently produced by Jack Anderson, Evans and Novak, Joseph Kraft, Mary McGrory, William F. Buckley, Jr., William Safire, Tom Wicker, James Reston, et al., but he created a dazzling one-ring circus, in which the brightest and most opinionated journalists then available each did their star turn.

Swope quickly enlisted as columnists, most of them on a three-times-a-week basis, Alexander Woollcott, Franklin P. Adams, Deems Taylor, Samuel Chotzinoff, Harry Hansen, Laurence Stallings, St. John Ervine, and later William Bolitho, the author of the classic *Twelve Against the Gods.* Heywood Broun joined the galaxy. He was not enlisted, but volunteered himself downtown from the *Tribune.*

Op ed page within a year became a combination of lively political comment and what would later be called cultural reportage, which fifty years ago was a daring departure for American journalism, the first principle of which was that a newspaper, to be successful, had to be designed to be read by a man hanging onto the strap of a subway car. It may not have been as stimulating and effulgent as it seems in retrospect; the interplay of journalistic ego is not always as fascinating as it appears to those involved. "At times it was flat," as Swope's biographer has remarked, "and at other times excessively cute, but for a daily commodity it was consistently good. And it was fresh in both senses of the word. Its contributors were encouraged by Swope, who never wrote a line for it himself, to say whatever they liked, restricted only by the laws of libel and the dictates of taste. To keep their stuff from sounding stale, moreover, he refused to build up a bank of ready-to-print columns; everybody wrote his copy for the following day's paper." Paradoxically, however, "while the op ed page attracted a devoted and enthusiastic following among New York's intellectuals, their delight in it seemed to point up ever more strongly the disparity between the *World*'s two main groups of readers—the urbane and cultured on the one hand, who for straight news, though, often preferred the *Times*; and on the other hand a larger body who seemed to prefer the rest of the *World* to its op ed page and who comprised what Ralph Pulitzer called 'the lower fringe of population.' "

Heywood Broun signed on as a member of that fiercely articulate and rampantly individualistic crew in the summer of 1921.

One day he called Swope and asked for an oar in the op ed page galley.

Why, Swope asked, did he want to switch from the *Tribune* to the *World*?

Because, Broun replied, there was more "freedom of expression" for a writer on the staff of the liberal *World* than the conservative *Tribune*.

It seemed a decent motive to Swope, whose attention had already been attracted by Broun's columns in the *Tribune*, so he told Broun to come down and discuss the matter. They quickly arrived at a decision: Broun would write a column titled "It Seems to Me" for the *World*'s op ed page as well as taking on other chores as a cultural reporter. Swope did not tell Broun what he should write, only that it be provocative, controversial, outspoken.

Swope and Broun became contemporary journalism's odd couple. Close as they were socially as well as professionally, Broun would always address him as "Mr. Swope," even when drinking his bootleg scotch. He was wary, as he made plain to Swope, of all men in positions of authority, even in the comradely atmosphere of a newspaper office, and he insisted with more than a touch of whimsy that a squire-varlet distancing between them was necessary to maintaining a proper relationship.

Swope would remain on the most affectionate terms with Broun until the latter's death, but could never stifle his repugnance for Broun's perennial leadership in the worst-dressed-man-of-Manhattan category. There were Bowery bums who rose from their slumbers in an alley more carefully groomed than Broun, who, he felt, should make some effort to dress up to his position as a star contributor to the *World*. It became one of the few unsuccessful causes of Swope's career to make over Broun into a well-groomed citizen.

Swope, who never had fewer than seventy-five beautifully tailored suits in his closet, once persuaded Broun to come to a first-class tailor's with him. A fine piece of material was selected, then cut to Broun's measure, which was that of a bear before going into hibernation. Swope hoped that expert piece of tailoring would encourage Broun to take some interest in his appearance. Instead, as with any off-the-rack garment, Broun wore it daily until it was ready for the ragpicker.

In tones ringing with despair, Swope would often recall how he and Broun once made a journey to Florida, where they shared a hotel room. One morning Swope awakened to find Broun standing at the window, holding up the baggy seat of his trousers to the sunlight streaming in. The sun was also streaming *through* the trousers, and only a few frayed threads stood between their owner and an arrest for indecent exposure.

"Looks as though they'll last another day," Swope heard Broun murmuring to himself.

If Swope was constantly appalled by Broun's total lack of interest in his personal appearance, Broun was often bemused by the supercharged aspect of the Swope persona.

Others had observed that a room charged with the Swope presence could be called a "Swope-filled room" (the pun was credited to book publisher M. Lincoln Schuster). Broun agreed that in any gathering Swope was likely to use up more than his share of the available supply of oxygen, particularly in the councils of the New York *World*'s high command. "Whenever two or more executives are gathered together," he remarked, "you have a group. Indeed, in my early days in journalism I always felt that when Herbert Bayard Swope gathered together this was group enough for me."

Several years after Broun signed as a *World* performer he compiled a list of the nation's greatest and most persistent conversationalists—an All-American Talking Team, as he styled it. Among its members were Swope, of course, Clarence Darrow, George Jean Nathan, Max Eastman, Irvin S. Cobb, Alfred E. Smith, Alice Roosevelt Longworth, Dorothy Parker, Alexander Woollcott, Will Rogers, and Floyd Dell. Discussing his team of raconteurs on a radio program, Broun admitted that he included Swope on his list with some trepidation because, even in such a lineup, the other members wouldn't be able to get a word in edgewise against the torrential flow from Swope. He recalled a dinner he had attended with Swope, H. G. Wells, and six Japanese newspapermen:

"These Oriental journalists were anxious to learn what the great English novelist thought about a number of topics, but they let him get all the way to his demitasse in peace. Then the spokesman for the Japanese began the interrogation. I forget what the question was. I think it had something to do with birth control, but it doesn't matter. Mr. Wells started to answer—and it was going to be at length, I guess—that is if one can judge by the writing of H. G. Wells. But this time he made a fatal mistake—he paused to clear his throat—erhem, like that—and no man can afford to take a chance like that while Swope's around. He's as quick as a Notre Dame halfback to see an opening. H. G. Wells never got started this time. He cleared his throat to no purpose, for the booming voice of my beloved boss cut through the respectful silence of the Japanese journalists, and he spoke up loud and clear, saying, 'I think Mr. Wells means to say about as follows.' And for the next half hour he held us all—including H. G. Wells—spellbound."

With a boss like that, one who was constantly protecting his op ed page stable from a business manager who objected to the relatively high salaries they were paid, Heywood Broun was a happy man. Undoubtedly his years under the *World*'s golden dome were, professionally, the happiest of his career. He and the rest of Swope's quasi-intellectual circus were quartered in cramped cubicles in the dome, on the thirteenth and fourteenth floors, just above the city room. Above them, on the topmost floor, were the *World*'s editorial writers, who included three future luminaries, the historian Allan Nevins, the novelist James M. Cain, and the playwright Maxwell Anderson, whose prose made the *World*'s editorial page rumble like a thunder sheet whenever wrongdoing was detected in the land.

Broun shared a cubicle with Deems Taylor, the music critic, and Alison Smith, the first wife of playwright Russel Crouse, who was the assistant music critic and assistant dramatic critic. When he first moved over to the *World*, Broun not only turned out three "It Seems to Me" columns a week but acted as dramatic critic and produced a book column for the Sunday edition, in addition to contributing regularly to *Collier's, Judge, Vanity Fair,* and the *Atlantic Monthly*. Soon, however, he was relieved of his drama critic's portfolio when Alexander Woollcott joined the group under the dome.

He was given all the latitude he required, at the moment, in expressing himself as the *World*'s chief gadfly. Even then his political stance was considerably to the left of the *World*'s editorial policy, which was that of the progressive wing of the Democratic Party, was anti-Tammany and proreform and was liberal to an extent modern liberals would find lacking. Under Swope's protective wing Broun, until a near-fatal collision with the *World*'s more conservative viewpoint, was able to write what he wanted on any topic he chose.

And there was a cheerfully ribald atmosphere in the cubicles under the dome which must have reminded him of beery nights in a Harvard dormitory. Franklin P. Adams, who conducted "The Conning Tower" on the opposite editorial page after following Broun over to the *World* from the *Tribune* several months later, wrote, "Never had I known such fun in a newspaper office as I had the first few years on the *World*. Whatever office politics there may have been, I was unaffected, for nobody wanted my job and I didn't want anybody's. . . . Often there were discussions and violent, abusive arguments lasting three hours. . . . There were fights—generally by telephone—with my technical boss, Mr. Swope, sir, who never changed a line, in or out, of mine, except once, when he saved me, by changing something that had become untrue between the time that I wrote it, at 3 P.M., and 8:30 P.M."

Samuel Chotzinoff, who succeeded Deems Taylor as music critic, recalled that in the *World*'s atelier "Everyone was charming and sympathetic. The place in its disorder and untidiness was a realization of what I had hoped it would be, and I was blissfully happy. . . ." The owlish and laconic Franklin P. Adams, as he remembered, was the only one of what less privileged members of the *World* staff called "Swope's prima donnas" who demanded a modicum of privacy, while the gregarious Broun wandered happily through the cubicles on the thirteenth and fourteenth floors. "F.P.A. was the only man on the floor who had a room to himself, and I caught a glimpse of that lanky sage at his typewriter, serenely oblivious of what I then thought was a vast disorder around him. In those days F.P.A.'s door generally stood half open. The partitions of his little room did not join the ceiling and he was constantly subjected to visits from his colleagues and the intellectual (?) noises that floated in from the dramatic-movie-music department. But his rebellion was not slow in manifesting itself, and presently carpenters had made his den air tight." Furthermore, Adams posted a sign on his closed door warning that "this is not the office of Heywood Broun, Alexander Woollcott, Quinn Martin, Laurence Stallings, Samuel Chotzinoff, Alison Smith, Herbert Swope, Louis Weitzenkorn or Mrs. Ober [the society editor]."

The talents of that group assembled by Swope are apparent to anyone familiar with the theatrical, literary, and journalistic history of the period between the world wars. Stallings soon wrote the Broadway hit and Hollywood film *What Price Glory?*; Weitzenkorn the definitive play about tabloid journalism, *Five-Star Final.* Chotzinoff became the country's leading music critic. In a late-blooming development of his career F.P.A. became a radio star as a member of the *Information, Please* panel. The city room on the floor below, too, was loaded with talent. One year after Broun joined the *World*, Frank Sullivan, a longtime friend of Broun's and a future luminary of American humor, walked across City Hall Park from the *Evening Sun* to congratulate executive editor Swope on having the wit to hire him away from the *Sun* and also, offhandedly, to ask for an advance on his salary. He never got in a word of his speech. He found Swope simultaneously—he swears—dictating to his secretary, firing orders at two other aides, and barking over the phone to Governor Al Smith in Albany. "My speech," he recalled, "was not delivered as planned. It was not delivered at all. H.B.S., however, gave me a trenchant address on the ethics of journalism in general, the place of the *World* in particular, my own good fortune in being tapped for that paper, the influence of Stanton in Lincoln's Cabinet, the best method for making raised biscuits, the Tacna-Arnica dispute, and the Schick test for scarlet fever. I went to work and immediately lapsed into obscurity."

Of all his colleagues, Adams found Broun the most fascinating, not only for his journalistic skill but for an "unfathomable" and elusive quality in his character; even those who knew him best, Adams believed, were aware that "he had depths that we never plumbed."

His unassuming quality, coupled with an all-conquering charm, made Broun the most attractive of men to Adams. "Broun was a debunker of any kind of pretentiousness," as Adams sized him up, "political, official, or literary. He hated bunk so much that he dressed carelessly and sketchily, because a man may be a fop and a villain still; he was the sort of man who would wear three hats in an elevator because he knew that some men would consider their entire duty and responsibility to women discharged when they removed their hats.

"He hated injustice and intolerance; seldom did he dislike those he considered unjust or intolerant. He was a lion in print, but a lamb in his personal relationships. Men whom he attacked in print would invite him to lunch; he'd go, and the victim of his wrath would fall to his charm.

"Heywood, for twenty years or so, must have earned lots of money. He cared less for money than anybody I knew; he was the most avaricious person I knew. If he won $100 in a poker game, he'd settle for $90 cash rather than wait until the next afternoon for a check. Yet he would say that he had to get home to Stamford at midnight, call a cab to drive him home, and keep the cab until 7 A.M. in the hope that by that time he would be even, or ahead. How many persons who had no claim on him were supported entirely, or in part, by him nobody will ever know. Certainly if he spent more than $100 on his apparel nobody will ever know. When he was earning at least $50,000 a year we used to say he looked like the 1904 *Puck* pictures of a Socialist."

Another recruit to the Swope think tank crowded into cubicles under the dome was Arthur Krock, who in his autobiography looked back on that association as one of the more amiable periods of his career. His colleagues, Krock believed, were a "more fascinating and gifted company" than had ever been assembled since the heyday of Fleet Street. Broun's column, he said, "set the Hudson afire almost every day."

To Krock, "the pleasure of association with this company was raised to an even higher level at lunchtime, when it was augmented by the gifted characters who occupied the floors just below the Dome. . . . The food in the lunchroom on the thirteenth floor was probably the worst in all New York City (at least it received that unanimous accolade from these patrons). But if the menu had actually been composed of the sawdust and ditch water that the group swore were its daily ingredients, this patronage would still have been preserved in full measure by the lure of the table talk. It was largely composed of banter, the sting of whose barbs was assuaged by the balm of admiration for their craftsmanship. The arsenal of wit and satire was free for all, and always open. So, those who didn't one day set the table in a roar, except for the victim, were pretty sure to do it the next." Krock recalled a mock feud between Stallings, a Georgian with a Deep South drawl, and Cain, a Marylander who was convinced that the Southern accent of all but Maryland natives was laid on with a trowel. One day the table was joined by Morris Markey, a Virginian, who so admired Stallings that he adopted his Georgia drawl. After listening briefly to Markey, Cain rose from the table in a rage and stalked away growling, "I *have* to listen to Stallings, but not to his stand-in on a road show!"

To other members of the *World* staff, observing the coziness of relationships between what Krock called Swope's "galaxy of stars," and nettled by what they regarded as Swope's excessive protectiveness toward them, it often seemed that they indulged in an unholy amount of logrolling, mutual backscratching, and public admiration of each other. "Broun would write about having played cards with F.P.A.," wrote E. J. Kahn in his biography of Swope, "and F.P.A. would write about Woollcott's neckties or Stallings' imprecise use of the English language. Lippmann [Walter Lippmann, who succeeded Frank I. Cobb as editor of the editorial page] thought that when they all began taking in one another's wash like that it was a 'ridiculous performance,' and Krock complained that 'our critical gentlemen are revolving around the others all the time.' He cited as a particularly whirly instance a long telegram that Adams ran—a message from Stallings replying to an Adams rebuke for a misapplied word in *his* department. Most of the op ed writers were close friends outside of the office, and since Broun's 'It Seems to Me' and F.P.A.'s weekly, Pepys-like diary were highly personal, their intramural references were perhaps inevitable. One day in 1926, separated by a thin single column of type, Adams was writing about Broun and Broun about Adams. . . ." Swope didn't object to the incestuous atmosphere of the op ed page, even less to F.P.A.'s references in his column to Swope's wife as "Mistress Margaret Swope" and word pictures of her as a glitteringly successful hostess.

It was true enough that Broun had greatly personalized his approach to column writing since moving from the austere *Tribune* to the more permissive *World.* The way to make a name for himself, he shrewdly noted, was to make the by-line more important than the heading over his column; otherwise anyone else could assume proprietorship of the space. He would speak to his readers in his own voice instead of the objective tone valued in contemporary journalism. He was determined that *World* readers would say "Broun said," not "the *World* said," when they discussed some calefactory essay of his, which may or may not have set the Hudson afire but was fairly certain to have started a number of intellectual conflagrations in the island city it flanked.

The early twenties was not the time for a flamboyant display of liberalism. Although the Attorney General's office had stopped rounding up aliens of suspected radical tendencies and deporting them to Russia and elsewhere, the so-called Red Scare still terrified a large part of the citizenry, an atmosphere of apprehension only compounded by anarchist bombs exploding and the Ku Klux Klan marching in unprecedented numbers, burning crosses and flogging those on their enemy list in Northern as well as Southern states.

It was a time for discretion, for carefully qualified statements of opinion, but Broun was outspoken in his contempt for anything that emanated from the antilibertarian forces. He ridiculed the KKK and those political figures who made political capital out of finding Bolsheviks under their beds. He campaigned for the release of Eugene V. Debs, the Socialist leader who had polled a million votes twenty years before in a Presidential election and had been imprisoned on charges of sedition during the war. Yet he could only deplore the fate of his Harvard classmate, John Reed, who had gone over to the Bolsheviks, had died of typhus in Moscow, and been entombed as a Soviet hero.

Under Swope's protection Broun and the other libertarians in the op ed page group prevailed in their free-swinging opinions despite front-office opposition. Florence D. White was the *World*'s business manager, a peppery Irishman who viewed the men in hutches under the golden dome with deep suspicion, if not loathing, and he swung a lot of weight with publisher Pulitzer. "Ideas of liberalism," White proclaimed at one council of *World* executives, "are in vogue on the *World* at present and are playing hell with the interest of the paper. Our readers do not share prevailing liberalism." If the Pulitzers wanted to buckle on the liberal crusaders' armor, why not subsidize another newspaper and let Broun, Stallings, Adams, and the other agitators "run riot" on its pages? "Let us save the *World* while there is still time," White ended his peroration.

But the *World* was still run, essentially, along the lines dictated by the senior Pulitzer, which meant the editorial high command would prevail over the business management.

With some private self-questioning Broun joined in the battle against the forces of censorship then being led by John S. Sumner, successor to Anthony Comstock as hetman of the Society for the Suppression of Vice. The antivice crusaders were especially worked up over the new candor in literature and the growing sensationalism of the Broadway theater, which was presenting such boob-catching melodramas as *A Good Bad Woman* and *Ladies of the Evening*. The *World*'s editorial page, being more directly under the supervision of the management, labeled them "gutter orgies." On the next page, however, the reader would find Broun defending literary and theatrical realism.

Such views ran counter to his own rather puritanical personality. Obscenity disgusted him, particularly when uttered in the presence of females. Disheveled though he might be in appearance, looking more bohemian than most denizens of Greenwich Village, he was old-fashioned in his personal morality. Inside the crusader for freedom of expression was a Christian moralist. Ineradicably a member of the pre-World War I generation, he could not bring himself to applaud the flapper with her knee-length skirts, rouged kneecaps, and bobbed hair, or "petting" in country lanes, or Scott Fitzgerald's beautiful and damned youth flourishing their silver flasks of bootleg whiskey. He was all for the booze, but felt it was better dispensed in the saloons of his youth. He winced at young women slouched over speakeasy bars.

A dichotomy developed. Secretly he could not entirely throw off the precepts of his parents' bourgeois home. As a public figure with a growing audience, however, he felt impelled to defend those who were attacking the code formulated during America's "age of innocence," of which Broun was inescapably a child, half a generation too old to be a legitimate member of the "lost generation." The use of four-letter words, he held, was permissible if it furthered the cause of literary realism. The arts could not be regulated by the constabulary. Freedom was more important than any offense which might be given prudes.

The *World* in a series of articles charged that, as one headline put it, OBSCENE MAGAZINES OVERRUN NEW YORK. The target of that crusade was a number of "art" magazines being published with nude photographs included on the premise that they would benefit art students (though any observer at a newsstand would note that buyers of the magazines included a large number of portly, middle-aged men whom no one would suspect of artistic tendencies). The *World* grew so indignant over the issue that Mayor Jimmy Walker, never noted for sympathy with the bluenoses, reluctantly promised to "clean up the newsstands." Broun took a whimsical approach to the art-magazine controversy slightly out of key with the editorial and news pages' stern moralizing. Some of his readers had written to inquire why he hadn't taken a stand on such an important issue. He had ducked it, he said, because he didn't know what his proper response should be; he was a Sunday painter himself with a fondness for doing nudes.

In a more serious vein he made it clear, in a column titled "Censoring the Censor," that policing the arts was repugnant to him. "If we should choose our censor from fallible folks we might have proof instead of opinions. Suppose the censor of *Jurgen* had been someone other than Mr. Sumner, someone so unlike the head of the vice society that after reading Mr. Cabell's books he had come out of his room, not quivering with rage, but leering and wearing vine leaves. In such a case the rest would be easy. It would merely be necessary to shadow the censor until he met his first dryad."

To any careful reader it was evident that Broun in his *World* phase was not entirely comfortable in the mantle of a crusader for or against anything; his disposition was too amiable, too easygoing to work up the necessary spleen. Even with Ruth Hale's help. (He often quoted Ruth Hale in his column without identifying her as his wife, which of course would have enraged her. Quoting her in one column on the subject of marriage and divorce, without stating that she was his wife, he commented, "We think that Miss Hale means to say that monogamy, far from being an impossibly high ideal, isn't good enough to stand as man's final solution of the problem of human relationships." He was always respectful of her views; domestic tranquillity depended on it, of course, but he was genuinely admiring of, and indebted to, Ruth's intellect.)

Often he turned from the larger issues, with an evident sigh of contentment, to the sports world. Nostalgia for the press box at the Polo Grounds, the press row's ringside at Madison Square

Garden would periodically overcome him. In considering the classic match between lightweight champion Benny Leonard and the challenger, Rocky Kansas, he threw in literary allusions and a few bits of philosophy to make the subject palatable for op ed page readers. Leonard was a beautiful boxer as well as a strong puncher, while Kansas was an unscientific whirlwind in the ring. To Broun more than a pugilistic championship was at stake. "Spiritually, Saint-Saëns, Brander Matthews, Henry Arthur Jones, Kenyon Cox, and Henry Cabot Lodge were in Benny Leonard's corner. His defeat would, by implication, have given support to dissonance, dadaism, creative evolution and bolshevism. Rocky Kansas does nothing according to rule. His fighting style is as formless as the prose of Gertrude Stein."

In the early rounds Leonard took a beating from the challenger, and "even though his hair was mussed and his nose was bleeding, Benny continued faithful to the established order." And when Kansas unstylishly and foolishly led with his right, Leonard dropped him for the ten count, thus vindicating, in Broun's somewhat playful view, all those who abided by the traditions of any art or craft. "There is still a kick in style," he concluded, "and tradition carries a nasty wallop."

His young son, Heywood Hale Broun, or Woodie, was a continuing delight which Broun shared with his readers. He wrote of taking the boy to see his first film, which was not a William S. Hart Western or a Keystone Kops comedy, but Nazimova in *A Doll's House*. Ibsen, he evidently felt, was not too mature a subject for a boy of four. When Nora walked out on her husband, however, young Woodie delivered the opinion that she was going to the grocery store. "The misapprehension," Broun wrote, "was not the fault of Nazimova. She flung herself out of the house magnificently, but Heywood Broun, 3d, insisted on believing that she had gone around the corner for a dozen eggs."

7. Poker Among the Olympians

SHORTLY after Broun moved over to the *World*, Ruth Hale decided that they needed a country retreat. She was a country girl and knew how much the spirit could be refreshed by communion with natural surroundings. On that point Broun begged to differ. Almost violently prourban, he preferred the clatter of the elevated railways, the roar of traffic, and the bustle of compacted humanity to any illusions of peace and quiet in the countryside. From his few brief immersions in rural life, he complained that it was filled with the bellowing of horned cattle and the cacophony of other beasts and birds. The cry of a night bird sounded ten times as loud as a quartet of drunks harmonizing outside the windows of his brownstone in Manhattan.

A delaying action was the only recourse when dealing with a strong-minded woman bent on fulfilling one of her ambitions. For months Broun trotted along with Ruth on inspection tours of rural properties within an hour or two of New York City; he summoned all his intellectual and imaginative powers to find drawbacks to each place they looked over, until finally Ruth was convinced that nothing would satisfy him.

She had savings of her own and decided to use them to buy part of an old farm in Fairfield County, Connecticut, not yet the territory of well-heeled commuters to Manhattan offices. It was a few miles north of Stamford and easily reached by train. And if Broun chose to make use of the place—which she christened the Sabine Farm, after Horace's retreat from the distractions of imperial Rome—he would have to regard himself as a paying guest.

There were two small houses on the property, the largest of which she reserved as her own headquarters, the smaller to be rented to Broun. Broun's accommodations were, to put the best face on it, modest. The place he used to meditate or write wasn't really much more than a woodshed. Around Park Row sped the rumor that Broun was spending his weekends in a chicken coop he had to rent from his wife. Furthermore, it was noted, any mail sent to him had to be addressed to the Sabine Farm or in care of Ruth Hale; she was determined to make it plain that he was only a temporary resident and could be evicted at the pleasure of the owner.

One reason Broun wasn't eager to invest in a country retreat, apparently, was a poker club of which Broun was a charter member. Poker was perhaps his greatest enthusiasm, which didn't mean that it was profitable. It kept him lean of purse; it also cut into the weekends Ruth believed they should be spending in the country, since his group convened at five o'clock on Saturday afternoon and stayed in session until dawn Sunday.

The poker club was probably the most publicized essay in gambling since the days of the Regency bucks. Its membership constantly referred in print to the Thanatopsis Literary and Inside Straight Poker Club—which was also known variously, in the heavily facetious style of its members, as the Thanatopsis Inside Straight Chowder and Marching Club, the Thanatopsis Pleasure and Literary Club, the Young Man's Upper West Side Thanatopsis and Inside Straight Poker Club—and praised each other's literary efforts.

Naturally the coziness of the relationships around that fabled poker table, not to mention the valuable publicity they accorded each other in a time when the newspapers were unrivaled as a medium of communication, attracted the envy of the outsiders. How could they crack a circle that included in addition to Broun, F.P.A., Herbert Bayard Swope, Alexander Woollcott, Laurence Stallings, and Deems Taylor as the original nucleus? All were part of the happy few who romped around on the *World*'s op ed page, though later the membership was cautiously enlarged to include such fashionable or talented fellows as Robert Benchley, George S. Kaufman, Russel Crouse, Harpo Marx, and others who drifted in and out of the Thanatopsis orbit on the way to Hollywood or London or the Riviera. It did not escape attention that, for all the professed egalitarian instincts of its founding members, they were extremely choosy, even snobbish about whom they allowed to draw a hand in their games.

Nobody would claim that they were as exclusive as the Union League Club, perhaps, but there was a sort of unspoken agreement among the Thanatopsis membership that some chaps simply weren't clubbable. It wasn't so much a matter of breeding or large bank accounts as the possession of wit, charm, and talent. Nevertheless, most of its members, who would have been appalled at the thought of racial or ethnic discrimination, who rarely expressed in print anything but the most impeccably liberal sentiments, were not above practicing a bit of social discrimination. What amounted to blackballs were bestowed on a number of men highly successful in the journalistic trade, presumably because they didn't fit into the Thanatopsis pattern: not only the ability to be amusing and lighthearted (not necessarily when one had just been bluffed out of a big pot) but the willingness to join in the mutual backscratching and logrolling, the joshing in print that added up to affectionate salutes to each other's talents. Mavericks like Burton Rascoe, presently the book reviewer of the *Tribune* and an outspoken fellow whose candid opinions would hardly foster the togetherness of the Thanatopsis circle, were excluded. Rascoe, a good hater, swore he'd destroy the club if he had to engineer a raid by the vice squad. O. O. McIntyre, who wrote a syndicated column which conveyed Manhattan sophistication to hundreds of newspapers out on the benighted prairies, constantly maneuvered for admittance. He was ignored as an overdressed rube who wore spats and carried a cane. Frank Ward O'Malley had long been regarded by his fellow craftsmen as the most brilliant descriptive and humorous writer on Park Row, the brightest ray in the New York *Sun*, but he received no invitations to join the club. O'Malley just wasn't with it; too much the cynical veteran with bar-callused elbows.

When the Thanatopsis nucleus also became the yeast which gave rise to the Algonquin Round Table, O'Malley blandly inquired of Frank Case, the manager of the Algonquin Hotel, "The boiler room of the hotel is right under the round table, isn't it?"

The early meetings of the Thanatopsis group took place in a private room at Papa Monetta's Tavern in Mulberry Street. They were not quite so self-consciously glamorous as later sessions at which more gilded personalities were invited to participate—just a bunch of the boys in shirtsleeves playing for modest stakes.

Arthur Krock recalled them in a suffusion of nostalgia—one in particular which ended in a stampede back to Park Row and the *World* building. "Our game, interrupted only by dinner, had progressed to about the hour when the *World's* op ed page was in type and ready for plating and printing. There burst in upon us a head office-boy whose usual imperturbability had given way to frantic distress.

"Two factors accounted for this. He had used up the time in locating us that the reason for his search made highly precious. The reason was that several articles already in type for the op ed page had suddenly been found to be obsolete: Stallings had reviewed a book the publishers had withdrawn, Broun had reviewed a play whose premiere had been incontinently canceled, and I forget whether another disaster had overtaken a concert of which Deems Taylor had written an advance critique.

"Anyhow, the op ed page was in ruins, and the night managing editor was desperately searching for substitute material of a relatively timely nature. A rush back to the *World* office, and the reviewers of non-events somehow provided it. Except for the facts that this op ed page was debased in quality by what are known as 'fillers,' the first edition was an hour or so late, and Swope was in a state approaching apoplexy, no damages to the paper were incurred by this unforeseeable contretemps."

When the Thanatopsis Club moved uptown to the Algonquin as a sort of gentlemen's auxiliary to the Round Table, Krock wryly noted that "their wit was on perpetual display." Scintillating socially became more important than the game itself; an outrageous pun was valued over a royal flush. The pun, in fact, was regarded as a high form of humor in that group. Krock recalled one uptown game in which Broun—who preened himself on his rapid-fire production of puns and would go to almost any lengths, it seemed, to provide the occasion for a play on words—and Harold Ross were the only two players left in contesting for the pot. "Ross had drawn three cards, Broun none," as Krock remembered. "Concluding that Broun's hand was a bluff, Ross called his raise every time. After a number of these calls Broun tossed his hand into the deck, excusing this violation of the rule that a called hand must be shown by murmuring, 'I have been tray-deuced.' The pun was clarified when a snatch of Broun's cards from the pile disclosed only a pair each of deuces and trays, to which the fifth card lent no assistance. Ross won with the three fives he had started with."

Krock observed that it was not often that the charter members of Thanatopsis encountered a superior wit among the newer players they admitted to their circle around the green baize.

A stockbroker named Gerald Brooks who was admitted to the charmed circle on qualifications that mystified the rejected applicants, unless it was true that the Thanatopsis clubmen were succumbing to the attractions of the Fifth Avenue and Wall Street sectors, once facetiously (it was believed) complained that he had fallen into the company of social inferiors. None of his fellow players, he charged, had a proper family tree. "For example," he added, "my ancestor Sir Belvidere Brooks fought in the Crusades."

"So did mine, Sir Roderick," came the put-down from George S. Kaufman. "He went as a spy."

The rather sober-sided Krock admitted he couldn't match the op ed page stars when it came to repartee. It seemed to him that they were using the poker table as an arena in which they "sharpened their skills and their tongues"; an emery wheel on which they honed the epigrams, puns, and put-downs later to be published with a lapidary polish in their various columns. He and others would find an atmosphere of preciosity over the Thanatopsis table, unseemly perhaps to purists who believed that poker was a solemn occasion devoted to testing the laws of chance rather than intellectual peacockery.

The quality of the poker played by the Thanatopsis members, by most objective accounts, did not come close to equaling the fame which attached itself to the games. According to one source—Kaufman's biographer—Adams, Broun, Benchley, Ross, and Woollcott were all inferior poker players. Swope and Harpo Marx were rated as pretty good, while Kaufman was "the best honest poker player in town."

The stakes were high enough, however, so that a participant in the weekend session could lose a few thousand dollars by the time dawn broke over Manhattan on a Sunday morning.

Broun, by all accounts, did not take his losses with any great show of stoicism. He bled all over the place. Amiable and easygoing as he was in all other aspects of his existence, he turned histrionic over the poker table, bellowed triumphantly when he made a killing, moaned piteously when he lost, and at all times called on heaven's protection against the wiles, if not downright dishonesty, of his adversaries. He may not have been the worst or the best player in the group, but he was the noisiest.

It was over the Thanatopsis table, by one account, that he lost the money he had been saving to buy a country house. One night at the table emptied his bank account. Ruth Hale, it was said, refused to speak to him for three weeks and then made the decision to buy the Sabine Farm on her own.

Broun's inability to suffer his losses with a gentlemanly shrug, a wry little smile, naturally made him the butt of some of his fellow players' prankishness. In one game he and John Peter Toohey, the theatrical press agent, were contesting for a sizable pot, the others having dropped out on the suspicion that Broun was bluffing and Toohey was holding the high cards. The playwright Marc Connelly intervened with the announcement that it was the "consensus of the group" that the raising stop, lest it go on forever, and both men were to show their hands. Toohey displayed his cards. Broun, enraged, flung his cards on the table, got up, and began majestically stomping toward the door, then reconsidered and came back to the table.

It was generally believed that Broun was not trying to be amusing when he lost his temper over the poker table. He was as careless of money as a Medici princeling, but it galled him to the depths of his psyche to lose money at cards. A psychoanalyst confirmed the lay impression that Broun's bad-loser syndrome was deep-rooted. Broun had gone to the doctor to rid himself of his medically unfounded fear that he was suffering from heart disease; increasingly he would suffer from galloping hypochondria which no professional opinion could eradicate. The psychoanalyst, making a detour in his exploration of Broun's psyche, probed into the reasons for Broun's obsession with winning at poker, which could not be laid to simple greed, and why he couldn't dismiss the game as a simple affair of fifty-two pasteboards being shuffled around a table. The psychoanalyst concluded—not entirely to Broun's satisfaction—that Broun in picking up a poker hand was sublimating a latent streak of sadism.

Even over a two-handed game of hearts, which he often played with Alexander Woollcott during the week, his obsession with winning was evident. One late-autumn night he and Woollcott were playing a game after dinner at Robert Sherwood's apartment. Broun was supposed to catch the midnight train for upstate New York to attend a football game. It was a raw and chilly night and he was supposed to quit the party early to go uptown to his own house to pick up his disreputable raccoon coat. But Broun was a few dollars behind in the hearts game, and he insisted on "one more hand" time after time until he barely had time to make a dash for Grand Central. Though constantly bedeviled by fears of catching pneumonia, he plunged into the night coatless and barely made the station in time to catch his train.

There was no doubt among his friends that if Broun were given the choice of role in reincarnation, it would have been as a highly successful riverboat gambler.

8. We Charming Few

AT the beginning of the twenties, to the discerning eye, there was an unprecedented liveliness, a yeasty ferment of rising expectations, in the literary, journalistic, and theatrical worlds. There were a dozen daily newspapers to serve the two million souls residing in Manhattan. The theater had moved uptown from Herald Square to Times Square and was the unrivaled medium of entertainment, with the movies still silent and only beginning to shake off the vulgarity inherent in their nickelodeon origins, radio still a hobbyist's pastime, and television undreamed of. Those who could move freely in one or more of those three worlds, in the early twenties, were giddy with self-enchantment. To be young was very heaven, no doubt, but to be young or youngish, talented, quick-witted, and ambitious in Manhattan was to experience a euphoria which would disappear when the various forms of communication were taken over by conglomerates and controlled by men who kept both eyes glued to corporate balance sheets. The promising beginner in any of the popular arts had a chance to prove himself. If he or she belonged to one of the cliques which made such opportunities easier, so much the better.

The inmost of the inner circles, the Algonquin Round Table, the "Vicious Circle," as Margaret Case Harriman (daughter of the Algonquin Hotel's manager) termed it in her definitive history of the clique, was the supreme arbiter of who belonged and who should be excluded. What was in and what was out. Who was worthy of notice and who wasn't. That feeling of being self-constituted arbiters was cogently expressed when one of Florenz Ziegfeld's *Follies* opened and Marc Connelly, playwright and charter member of the group, inquired in the manner of the moderator of a town meeting, "Shall we let it run?"

The query was not entirely facetious. His companions at the

luncheon table in the Algonquin dining room could indeed patronize or decree a killing frost for any venture in the field of popular literature, drama, or the cinema.

They made up a powerhouse of critical evaluation. In combination they could often, if not invariably, make a best seller or a long-running play. "We all lived rather excitedly and passionately," as Marc Connelly would recall when he was one of the junta's few surviving members. "In those days, everything was of vast importance or only worthy of quick dismissal. We accepted each other—the whole crowd of us. I suppose there was a corps of about twenty or so who were intimate. We all ate our meals together, and lived in a very happy microcosm."

The Round Table was never officially organized, never elected officers or drew up a membership list. Like Topsy, it just growed. The Thanatopsis Poker Club had begun holding its sessions at the Algonquin, and then the members and others who gravitated toward the power they represented began having lunch together daily. The Algonquin's manager, Frank Case, who had long catered to literary and theatrical people, quickly recognized that they would attract a large volume of business simply because they publicized all their doings. He moved their large round table from the Pergola Room to the larger Rose Room and displayed them like gems in a jeweler's window. Within a year the restaurant was crowded daily at lunchtime by people curious to see the people they were reading so much about, try to overhear their persiflage, hope for a chance to rub elbows with them.

It was a perfect midtown setting for what soon became a fabulous echo chamber. "The Algonquin Round Table," as Margaret Case Harriman wrote, "came to the Algonquin Hotel the way lightning strikes a tree, by accident and mutual attraction."

In a manner so shameless that it was beguiling to all except those who had suffered the pangs of exclusion or rejection, the members of the Round Table praised and quoted each other; through self-proclamation it became the fountainhead of metropolitan wit, the recrudescence of the Cheshire Cheese, though to envious outsiders it seemed no less a commercial lunch club than the Rotary of Kankakee, Illinois. As the biographer of one of its charter members has observed, "Not since the days of Artemus Ward, William Cullen Bryant, and Walt Whitman had Manhattan such a merry group of writers lunching together and making talk that those outside the semi-magic circle imitated, told, retold, and committed to print."

All that self-promotional effort on the part of its members might indicate that the Round Table was sort of a conspiracy, but actually its primary purpose was amusement. Indubitably the members liked each other's company, and if they profited from the self-glorification, the constant publicizing of each other's efforts, that was only an extra added attraction.

Yet it must have been a constant strain on those less endowed as quip makers to feel that they must contribute to the brilliant ripostes that streaked around the Round Table. Several of its members were masters of what would later be called the put-down, and those less adept at ad-lib cross fire must have left the table on frequent occasions with lacerated egos. If the quality of the wit produced over the luncheon table now seems a bit precious, if not grossly overrated, possibly because it has been endlessly recycled, it still didn't pay to tangle with the more formidable jesters who gathered at the Algonquin. Marc Connelly, who had been a reporter on the *Morning Telegraph* and who became George S. Kaufman's first successful collaborator, was a rotund, good-natured fellow but it was ill-advised to take liberties with him. An acquaintance strolled past the Round Table one day and caressed Connelly's shiny bald dome, remarking, "That feels just as smooth and nice as my wife's behind." Connelly glanced up and replied, "So it does."

The unofficial roll call of the Round Table in the years before the Wall Street crash and consequent Great Depression blighted even the blithest spirits and turned many of them toward cultivating a "social conscience" (the prime cliché of the following decade) or to more or less radical causes still glitters across the half century which has passed. Few of them, naturally, seem as brilliant as they did to their contemporaries. Time darkens everything, including legends. Still, their combination of talent and personality, of charm and opportunism, does have a continuing appeal if you can judge by the number of successful biographies which have been written about them.

Initially, at least, the leading spirits of the Round Table were F.P.A., Broun, Alexander Woollcott, Marc Connelly, Harold Ross, Art Samuels of *Harper's Bazaar*, and George S. Kaufman.

Soon the regulars included Robert Benchley, Robert E. Sherwood, and Dorothy Parker, who had been working together on magazines. In addition to Miss Parker, the ladies' auxiliary included Jane Grant and Ruth Hale, who turned belligerent if addressed as Mrs. Ross and Mrs. Broun; the novelist Edna Ferber, Beatrice Kaufman, Margaret Leech (who was married to a Pulitzer and would collaborate on a book with Broun), the artist Neysa McMein.

Others made welcome from the theatrical world, whenever they weren't on tour, in London or Hollywood, were Harpo Marx (but not Groucho, Chico, Zeppo, or Gummo), Alfred Lunt and Lynn Fontanne, Peggy Wood, Tallulah Bankhead, Margallo Gilmore, Noel Coward. Ring Lardner occasionally dropped in. Ben Hecht and Charlie MacArthur, two uncurried Chicago journalists, were adopted after their play *The Front Page* became one of the great Broadway successes of the twenties.

Other frequent droppers-in on the luncheon sessions included Donald Ogden Stewart, Murdock Pemberton (then a theatrical press agent but later a distinguished producer), Herman J. Mankiewicz (then also a press agent but later renowned as the author of the screenplay of *Citizen Kane*), Douglas Fairbanks, Sr., the acrobatic film star, Ina Claire, and Jascha Heifetz. The humorists Frank Sullivan and Corey Ford were also peripheral members of the Round Table.

They were the bright and beautiful people of the Jazz Age, who rightly felt that they stood at stage center during a literary and theatrical renaissance, during a time when the popular arts were booming and many believed that even Hollywood in all its gauche splendor might provide an art form for the twentieth century. Their self-satisfaction was etched in acid by Anita Loos in *But Gentlemen Marry Brunettes*, the sequel to her famous *Gentlemen Prefer Blondes*, in a scene laid in the Algonquin dining room. "The first genius who came in was Joel Crabtree [evidently a stand-in for F.P.A.], the great writer who writes a long collum every day on the subjeck of everything. I mean, providing it happened to some friend of his. Because it makes Mr. Crabtree feel very good to have everybody think that *his* friends are greater geniuses than anybody elses friends. So the day never goes by that every one of his friends are not mentioned in his literary collum, and all of the public that is interested in literature enough to read it, can find out what they have been doing every hour of the day or night. So naturally they are always trying to do something readable on purpose, like a match game of amuseing tideldywinks, or sharades at one anothers parties, or some laughable crokay championship in Central Park where you can draw a crowd with almost anything. . . .

"So then they all started to tell about a famous trip they took to Europe. And they had a marvelous time, because everywhere they went, they would sit in the hotel, and play cute games and tell reminiscences about the Algonquin. And I think it is wonderful to have so many internal resources that you never have to bother to go outside yourself to see anything. . . .

"And I really don't know why the geniuses at the Algonquin should bother to learn about Europe any more than Europe bothers to learn about them. So they came back, because they like the Algonquin best after all. And I think it is remarkable, because the old Proverb tells about the Profit who was without honor in his own home. But with them it is just the reverse."

Sour grapes, the Algonquinites would reply to such scatter-gun satire. So also to Beatrice Ames, then married to Donald Ogden Stewart, who sneered that they were "Broadway people, Forty-second Streeters." Self-promoting theatrical types, in other words. And Mr. Stewart, after deserting New York for the greenback pastures of Hollywood, would come to share Mrs. Stewart's opinion.

The Round Table, like King Arthur's original model, like the later representation jerry-built for the Kennedy Administration, like in fact all vainglorious metaphors for self-perceived excellence, would sunder and vanish. Camelot, it seems, cannot be transplanted in space and time. At the Algonquin, perhaps, there was too violent a clash of egos, too free an exchange of candor. "Far from boosting one another they actually were merciless if they disapproved," Edna Ferber observed in her autobiography. "I have never encountered a more hard-bitten crew. But if they liked what you had done they did say so, publicly and wholeheartedly. Their standards were high, their vocabulary fluent, fresh, astringent and very, very tough. Theirs was a tonic influence, one on the other, and all on the world of American letters. The people they could not and would not stand were the bores, hypocrites, sentimentalists, and the socially pretentious. They were ruthless toward charlatans, toward the pompous and the mentally and artistically dishonest. Casual, incisive, they had

a terrible integrity about their work and a boundless ambition."
Those they proscribed, according to their high standards, thus
included about ninety-eight percent of the human race.

For all the seriousness of attitude toward their work and that of
others, they were also the "most hilarious, gay, rowdy, charming,
laughing" people she knew. "They were a hard-boiled crew;
brilliant, wise, witty, generous and debunked. . . . About their
own work hours they were hard as nails. But when work was
finished they had more fun than any other group I've ever seen.
They played like children. . . ."

Samuel Hopkins Adams, a literary figure in his own right but
not a member of the Round Table, took a fairly balanced view of
its transient brilliance. It was true, he thought, that "the
Sophisticates were pleasurably aware of their sophistication."
But in his opinion they didn't deserve all the calumny they
attracted from the excluded and envious, who might figuratively
be viewed as hungry children pressing their noses against the
plate glass of a bakery shop window.

"Libelous and presumptively jealous outsiders accused the
association of group posing. A contemporary denounced them as
the 'most determinedly coruscating bunch of self-igniting fire-
works that ever sat around a table, touching each other off.'
There may have been some foundation for the charge that their
more pungent epigrams were likely to be delivered in accents
sufficiently penetrating to reach the ears of the outer populace.

"It is certainly true that the regulars hoarded their 'smarties,'
watchfully waiting or, if necessary, maneuvering for opportunity
to slip them in to the best advantage. Dave Wallace complained
that he once lay in wait for five sessions before being able to
swing the talk to prehistoric man, upon which he had prepared a
specially snappy jape. Subsequently these scintillations would
appear in one or another of the newspaper columns, which
prompted an outsider to suggest that the members lived by
taking in each other's joshing." Adams also cited George M.
Cohan's remark that it was "a Round Table without a square
man at it." The presence of so many critics, none of them
intellectually attuned to Mr. Cohan's flag-waving and sentimental style, undoubtedly honed to a finer edge his opinion of the
group.

It was absolutely *de rigueur*, of course, for the members to decry
unanimously such commercially successful but artistically de-

plorable offerings as *Abie's Irish Rose*. To a man, and woman, they predicted its immediate closing. Broun was among the first-nighters who wrote that *Abie's Irish Rose*, with a Jewish boy and an Irish girl maladroitly cast as Romeo and Juliet in a contemporary setting, wouldn't last a month on the boards. "At the end of the first year," as he later confessed, "I had to switch and take the stand that it wouldn't run forever. But for a long time it seemed possible that I might be wrong a second time. I am still aware of the fact that it was a cheaply conceived and crudely executed story, full of gross sentimentalism and standard-ized humor. . . . And yet, in retrospect, I am not at all sure that *Abie's Irish Rose* did not more or less fulfill the function of *Uncle Tom's Cabin*. And that didn't happen to be a very good novel, either." The reason for his change of heart, as he would explain some years later, was that *Abie's Irish Rose* impressed on a mass audience, on both stage and screen, that discrimination against Jews was cruel and "that racial prejudice was comic."

Despite such miscalculations on the part of its membership, it did seem that during most of the twenties the Round Table seated the most promising young writers, critics, artists, and performers in postwar America—and much of that promise was fulfilled, at least in the eyes of their contemporaries, even if much of the work they produced no longer possesses the luster of its original success. They believed, with some reason, that they could do anything superlatively. And on occasion, almost ad-lib, they offered to prove it. If they sneered at *Abie's Irish Rose* and Cohan's sentimentality and Flo Ziegfeld's vulgarity, they were ready to demonstrate that they could, by a spontaneous combus-tion of their combined talents, do better.

The decision to rise, as a group, to the challenge came one day after the Irish actor J. M. Kerrigan, disgruntled by comments on a recent performance offered by Woollcott, Benchley, and Broun, threw down the gauntlet and told the Algonquinites, "You fellows are all so smart. If you don't like the plays you go to see, why don't you put on a show yourselves?"

Most of the Round Table membership were stagestruck, if untrained in theatrical disciplines, and they agreed to put on a revue titled *No Sirree!* as a takeoff on the successful import from Paris, the *Chauve Souris*. They assured each other that they could demonstrate performing talents even before a hypercritical audience. At musical evenings in Neysa McMein's apartment

Deems Taylor would play the piano, Benchley the mandolin, F.P.A. the flute, piccolo, and harmonica, and Dorothy Parker the triangle. The six-foot-seven Robert Sherwood had perfected a song-and-dance act in which he imitated Al Jolson's hit "When the Red, Red Robin Comes Bob, Bob, Bobbin' Along." Marc Connelly's recitation of "Barbara Frietchie," with dramatic gestures, was highly regarded by his friends. Benchley also had a one-man skit, "The Treasurer's Report," in which he impersonated an excruciatingly dull-witted country-club treasurer reporting on the money taken in by a charity bazaar, which eventually would lead him to a lucrative career as a comedian in Hollywood films.

It was in the spring of 1922 when the Algonquinites presented the entertainment billed as:

NO SIRREE!

An Anonymous Entertainment
by the Vicious Circle of
the Hotel Algonquin

It ran for one night, a Sunday, at the 49th Street Theater, the playhouse having been donated for the occasion by the Shuberts. In addition to the amateurs, the cast included Lenore Ulric, Helen Hayes, Reinald Werrenrath, Louise Closser Hale, Sidney Blackmer, June Walker, Winifred Lenihan.

Broun, as stagestruck as any of the rest, made his debut in *No Sirree!* on the night of April 30, 1922. He opened the show, in fact, appearing before the curtain, looking much like a dancing bear who had escaped from his trainer, as Spirit of the American Drama. Aside from Robert Sherwood's vocalizing and Marc Connelly's recitations and some dancing by a chorus of young actresses which included such future luminaries as Helen Hayes, Tallulah Bankhead, Lenore Ulric, and June Walker, the revue consisted of a series of satires on Eugene O'Neill, A. A. Milne, Zoë Akins, and other dramatists then making a stir in the New York and London theater. It was observed, snidely perhaps, that the people onstage seemed to be having more fun than the audience. The drollery of Alexander Woollcott appearing as "Dregs, a Butler," and John Peter Toohey impersonating "Coal-Barge Bessie, a retired waterfront prostitute," in a takeoff on an O'Neill drama convulsed their fellow cast members.

The New York *Times* assigned Laurette Taylor to review the show, while the New York *World* appointed Wilton Lackaye as its one-shot critic, apparently on the theory that the acting profession deserved the chance to take a few swipes at their occasional tormentors.

Miss Taylor bluntly advised the lot of them to give up any theatrical ambitions, but if they persisted in placing themselves on public view, "I would advise a course of voice culture for Marc Connelly, a new vest and pants for Heywood Broun, a course with Yvette Guilbert for Alexander Woollcott." She noted that at one stage in the proceedings Broun, as interlocutor, commented to the audience, "We have had a lot of fun, but so far the show has lacked charm," and elaborated on that point:

"Heywood Broun, appearing in front of the same curtain that held up Balieff [who had presided over the *Chauve Souris*], made me grateful that they had a resemblance at least in size. I had lost my program in the dark, and I couldn't stay for the finish, and I was late arriving. I realize that this conduct would not be tolerated on this particular paper, but I have seen it done on one other. . . .

"The first beautiful sight that met my eyes was Woollcott, Toohey, Benchley, Kaufman, Connelly and Adams in dishabille and, believe me, Mabel, it was terrible. . . . Everything was made fun of, from O'Neill to William Brady's scenery. It really made me rather sad, but I am sure it was sitting in my seat and thinking the way I had always seen the critics look. I suppose there must have been some suppressed indignation in my heart to see the critics maligning my stage, just as there will be at my daring to sit and judge as a critic."

Mr. Lackaye was much kinder in his notice and declared that "the burlesques were admirably written. . . ." He also singled out Heywood Broun for particular attention:

"Mr. Heywood Broun was the Joe Humphreys of the occasion [Humphreys was the then-celebrated announcer of fights at Madison Square Garden]. His patter was more consciously funny than Mr. Humphreys', his elocution not so good. However, this was atoned for by his personal charm, which not only captured the audience but aroused such enthusiasm in Miss Ruth Hale, who sat in front, that she was almost willing to acknowledge herself Mrs. Heywood Broun."

After wiping off his "Dregs, a Butler," makeup, Woollcott also produced a review for the New York *World*. If his coconspirators thought he'd smother them in flattery, they were abjectly disappointed. Great expectations had been fostered for the show, he noted, but "It wasn't fun. Not at all. It is not too easy to say just why. It is true that there was a hit-or-miss showmanship about it. It is true that, like the precious *Zuleika Dobson*, of which any twenty pages was always enough for us, it ran too much in the single vein—rather like a dinner consisting of five courses of perfectly splendid lemon meringue pie. . . ."

To lesser mortals the Algonquin clique by flaunting themselves in a homemade revue in a Broadway show house, as well as in their other much-publicized activities, were only exhibiting a joint affliction of hubris which was assuming startling proportions. To Dorothy Parker's recent biographer they indicated an evident belief, "like so many Renaissance men, or graduates of Eton, that any of them could do anything easily—write books, write satires, write plays and act in them, sing, dance, make music, found magazines and publishing houses, act as editors, write columns of opinion, serve as critics, be poets. The amazing thing is that so many of them did several things so well. Their mutual friendships reinforced one another's talents, and they were, many of them, becoming important to New York and to the nation."

Their importance, he added, was bolstered by the fact that New York City was just then becoming the capital of the proliferating mass-media communications industry. Broun's growing popularity as a columnist, with national syndication in the offing, greatly helped in spreading the Round Table's influence because "what his friends thought colored Mr. Broun's own thinking. When he therefore spoke to his several million readers, Mr. Broun was not giving them just an Eastern seaboard point of view, but a specifically Round Table point of view. . . . The Algonquinites could cause to be published, and could comment on, such new writing as, for example, that of the Paris group, and thereby help to create a climate in which it would find accepance. . . ."

That perceptive estimate of Broun's journalistic influence by John Keats, placing him in the forefront of those increasingly liberal and antiestablishment commentators whose combined efforts decades later would arouse a bitter antagonism in the heartland west of the Alleghenies, suggests his value as a member of the Algonquin junta. But he won his seat at the Round Table and his place in its inmost councils—if that is not too formal a word for what was an association based more on fun making than conspiracy—through other qualities. Certainly he was odd man out in a group that prided itself on a finicking sense of good taste, on excellence in all things, on a casual sort of elegance epitomized by the group's obsession with playing that most sedate and nonviolent of all games, croquet, on the sweep of country-house lawns. Certainly he didn't have Kaufman's razor-like wit or Dorothy Parker's mordant humor or Sherwood's talent or Woollcott's cultivated malice.

His comrades, it seems, simply found him lovable. He was also fascinating in his complexity and unpredictability, as was suggested by Margaret Case: "At thirty-three, Broun was a bewildering and bewildered, but peculiarly lovable, mass of contradictions. He was gently bred, slovenly of person, soft-hearted, steel-minded, evasive and direct, brave and terrified, considerate and tough, gregarious and solitary. His face, under its tangled crown of matted curls, had an intangible beauty of feature, and the soul enclosed in last week's laundry was, of course, the soul of a shining knight. Broun was the greatest of infracaninophiles, or lovers of the underdog." That girlhood view of Margaret Case, observing the Round Table's membership as the daughter of the manager of the Algonquin, summed up the impressions of most of his friends.

Down on Park Row in his more youthful years he may have seemed simply a lovable slob, a type which flourished and became legendary in the Old Journalism and was memorialized in Hecht and MacArthur's *The Front Page*, but he had advanced, almost effortlessly, from sportswriter to licensed essayist, from the rackety *Morning Telegraph* to the august *Morning World*. The character and intellect behind that progress, though encased in the persona of a singularly unprepossessing police reporter, were divined and honored by his comrades of the Round Table.

They appeared to the outsider to be totally preoccupied with the production of epigrams, insults, quips, sallies, flippancies, wisecracks, puns, and put-downs. Samples of such have been common currency ever since they were first issued, and there is no point in repeating who said what to whom, in jest or outrage, when they have so often been exhumed from the time capsule of the Jazz Age.

Broun's contributions to that body of impromptu humor seem to have been inconsiderable. He wisely saved his best stuff for the typewriter, and in any case he wasn't the wit-raconteur type. His persiflage was likely to be a bit labored. He lacked the malicious insights which made the tongues of his confreres so justly feared. Thus few samples of his spoken humor survive in the repetitive records of the Round Table's endless joshing and jousting. Viz.:

"The only real argument for marriage is that it's still the best method of getting acquainted."

"Repartee is what you wish you'd said."

He also composed a limerick on his hospital bed following a minor (to his surgeon but not to Heywood) operation:

> There was a young man with a hernia
> Who said to his surgeon "Gol-dernya,
>   When carving my middle
>   Be sure you don't fiddle
> With matters that do not concernya."

Nothing, certainly, to convulse any connoisseur of American humor.

His role among the more slashing minds of the Round Table fellowship was passive and presumably appreciative—a moth in a wasps' nest—a leavening influence amid so many clever people maneuvering to find a place for some apothegm concocted long in advance for insertion at the right moment. Oh, to have a clever remark repeated in F.P.A.'s column; to deflate someone else's overblown reputation; to sting the hide of someone infatuated with his own importance; to be known as one of the tastemakers and pacesetters of the lunchtime Algonquin. It says something for Broun's character that he did not join in that sort of competition. Something too, perhaps, for his intelligence in sensing the evanescence of the Vicious Circle and its verbiage. It could be said that he got more out of that fellowship, in that he shared in the profits of mutual admiration, than he invested in the way of prankishness.

Broun was the target rather than the archer in that tournament.

His style of dress, or complete lack of it, provided endless material for the production of witticisms. His hypochondria, too, was the subject of endless quipping, hypochondria being extremely amusing to anyone except the victim. Certainly it was a textbook case of that syndrome. E. B. White, who contributed so much to the success of *The New Yorker* as a commentator on the follies and glories of the metropolis, remembers only a few chance meetings with Broun. "He once bought me a drink and kept taking his pulse to see whether he was still alive." Broun was tormented by the conviction, for which his medical advisers could find no physiological proof, that he was going to suffer a fatal heart attack at any moment. He had a whole library of cardiograms which he shuffled through, like a riverboat gambler looking for the queen of spades, and which he displayed to his friends despite their facetious attitude toward his health. Once he showed up at the Round Table with a new batch of the graphs and insisted that Woollcott inspect them for new signs of deterioration. "Why," asked Woollcott, "don't you hold a one-man show of these things some time?"

Mere affection never stopped a member of the Round Table from using Broun as a target. Once he and George Kaufman were standing in the wings and watching the Marx Brothers romping through *The Cocoanuts*, a musical for which Kaufman had provided the sketches. Kaufman was trying to listen closely to the dialogue because Groucho, in particular, loved to toss away the script and ad-lib, a practice which its author naturally deplored. Kaufman edged away from the talkative Broun to get closer to the stage and check Groucho's dialogue against the script. A few moments later he returned to Broun's side.

"Now," said Kaufman, "what were you saying?"

"Why did you stop me in the middle of a story?" Broun demanded.

"Well, I had to," Kaufman replied. "I thought I heard one of the original lines of the show."

His friends also enjoyed testing the mettle of Heywood Broun whenever he donned the armor of a journalist-crusader. In the spring and summer of 1924 the activities of the Ku Klux Klan in the South and Middle West, the terrorism it practiced and the pre-Fascistic methods it used, had aroused Eastern liberals to a state of high alarm. The New York *World* launched a lengthy and exhaustive investigation of the Klan's activities, particularly its unconcealed campaign against Jews and Catholics, naturally a matter of great concern in New York City with its large Jewish and Catholic factions.

Broun joined the crusade and wrote in his column slashing denunciations of the KKK as a cowardly and un-American organization. If it reared its fiery head in the East, he promised, he would smite it unmercifully.

It looked as though he might be given that opportunity on the evening of the Fourth of July, 1924, when he and Ruth Hale returned to their Connecticut retreat from attending a play in Stamford. A fiery cross, the token of the Ku Klux Klan's displeasure, was burning in a field between the Sabine Farm and the country house of Newman Levy, a lawyer-litterateur with Round Table connections. Broun was certain the warning was meant for him, while Levy pointed out that since he was Jewish it was more likely directed at him.

Broun immediately wrote a column thundering with defiance. He would appear at the Sabine Farm the following Saturday midnight and be prepared to meet the KKK hand to hand. Wasn't that a bit foolhardy? his friends at the Round Table inquired. Not at all, Broun grinningly replied. Come Saturday midnight he'd be playing poker at the Algonquin as usual. Some of the Scottish border chieftain's blood in his ancestry stirred to the challenge, however, and he waited at the Sabine Farm at the appointed hour to grapple with his enemies. None appeared. A short time later Ruth Hale caught Mr. Levy and another prankish neighbor, Gilbert Gabriel, the dramatic critic for the New York *American*, hauling a kerosene-soaked cross onto the Broun property late one night. His friends, it developed, had merely been testing his resolve.

Inevitably the Round Table eventually faded into the realm of legend, as misty if not quite so fabulous as the towers and banners of Camelot. Its influence and the camaraderie which fostered it began declining in the mid-twenties, and a half-dozen years later it was only a memory. "I didn't even know that the group had sort of melted away," Edna Ferber recalled, "and one day, having finished a long job of work, and wishing to celebrate, I flounced into the Algonquin dining room, sat down at an empty place at the Round Table—and found myself looking into the astonished and resentful faces of a family from Newton,

Kansas, who were occupying the table on their New York stay. I mumbled an apology and left."

What happened? Manager Frank Case's answer was, "Whatever became of the city reservoir at Fifth Avenue and Forty-second Street? It gave place to the Public Library. These things do not last forever."

There were more definitive explanations. Rivalry festered into jealousy. All those satirical darts hurled around the table were bound, sooner or later, to leave their marks on the more sensitive spirits. Some members, as the joy went out of the twenties and curdled into the despair of the thirties, thought they should occupy themselves with something more serious than chitchat. Others had moved to Hollywood or had been dislodged from their corner in the marketplace; failure was never viewed with sympathy by members of the Round Table; it was an understood thing that they were all shareholders in success.

One of the early dropouts, Donald Ogden Stewart, explained, "It wasn't much fun to go there, with everybody onstage. Everybody was waiting his chance to say the bright remark so that it would be in F.P.A.'s column the next day, and there was a kind of—well, it wasn't friendly. There was a kind of strain about it—at least there was for me—and I don't think Dottie [Parker] ever enjoyed going there. But what the hell else was there to do? Who else was there? They weren't friends, and yet they were much more than acquaintances. . . ."

To Margaret Case it seemed that "the emotional lives of many of them had grown so complex as to interfere with their gags. . . . Perhaps it was politics, and a broadening sense of public issues, that helped to break up the Round Table. . . . As the small, independent worlds we all used to live in gradually expanded and fused into One World with its one vast headache, there was no longer any room for cozy little sheltered cliques of specialists. . . . The day of the purely literary or artistic group was over, and so was the small, perfect democracy of the Algonquin Round Table." She also pointed out that early death was the fate of many of its members, that only one of those she cited had reached the age of sixty.

But undoubtedly it was seriousness, matching the times, that killed the spirit which had infused the fellowship.

And it was Heywood Broun who epitomized the changing mood which caused the breakup. One day in 1932 the Algonquin employees, having suddenly been unionized, walked out on strike. Some members of the Round Table, including George Kaufman and Ina Claire, filled in as waiters in the dining room. Broun, by then a flaming activist who was marching in a picket line in Pennsylvania, was outraged by his friends' desertion of the proletariat. He wrote them letters in which he denounced them as "scabs" for coming to the aid of the "capitalist," his old friend Frank Case. They would serve as the epitaph of the Round Table. When Heywood Broun lost his temper, the times were indeed out of joint.

9. A Few Flings at Literature

EVEN to their more unconventional friends the Hale/Broun ménage and their style of living were things of wonder. Their household was ruled by Ruth Hale's insistence that they must live separate, independent lives; thus the invitations that went out with the heading "Ruth Hale and Heywood Broun invite you . . ." and gave the misleading impression that they were, as the current phrase had it, living in sin. If not entirely bohemian, given the presence of a young son, their life-style was, to say the least, haphazard.

Each had his/her separate career and some separate friends; each came and went at all hours as he/she pleased. After becoming one of the big guns of the *World*'s op ed page and attaining the then-princely salary of $25,000 a year, Broun rarely went down to the *World* building but wrote his column either in the house on West Eighty-fifth Street or in the office he shared for several years with Alexander Woollcott in an uptown hotel. Propinquity did not interfere, on at least one occasion, with Broun's pursuit of integrity as a critic. He still wrote occasional book and theater reviews. And when he was given Woollcott's *The Woollcott Reader* for review, he did not spare his old office mate's feelings. Woollcott was highly offended and wrote a friend regarding the review and the reviewer, "It seems to me childish, spiteful, and (even to one who had known for some years that he was a phony) surprisingly unscrupulous." This view of Broun, though written in a moment of passing irritation, was shared by another contemporary who was Woollcott's opposite in almost every respect. Sinclair Lewis considered Broun an arrant sentimentalist who capitalized to the hilt on his liberal-humanist attitudes.

Almost invariably Broun wrote at night on the premise that the toxins of fatigue were a mental stimulus and allowed him to tear off his column in thirty or forty minutes. Often he tried out the thoughts he intended to express in his next day's stint on the people he met during the day and earlier in the evening. Most of them were encountered on his rambles through the midtown speakeasy belt, which was a wide belt indeed and provided a cross section of opinion against which he could play off his own opinions and fancies. By then Broun, disregarding the effect of alcohol on what he was certain was a congestive heart condition, was striking many blows for liberty every day; the liberty entailed, that is, in consuming ardent spirits against the law of the land.

The brownstone on West Eighty-fifth Street, which seemed to have been furnished in the style of Broun's haberdashery, was hardly a model of domestic comfort or felicity. E. B. White recalls visiting it for a late-night party and retains only an impression of its untidiness and of "seeing little Heywood Hale Broun wandering around in his nightie at 2 A.M., pale and skinny."

Another guest's memory of the Broun household also recaptured its general decrepitude, its downright grunginess. "The bedroom which he used as an atelier was furnished with a big double bed in the center with two bridge lamps and a row of ashtrays on each side of it, and Broun worked mostly in or on this bed, refreshing himself now and then from a flask of his favorite gin-and-bitters. Across the room, a large bookcase was crowded with partly opened packages of books from publishers, and there was no other furniture in the room at all. Both Broun and his wife had their minds on higher things than interior decoration, and Murdock Pemberton now insists that there was a long period during which the living room in their Eighty-fifth Street house had no furniture whatever. Other friends of Broun's recall with some nostalgia that, for a whole year, the bathroom had no door on it."

Amenities were equally lacking at the Sabine Farm up in Connecticut, as their more Sybaritic guests kept pointing out. Not only was the bathroom door missing, there was no bathroom, only a ramshackle outhouse. Ablutions were performed in the nearby pond, which was rimmed with scum and amphibious insects, or in a battered tin basin on the back porch. The Algonquin's manager, Frank Case, once returned from a week-end at the Broun's country retreat pale and shaken from the ordeal of living through the primitive conditions there for several days. "I give you my word," he told his daughter, "there is *one* towel, hanging on a nail on the back porch, for everybody to use. And that towel must have come with the house."

Despite the rudeness of its accommodations, the Brouns eventually abandoned their town house and made the Sabine Farm their more or less permanent headquarters. In the summertime the place swarmed with flies, but Broun could be moved to put up a screen only on the back door. "Flies are dumb, haven't you noticed?" he explained. "They all congregate in one place, usually the place they can't get in. And when they can't get in there, they haven't got brains enough to try anywhere else."

Perhaps the most remarkable feature of the Broun households, however, was Ed McNamara, widely publicized as "the singing cop," a bachelor who came for dinner one night and stayed for a number of years. McNamara was indeed a former member of the constabulary, but was persuaded to give up his nightstick in favor of cultivating his magnificent tenor. Otto Kahn, the banker-philanthropist and Lorenzo of the Jazz Age, had adopted him as a protégé for a time. So had the great Caruso. Though Caruso had never cast himself in the role of a vocal coach and had no intention of raising a crop of rival tenors, he took a liking to the amiable McNamara and gave him voice lessons in his apartment at the Knickerbocker Hotel. Commanded to sing *fortissimo,* McNamara once shattered a crystal vase standing twenty feet away in Caruso's living room.

McNamara was a large, easygoing man whose temperament, with Celtic variations, almost exactly matched Broun's. Only inert ambition, his friends believed, prevented him from a successful operatic career; instead of making the most of his voice, he was content with playing small roles on Broadway and in motion pictures, a considerable number of which were still being produced in New York. The Irishman not only contributed his share of the haphazard Broun household budget, but at their celebrated Sunday evening parties cooked and served the huge, salt-caked steaks which made their guests forget the lack of other amenities. He also served as Broun's gentleman companion. Whenever Broun wearied of making the speakeasy rounds, playing poker and attending parties incessantly given by members of the Round Table, he sat at home and debated with McNamara on politics, literature, the theater.

Once they got into an argument about the upper echelons of capitalism at a time when McNamara, having evidently forgotten the patronage of Otto Kahn, was politically somewhat to the left of Broun. His beefy face turning scarlet, one large hand which had collared malefactors in Hell's Kitchen pounding the arm of his chair, McNamara roared denunciations of the superrich. At a pause in the tirade, Broun softly commented, "Mac, it's a shame that with a voice like yours you don't ever know what the hell you're talking about."

McNamara, though neither as tall nor as portly as Broun, also provided a sort of backup wardrobe for his longtime host. One evening Broun was invited to attend a dinner party of the utmost elegance at the home of Mrs. William Randolph Hearst. White tie and tails were mandatory. Broun, who was hard put to find a coat and pants that matched, borrowed the required costume from McNamara. Because of the differences in their sizes, Broun and his sartorial adviser took grave note of the gap that appeared, showing a band of pale protruding belly, between the bottom of the white waistcoat and the waistband of the trousers. McNamara shook his head and suggested, "I wouldn't show off any ballroom steps if I was you."

For once discomfited by his failure to approximate the well-dressed man, Broun spent an awkward evening among the dowagers grazing at Mrs. Hearst's dinner party. He spent most of the evening partly bent over, in a sort of arthritic crouch, so the space between waistcoat and waistband wouldn't be apparent. He gave the appearance of constantly bowing, almost of cringing in Uriah Heep fashion, whenever anyone approached.

One person so impressed by his resemblance to one of Metternich's ambassadors was Mrs. Norman de R. Whitehouse, who later commented to F.P.A., "Mr. Broun has the courtliest old-world manners. I can't understand how he got the reputation for being such a great rude bumpkin."

F.P.A., who was invited to the same stately board, found Broun sitting beside an elegant and dignified old lady during the musical portion of the evening.

"Who's the babe?" F.P.A. bent over and whispered in Broun's ear.

"The babe," Broun somewhat haughtily replied, "is Mrs. Vincent Astor."

Ed McNamara's tenure as a member of the Broun household ended abruptly later in the twenties, for no reason he was able to divine. One night he came home from playing a bit role in a film being made at the old Famous Players Studio uptown and found his trunk standing in the hallway and a note from Broun asking him to call a number unfamiliar to McNamara. When he rang the number, Broun told him, "I forgot to tell you, Ed. We've sold the house." But his friendship with Broun continued, even though mystery would continue to envelop the termination of his status as a household fixture.

It may have been that Broun, if not Ruth Hale (who preferred to spend her weekends at the Sabine Farm and any spare social time with fellow crusaders in the Lucy Stone League and other causes), was becoming more social-minded and felt he could dispense with McNamara's anomalous presence on the domestic scene.

He was beginning to spend more time with the upper classes, often at country-house weekends with Otto Kahn and the Ralph Pulitzers. Pulitzer, of course, was the publisher of the New York *World*. His wife, Margaret, usually called Peggy, was an aspiring writer. As Margaret Leech she would produce her first book in collaboration with Heywood Broun—a biography of Anthony Comstock—and before her death in 1974 she wrote two massive but vividly readable histories, *Reveille in Washington* and *In the Days of McKinley*. Both, fittingly enough, were awarded Pulitzer Prizes. More often, on the long, carefree weekends so nostalgically celebrated in recapitulations of the twenties, in Scott Fitzgerald country on the Long Island shore, amid the flash of white flannels and pleated tennis skirts and the music of cocktail shakers, he and other members of the Algonquin Round Table disported themselves at the Herbert Bayard Swopes' summer house at Great Neck.

Most of those weekends were devoted to verbal jousting and cardplaying, the Algonquinites being a sedentary group. Their host, however, often insisted that they bestir themselves for a game of croquet on the Swope lawn. Croquet, it was felt, was not too strenuous a pastime for people whose most athletic exercise was lifting a pale hand to summon a speakeasy waiter.

Eventually it became a passion among the Round Table

membership. One of its attractions, doubtless, being its aura of exclusivity. It wasn't everyone who had playing privileges on a stately sweep of country-house lawn, and there were fine points to the game which provided endless opportunities for the bantering and insult trading in which the Round Table delighted. The group delighted in taking up some sport or pastime, otherwise regarded as banal or trivial, such as anagrams or tiddlywinks, and then raising it to a highly competitive and sophisticated level.

Swope's guests, as it would be recalled by John Baragwanath, the husband of Neysa McMein, started out by playing with their host's short mallets, old-fashioned wire wickets and wooden balls, the equipment which had served players of the dowdy American version of the game for several generations. Then equipment for the livelier English style of croquet was imported, including cast-iron wickets, long and heavy mallets, and composition balls. Baragwanath noted, "This changed the game from a child's pastime to a tough, acrimonious sport which was played bitterly, for rather high stakes, with antipathy for one's partner and hatred for the opponents. We gradually doctored the basic American rules which made the game much harder and more conducive to mayhem. Even frail women like Neysa, Vincent Astor's wife Minnie, Dorothy Rodgers, Ellen Doubleday, Alice Gates, and a number of others became monsters to whom a man would scarcely speak until after the first cocktail."

During the autumn months, when the Long Island pitches weren't available, the male section of the group gathered at the croquet ground in Central Park, near the zoo, where their outcries of frustration and foul play were said to disturb the sensitive ears of the hyenas. During those crisp months Broun usually appeared in his tentlike raccoon coat. The first time Broun showed up in Central Park under that deplorably unathletic garment, George Kaufman glanced at him and offered the advice, "Don't bend over in Central Park."

If Heywood Broun ever suffered the spur thrust of ambition, literary or otherwise, it was not visible to his friends of the Round Table, perhaps because he regarded it as what Norman Podhoretz would call a "dirty little secret." There was no doubt of his appreciation of others' efforts; he beat the drum for John Dos Passos, Ernest Hemingway, Scott Fitzgerald, Floyd Dell, John

V.A. Weaver, and other contemporary writers. Sometimes he went to considerable lengths on behalf of a writer he felt was being ignored or unjustly treated. He made Dos Passos a personal cause when that writer's first novel, *Three Soldiers*, which happened to be ideologically in tune with Broun's thinking, particularly its antiwar attitude, was given an unfavorable review in the book section of the Sunday *Times*. Broun did not hesitate to cross journalistic boundaries to prevail on the *Times* to publish a highly favorable review, under his own by-line, on page one of that section.

But he seemed to lack the egocentricity which propelled other members of the group into such prolific careers. Underneath the layers of amiability, the endearing eccentricities, the social concerns, and the stated disregard for fame and success, however, was a different man from the one his friends fancied they knew. His son remembers him as a most reticent and private person, as viewed by a child (not the least discerning viewpoint), and doubts that anyone ever knew him very well. He seemed to drift, yet he often drifted in the direction of the main chance. His career advanced without noticeable propulsion, yet it passed up most of his contemporaries on Park Row. Broun operated undercover; greed, naked ambition, and maneuvering openly for position simply weren't his style.

So with all his rudderless qualities, his apparent aimlessness and indifference, he was still determined to make his name count for more in the literary sense than writing a column which people read once and then forgot. The best of his columns were regularly collected in such volumes as *Pieces of Hate and Other Enthusiasms, Seeing Things at Night, Sitting on the World, It Seems to Me*—certainly not the gesture of a man who neglected to leave his benchmark on his times.

Despite the fact that his friends had the impression that he spent most of his time in speakeasies—and it was true enough— he still sequestered himself long enough, both in the West Eighty-fifth Street house and on the Sabine Farm, to produce several books during the twenties in addition to the collections of his newspaper work.

As a part-time novelist Broun was governed by a tendency toward whimsy (in *The Sun Field*) and fantasy (in *Gandle Follows His Nose*).

In *The Sun Field*, published in 1923, he also demonstrated a journalist's appreciation of topicality as a stimulus to book sales. Just then the home-run-hitting career of Babe Ruth and his gargantuan personality were expanding from the status of a local baseball hero to that of a national idol, one of the authentic legends of the twenties. Broun seized on the outsize Ruth persona and made him the hero of *The Sun Field.* The heroine, Judith, was a militant worker for female equality and could be readily identified as Ruth Hale. The narrator, George Wallace, was a sportswriter with a heart condition, an obvious self-portrait. Along the way Broun also found space to include other real-life portraits disguised, of course, under other names. There was a sideswipe at Walter Lippmann, whom he had alternately admired and disliked (or envied for his Olympian certitudes) ever since they attended Harvard. In the novel Lippmann was disguised as a magazine editor, of whom Broun wrote, "He knows so much, so many facts I mean. We were in college together and even then it seemed to me that he was all finished. There wasn't room to put any more education on him. That is one of the things there ought to be a law about. A city ordinance or a federal statute should lay down the principle that nobody should be educated above the twenty-third story."

The plot of *The Sun Field* could have been concocted by the late O. Henry on a hungover afternoon. Tiny Tyler, the Ruth-like ballplayer, falls in love with Judith, the feminist. They get married just as Tiny's home-run production slackens and his baseball career is rapidly waning, while Judith is gaining fame as a novelist. Tiny recoups and a happy ending is ordained when—incredibly enough, if Tiny was supposed to be anything like Babe Ruth—he takes up a political career and runs for Congress. In a day when every politician in the land was a professed churchgoer and any backsliders were closely watched by the electorate (President Harding's peccadilloes in White House closets were infinitely more shocking than the Teapot Dome scandal), Tiny wins over the voters by making a speech in which he denies the existence of hell.

Ramshackle though the plot, *The Sun Field* still displays some of the merits of Broun's style and personality. He did have a nicely humorous outlook, most of the time, and one of the liveliest parts of the novel is his observations on the rivalry between the wives of the baseball players. Their little world beyond the locker rooms is as socially rigid as the pecking order in Newport, Rhode Island.

Mrs. Second Baseman's standing with her rivals among the team wives rises when her husband hits a home run, falls when he boots a grounder and lets in the winning run. Thus *The Sun Field* was received with rejoicing by his friends of the Round Table, who could identify the real-life models for his characters and assure themselves they were among the cognoscenti, by the critics generally, and in the book stores.

Three years later, in 1926, he published *Gandle Follows His Nose*, a sort of fairy tale which Broun used to convey his dark and private view of life. It details the adventures of Gandle, a shepherd boy who tends his flock in a countryside menaced by dragons. Perhaps it owed something of its fabulous quality to James Branch Cabell's *Jurgen*, which Broun had extravagantly admired.

Those who considered Broun a happy-go-lucky fellow could find plenty of evidence to the contrary in *Gandle*, which was threaded with Broun's preoccupation with death and the futility of the human struggle. It would be bootless to retrace the peregrinations of his young hero and the adventures which befell him in a landscape fairly familiar to those who have read the Grimm brothers' tales. In relation to his own character, however, it was interesting to note that *Gandle* conveyed his personal philosophy to a degree that would surprise those who knew him through his newspaper columns as a master of the light touch or a man of such affirmative convictions that he steamed with indignation over the injustices and inequities of the human condition. The real Broun, in the role of Gandle, believed that man runs a circular course, that he always catches up with himself, that experience—good or bad—is the only worthwhile thing he can get out of life. To be your own man was the paramount aim. In *Gandle* the villainous Baoz tries to convince the shepherd to choose one of two roads at a fork in his journey. "The left was the road of danger and misfortune. Baoz had said that he should by all means take the right. Baoz was an unpleasant man and Gandle swung resolutely to the left. Evil it might be, but it was also the road upon which Baoz would not expect to find him if he took up the pursuit. But most of all Gandle turned left because this road was his own idea. He himself chose it. That made it his."

There were other indications of Broun's private philosophy in *Gandle*, as when he loses the magic genie-producing lamp: "It's my belief that nobody ever got much good out of the lamp. Somehow none of them could think up many things to wish for. A girl, a palace, a bag of gold and that's the end of it. Wanting things is fun. Getting them ruins your appetite.''

The fantasy proved more popular among his friends, who thought it pretty deep stuff, than the ordinary book-buying public. Deems Taylor, venturing from criticism to the creative role as a composer, was so taken by the extended fable that he used it as the basis of an opera. The Met, however, decided against producing it.

By then Broun, in collaboration with Margaret Leech (his publisher's wife), was tasting the fruits of his greatest literary success. The book they produced in tandem, each uniquely writing alternate chapters, was *Anthony Comstock: Roundsman of the Lord*, which became the first selection of the newly founded Literary Guild and thereby earned them a wide readership. The biography of Comstock, who devoted most of his life to crusading against pornography in print and on the stage, the catchpole who read doom in a bawdy postcard and descried the rush of Gadarene swine in the painting "September Morn," gave Broun the opportunity to inveigh, as he often did in his columns, against the perils of censorship. "This," as Broun wrote in one of his chapters, "is the spirit that lighted the fires of the Inquisition."

Comstock stands the test of time. It accurately delineated the career of the old sin killer because Margaret Leech had persuaded John S. Sumner, Comstock's successor as chief beadle of the Society for the Suppression of Vice, to turn over Comstock's diary and other papers to her, and they were self-revealing documents indeed, showing Comstock's unholy lust for publicity and his lack of compassion and charity. To civil libertarians like Broun and Leech, the Comstock persona was hateful. Yet their joint effort succeeded just because they showed Comstock to be a human being, after all, who dedicated himself to the welfare of a mentally defective adopted daughter and whose pockets bulged with small toys to give away to slum children.

The course of collaboration did not always run smoothly. Leech continually had to prod Broun to produce his allotted chapters in time to satisfy their contract with the publishers. And Broun was careless about keeping track of the documentary material his collaborator had wheedled out of John S. Sumner.

One day Miss Leech phoned George Oppenheimer, then an editor for a book publisher (not the one bringing out the Comstock biography), panickily reporting that Broun had taken much of the research material home and it had disappeared into the maw of the Broun household. Miss Leech tearfully wondered how she would be able to explain the loss to Sumner. Oppenheimer tried to soothe her fears and suggested that they meet later that afternoon in front of the Brouns' West Side house. Its occupants were out of town but, Oppenheimer related, "I was sure that the maid would let us in without a search warrant. There was no trouble on that score and I promptly led the bewildered Peggy to Heywood's bedroom.

"Once when I had gone to his bathroom during a party [the downstairs lavatory was off the pantry and separated from it only by a curtain of beads], I had leaned over to pat Captain Flagg, Heywood's setter [named for one of the leading characters in his friend Laurence Stallings' play *What Price Glory?*], and caught a glimpse of the repository of books that lay under the bed. Sure enough, under thick layers of dust and piles of volumes, including three copies of *The Case of Sergeant Grischa*, which we had published and which Heywood swore had never been sent to him, was the Comstock lode. By the time I had pulled it out, I was suffering from silicosis, but I had retrieved Peg's honor."

When *Anthony Comstock* was published to general acclaim and robust sales, Broun had good reason to believe his career was flourishing. Yet there were discomfiting signs that he was being overshadowed by his showier contemporaries. One night in 1927, shortly after *Comstock* was published and Broun was dining out on its success, he was invited to attend a dinner party Bernard F. Gimbel was giving at his Westchester estate in honor of heavyweight champion Gene Tunney. Herbert and Margaret Swope were also invited, and they offered to give Broun a lift. (Broun himself never drove. He had a taxicab driver named Charlie Horowitz under long-term contract. Horowitz drove him around the speakeasy circuit in Manhattan and wherever else he wanted to go, often spending the whole day and part of the night with the meter ticking away. Since Broun distrusted trains almost as much as automobiles, he also had Horowitz take him out to the Sabine Farm. A good part of Broun's income went into cab-leasing arrangements.)

En route to the Gimbel mansion, the Swopes' chauffeur-driven limousine collided with a lesser vehicle with minor injuries resulting.

Broun devoted a rueful column to the incident, beginning, "For ages I have been curious to know what would happen if the nose of a great editor was shattered. I find that it bleeds."

He confessed that he was piqued by the headline over the story in the Yonkers *Statesman* reporting on the accident:

WORLD EDITOR,

WIFE HURT

IN CRASH

Swopes Are Injured on
Central Avenue—
Broun Shaken

Broun was convinced and so (he claimed) were his admirers that the headline should have read:

HEYWOOD BROUN

ESCAPES DEATH

IN AUTO CRASH

Columnist Has a Narrow
Call on Central Ave.,
Swopes Hurt Too

10. Exile from the Golden Dome

DESPITE the disheartening evidence that an editor out-ranked even a highly popular columnist—that would be changed in the next decade—Broun by 1927 was the brightest star in Manhattan journalism. F.P.A. went so far as to say, in print, that he was "one of the great journalists of all time." That could be dismissed as logrolling by a longtime associate. Still it was the Broun column which exerted a superior circulation pull in all the *World*'s galaxy of special writers. His social and political stance accorded most exactly with the enlightened people who bought or subscribed to the *World*, if not the sweaty proles hanging to straps in the subway—the under class over whom Broun endlessly yearned and appointed himself its defender—who preferred the tabloids, the *Daily News*, the *Graphic*, the *Daily Mirror*, and their redder meat.

Broun had become an influence, a molder of opinion. And a nay sayer. Calvin Coolidge resided in the White House, and to most of his fellow citizens he seemed just the sort of President to lead the American democracy, but not to Broun. It was Broun's chosen role to represent the Eastern liberal viewpoint, the type later known as limousine liberals, to whom even New York's Governor Alfred E. Smith was not quite progressive enough. The underdogs on whose behalf Broun and his allies labored might be satisfied with a choice between Smith and Coolidge or, a year later, Smith and Hoover; but Broun believed there were better alternatives.

When Eugene V. Debs, once the hope of American Socialism and its standard-bearer in several national elections, died in the autumn of 1926, Broun wrote a balanced review of the Debs career, but it was weighted with regret for all the country had lost through rejecting him. "Eugene Debs was a beloved figure and a tragic one. All his life he led lost causes. He captured the

Heywood Broun's father, Heywood Cox Broun.

ɔun's mother, Henrietta, whose .iden name was Brose.

Heywood Broun as editor-in-chief of the Horace Mann *Record* surrounded by his editorial staff.

Heywood and Connie Broun, on vacation in Miami Beach, with
Heywood Hale Broun. *Wide World Photos*

Heywood Broun, appearing voluntarily before the House Committee
on Un-American Activities. He had been charged as a follower of the
Communist party line, but he emphatically stated that he was not
and had never been a Communist.

Wide World Photos

Mr. and Mrs. Broun crossing the little bridge at the pond behind their house in Stamford.

Photograph by
Eric Schall

impact on the commission, Benchley then sought an interview with Governor Fuller and repeated his story for a third time. The governor heard him out, then leaned back in his chair and said, "Mr. Benchley, when I hear a good story and then when I go back and tell it to my wife, she often says, 'Alvan, haven't you fixed it up just a little?' And sometimes I have, just to make it better telling."

Despite those rebuffs, despite previous disinclination to become involved in weighty issues, Benchley joined the crusade to save the two men in their Massachusetts death cells.

Even with his personal if tangential involvement, Benchley could not match the indignation displayed by Broun in his commentary on the thumbs-down decision of the commission headed by the president of his alma mater.

"What more can the immigrants from Italy expect?" Broun demanded. "It is not every person who has a President of Harvard University throw the switch for him. If this is lynching, at least the fish-peddler and his friend, the factory hand, may take unction to their souls that they will die at the hands of men in dinner jackets or academic gowns, according to the conventionalities required by the hour of execution."

He also inquired, "Shall the institution of learning in Cambridge, which we once called Harvard, be known as Hangman's House?"

The executives under the golden dome on Park Row were shocked at what they regarded as the intemperance of Broun's comments, which could only stir up more ideological passions. They remembered riots in Union Square over the issue, the package of dynamite found in Governor Fuller's mail. If Sacco and Vanzetti must be dispatched, it should be done in a chilled and objective atmosphere. Broun, tossing firebrands, from their viewpoint, was making a deplorable spectacle of himself and the newspaper which provided him with a podium.

They were hardly comforted by an editorial in that other moderately liberal organ up on Times Square, the New York *Times*, which stated: "If we are to measure out condemnation for cowardly bomb throwers, we should not overlook men like MR. HEYWOOD BROUN, who asks in the *World* whether 'the institution of learning in Cambridge, which we once called Harvard, will be known as Hangman's House.' Such an educated sneer at the

President of Harvard for having undertaken a great civic duty shows better than an explosion the wild and irresponsible spirit which is abroad."

That summer Broun had been sending his columns down to Park Row from the Sabine Farm. Most of the time he spent painting, an avocation he had taken up several years before after the sculptor Jo Davidson remarked on his excellent sense of color. Most of his columns had expressed a genial mood, and he had recently praised President Calvin Coolidge for the cool style in which he had announced "I do not choose to run" for the White House again. Meanwhile Ruth Hale, abandoning feminism for the moment, was working as a volunteer propagandist in the offices of the Sacco-Vanzetti Defense Committee in Boston.

The blue-ribbon panel's report advising against clemency for the two men under the death sentence spurred Broun into taking a more active part in the effort to persuade the Massachusetts authorities to be merciful. He hastened to New York to confer with publisher Ralph Pulitzer and argue that even if his columns veered to the left of the *World*'s editorial policy, they didn't commit the newspaper or persuade its readership that he was expressing its opinions, only his own. He also pointed out that his column was headed "It Seems to Me" and that he was entitled to debate his views on the case.

Politely enough, Pulitzer informed Broun that he was mistaken if he thought he could write anything he pleased in his column and expect the *World* to publish it. "A separate entity within an entity is what we call a cancer," said Pulitzer. "Anyhow we've been over it before. It's the duty of writers to write and editors to edit. After all, in your contract you agreed, if I recall the words correctly, to 'carry out the directions of the party of the first part or its executive editors in the discharge of their duties.' "

Broun, nevertheless, signified his intention of going up to Boston for a closer look at the clemency situation and of continuing to express himself as he pleased on the Sacco-Vanzetti case.

He had hardly arrived when it was announced that executive clemency had been refused and the court had ordered that the executions were to be carried out in accordance with Judge Thayer's original sentence.

From Boston, Broun immediately dispatched a flamethrower of a column to be published in the *World* the next morning. That column, which appeared on August 5, 1927, is still regarded as one of the polemic masterpieces of American journalism. It began:

"When at last Judge Thayer in a tiny voice passed sentence upon Sacco and Vanzetti, a woman in the courtroom said with terror: 'It is death condemning life!'

"The men in Charlestown prison are shining spirits, and Vanzetti has spoken with an eloquence not known elsewhere within our times. They are too bright, we shield our eyes and kill them. We are the dead, and in us there is no feeling nor imagination nor the terrible torment of lust for justice. And in the city where we sleep smug gardeners walk to keep the grass above our little houses sleek and cut whatever blade thrusts up a head above its fellows."

Both Governor Fuller and Judge Thayer were "good" men in the accepted sense; they only served the brutal machinery of American justice, "hate-clotted from centuries of angry verdicts." To Broun it seemed a pity the sentences hadn't been imposed by crooks and knaves. "In that case we could have a campaign with the slogan 'Turn the rascals out,' and set up for a year or two a reform administration. Nor have I had much patience with any who would like to punish Thayer by impeachment or any other process. Unfrock him and his judicial robes would fall upon a pair of shoulders not different by the thickness of a fingernail. Men like Holmes and Brandeis do not grow on bushes. Popular government, as far as the eye can see, is always going to be administered by the Thayers and Fullers."

He scorned the theory, popular among radicals, that Sacco and Vanzetti had been railroaded to the electric chair. "This is a thing done cold-bloodedly and with deliberation. But care and deliberation do not guarantee justice. Even if every venerable college president in the country tottered forward to say 'guilty' they could not alter the facts. The tragedy of it all lies in the fact that though a Southern mountain man may move more quickly to a dirty deed of violence, his feet are set no more firmly on the path of prejudice than a Lowell ambling sedately to a hanging."

At that point Broun could have drawn back from his jeremiad without doing further damage to his standing at the *World*. He had done his duty, had his say, and further fulminations were not going to rescue Sacco and Vanzetti from the electric chair.

Since Broun left no diaries, journals, or records of any kind, it is possible only to guess at what governed him during those several hot days in August amid the passions and despair of the Sacco-Vanzetti Defense Committee.

Dwight Taylor, the writer-son of Laurette Taylor, recalls that he first met Broun one of those early August evenings at the apartment of Herbert Bayard Swope. Broun was waiting to plead his case with the executive editor and looking woebegone because he couldn't join the Thanatopsis Poker and Inside Straight Club holding its weekly session across the room. Then and always, Taylor recalled, Broun "looked like a man sitting on a bridge with a fishing line which he had forgotten to bait." And he "seemed to be looking over at his fellow clowns with an air of fresh appraisal; and yet there was a grudging jealousy in his eyes, too—of the warm apartment, the easy laughter, and the comparative security of their positions in contrast to his own."

Broun fidgeted for a while, as Taylor observed, and then found himself unable to resist joining in the camaraderie and joking at the poker table. He ambled over and asked his friends, "If Will Durant, who wrote *The Story of Philosophy*, should go up to Elmira, which is a reform school for delinquent girls—in order to give a lecture on the French philosophers—do you know what I would say?"

Most of the players ignored him, but finally one of them volunteered to act as straight man and asked, "What would you say?"

"I would say," Broun said, pausing at length to lend weight to his punch line, "that Will Durant is putting Descartes before de whores!"

His pun was greeted by a frowning silence, until someone suggested that a window be opened to air out the room.

From their attitude it must have been apparent to Broun that his recent crusading was not enlisting the support or sympathy of his colleagues from Park Row.

Nor, from Taylor's observations, was Broun able to win over his old friend and supporter. "A short time later Swope arrived and they both retired to the study. I have no idea what they talked about, but I do know Swope was genuinely fond of Broun and was doing his best, during this difficult period, to convince him that no paper in its right mind would retain a man on one page who was blasting away at the editorial page opposite. All Swope and Pulitzer were asking him to do was lay off the Sacco-Vanzetti case. When Broun came out he looked considerably more sober than when he went in, and as he headed for the private elevator in the outer hall, I jumped up to say good-bye." Obviously Broun's mood had been darkened by his talk with Swope, because when Taylor addressed the older man as "sir," Broun growled, "If you ever call me 'sir' again, I'm going to punch you right in the nose."

Nevertheless, a short time later Broun invited Taylor to his home, where the latter noted a punching bag "hanging like a withered fig on a hook behind the bathroom door."

To Taylor, recalling his impressions of Broun many years after Broun's death, that deflated punching bag seemed to symbolize his aspirations as a crusader. No matter how just the cause, Broun seemed to have difficulty in whipping up his combative instincts. Taylor viewed him as "a man preparing himself for conflicts which never quite came off. The air seemed to go out of him before he could get properly strung up, and yet he would continue to hang on, hoping that some vitalizing breath of life would inflate him sufficiently again to fulfill his purpose. In spite of this inherent weakness, he looms as far above most of his contemporaries in my memory as his tall figure actually loomed above them in theatre lobbies on first nights. He was a good and kind man."

Broun evidently felt less certain of his stamina in carrying on the lonely fight to save Sacco and Vanzetti—lonely in the sense that he was isolating himself from the powerful patronage of the Pulitzers and other established forces—than of the purity of his cause. It would have been easy enough to back away from the commitment; there was only his conscience and Ruth Hale's to bolster his conviction that he was doing the right thing. Yet he was determined to stay the course.

Perhaps he was carried away by the role he had chosen for himself. Possibly he felt that as the successful collaborator with his publisher's wife he was immune to any reprisals from the *World*'s editorial board, which, he suspected, was then controlled by Walter Lippmann, whose blood ran a degree cooler than most men's and who had an intellectual patrician's distaste for extreme positions. It was unfortunate that Herbert Bayard

Swope was vacationing at Saratoga, to which he repaired every August for the racing meet. Swope would not have defended Broun to the hilt, perhaps, but he might have worked out a compromise.

At any rate, he had been clearly warned off undue vehemence in expressing his opinions on the Sacco-Vanzetti case by Pulitzer himself, and he must have realized that he was endangering his cushy position on the *World* by pursuing the matter.

In the absence of any more positive proof, it must be accepted that Broun was demonstrating a considerable measure of moral courage in refusing to stop worrying the issue. On August 6 he followed up the first fusillade with another, in which he dissected Governor Fuller's decision against clemency.

The governor had vindicated Judge Thayer of prejudice, Broun pointed out, only on the basis of the court record of the trial. "Apparently he overlooked entirely the large amount of testimony from reliable witnesses that the Judge spoke bitterly of the prisoners while the trial was on. The record is not enough. Anybody who has ever been to the theater knows it is impossible to evaluate the effect of a line until you hear it read. It is just as important to consider Thayer's mood during the proceedings as to look over the words which he uttered."

Popular opinion in Massachusetts, he conceded, was all for removing Sacco and Vanzetti from the face of the earth. (Five times as many telegrams praising Governor Fuller's decision as those opposing it had been received by the governor's office.) Broun confessed that he was puzzled by the thirst for judicial vengeance. "Clearly it depends upon no careful examination of the evidence. Mostly the feeling rests upon the fact that Sacco and Vanzetti are radicals and that they are foreigners. Also the backbone of Massachusetts, such as it is, happens to be up because of criticism beyond the borders of the State. 'This is only our business,' say the citizens of the Commonwealth, and they are very wrong."

The *World* reluctantly published the first two columns on the Sacco-Vanzetti case, but by then a backlash had formed in the executive offices under the golden dome. There were many Harvard men on the *World* staff who were outraged when Broun, the professional mucker, referred to their alma mater as Hangman's House. A meeting of the editorial board, minus executive editor Swope, was convened with the principal item on the agenda the question of how to handle Broun. Many of its members thought Broun, as the spoiled darling of the uptown literati, had suffered an inordinate expansion of his hatband. Editorial discipline was indicated. The august pages of the New York *World* were not designed to be the personal sandwich board of any person, let alone a man who prided himself on disturbing the peace.

The board met on August 11 and quickly decided to spike any Broun columns that dealt with the Sacco-Vanzetti case. Purely pusillanimous? as hundreds of Broun admirers believed. No, the *World*'s record of moral courage could not be challenged; it had never aimed to be merely a sounding board of public opinion, but was dedicated to leading it.

The editorial board's decision certainly was defensible if one takes into account the climate of the twenties. In nostalgic recollection the decade glitters with the overlay of a literary myth that the whole country, the whole time was frenziedly dancing the Charleston, tooling around the countryside in motorcars, swigging from hip flasks, keeping score in the bloody wars of the bootlegging gangs, and in general relaxing from the strains of the First World War. Actually it was a very troubled time. The country was acutely aware of what some newspapers termed the Red Menace, now that all hope that the Bolshevik dictatorship in Moscow might crumble or be overthrown had vanished. The anticommunism of the twenties was much more fervid than that of the cold war years in the fifties. Thousands of foreign-born radicals had been deported with scant regard for any civil rights they might have possessed. They were sped on the way by a number of bombings throughout the country, which did considerable damage to life, limb, and property and which were (rightly, one supposes) attributed to radicals with an anarchist bent. One had only to read the proclamations of the American Communist Party to believe that there was a Red Menace.

The *World* editorial board evidently felt that political tranquillity was more important than continued debate over the guilt or innocence of Sacco and Vanzetti; it urged a new trial but only on "the grounds of mercy." More important, too, than the ideological passions of its star columnist. It refused to publish two further Broun columns on the Sacco-Vanzetti case, it carried an editorial which contained a backhander at Broun (repudiating the "notion that they [the governor and his advisers] could decide to send these two men to their death were they not convinced the men are guilty"), and on August 12 published a statement signed by Ralph Pulitzer in the space formerly occupied by the Broun column:

"The *World* has always believed in allowing the fullest possible expression of individual opinion to those of its special writers who write under their own names. Straining its interpretation of this privilege, the *World* allowed Mr. Heywood Broun to write two articles on the Sacco-Vanzetti case, in which he expressed his personal opinion with the utmost extravagance.

"The *World* then instructed him, now that he had made his own position clear, to select other subjects for his next articles. Mr. Broun, however, continued to write on the Sacco-Vanzetti case. The *World*, thereupon, exercising its right of final decision as to what it will publish in its columns, has omitted all articles submitted by Mr. Broun."

On reading that pronouncement from the publisher's office, Broun, who had returned to the Sabine Farm from Boston after making a detour to Otto Kahn's summer estate (the irony of that pilgrimage apparently lost upon him), decided that his honor could not be satisfied without a termination of his association with the *World*. Many of his friends argued that such a course would be foolhardy, but anybody who is half Scottish and half German can find deep reserves of stubbornness. If he couldn't write what he pleased, Broun affirmed, he wouldn't write at all for the *World*. It was a standoff. The newspaper's executives maintained they had the right not to publish anything of Broun's that too greatly offended the editorial policy of the *World*.

Broun called on the services of Max Ernst, his old schoolmate at Horace Mann and now an eminent counselor. Ernst suggested to the *World* that his contract be torn up and Broun become a free agent.

The contract, replied the *World* management, could be terminated, but one clause would remain in effect. That proviso stated that if Broun quit the *World*, he couldn't work for another newspaper for three years.

So Broun had to accept that—no journalism for three years except what could be published in magazines—or stifle his outraged sense of honor. Honor won, though poverty might be its handmaiden. All that Broun asked, in a letter to Ralph Pulitzer, was the space of one more column to explain his position to his presumably bereft readers. The letter evidently was composed by Ernst, legalistically stating that Broun would "hereby waive any rights which may so accrue to me, it merely being my intention should you use this material in your column, that I, of course, shall not be entitled to compensation therefor, but that you would be extending me the courtesy of giving me the same publicity which you received concerning the cause of my failure to appear as special writer in the *World*."

Pulitzer allowed Broun his say under the old column heading of "It Seems to Me." The Broun manifesto was not calculated to soothe ruffled feelings among the newspaper's brass hats—the free-swinging days of "advocacy journalism," of newspaper writers venting their personal beliefs as a principle of freedom of the press, being as far in the future as the old "personal journalism"—which was reserved for editors, not staff members —of Greeley and Dana and the Bennetts was in the past.

Broun began by briskly denying that he had been officially warned against overdoing the Sacco-Vanzetti controversy, then held up the biblical example of Pontius Pilate: "When Pilate saw that he could prevail nothing, but that rather a tumult was made, he took water, and washed his hands before the multitude, saying, I am innocent of the blood of this just person; see ye to it." So with the *World*, Broun implied, in not pressing the fight for Sacco and Vanzetti.

He pleaded guilty to having a passionate interest in the condemned men's case and to an inability to pull his punches when his conscience was aroused. He cited the example of a Giants pitcher who had been sued for breach of promise and whose love letters had been placed on the court record. "The memory of one of these I have always treasured. He wrote, 'Sweetheart, they knocked me out of the box in the third inning, but it wasn't my fault. The day was cold and I couldn't sweat. Unless I sweat I can't pitch.'" Broun couldn't write, he indicated, unless he was granted the privilege of working up a sweat over just causes.

He insisted that he was justified in pressing the campaign for Sacco and Vanzetti even if the *World*'s editors had given up the struggle. Because such liberal organs had failed to carry through and exert an overwhelming pressure for a pardon or a new trial, a "general apathy" toward the case had resulted. He concluded: "By now I am willing to admit that I am too violent, too

ill-disciplined, too indiscreet to fit pleasantly into the *World*'s
philosophy of daily journalism. And since I cannot hit it off with
the *World* I would be wise to look for work more alluring. . . . In
farewell to the paper I can only say that in its relations to me it
was fair, generous and gallant. But that doesn't go for the
Sacco-Vanzetti case."

Publisher Pulitzer reserved for himself the right to have the
last word. After all, it was his ball park, which some of the more
pampered players sometimes failed to remember. Broun's "un-
measured invective" against Governor Fuller and his blue-ribbon
advisory panel were considered "inflammatory" by the *World*,
and "to encourage those revolutionists who care nothing for the
fate of Sacco and Vanzetti, nor the vindication of justice, but are
using this case as a vehicle of their propaganda" would be
foolhardy.

Broun, he added, could not claim that he had ever been
ordered to write anything that conflicted with his principles.
"The issue is simply whether or not he may direct the *World* to
publish his column against its conscience." He concluded with a
paragraph that indicated the *World* management hoped, once
passions had cooled, to lure its maverick back into the Park Row
stable.

"The *World* still considers Mr. Broun a brilliant member of its
staff, albeit taking a witch's Sabbatical. It will regard it as a
pleasure to print future contributions from him. But it will never
abdicate its right to edit them."

The flattery didn't work with Broun. He couldn't see himself
trotting down to Park Row with a "contribution" in his hand
and waiting humbly to see whether the brass hats would deign to
publish it. Instead he retired to his bedroom in the house on West
Eighty-fifth Street and amid its familiar squalor tried to figure
out what to do next.

11. Back on Top of the World

AN Achillean sulk in his West Eighty-fifth Street tent wouldn't solve any of his problems, mainly financial in nature.

After brooding a few weeks, Broun decided to resume his writing career with the magazines as his new medium of expression. Years on the payroll of the New York *World* and other newspapers had not, of course, prepared him for the hazards of a free-lancer's career and its frequent fiscal droughts. But at least it would give him something to do while efforts were made to patch up a reconciliation with the *World*. Apparently unconcerned by what had happened to the star of his page opposite editorial, executive editor Herbert Bayard Swope had not only stayed in Saratoga until the last race was run but had then journeyed to Europe for a continuation of his vacation. Now Swope was back, but it would take weeks, possibly months before he could prevail over the anti-Broun contingent in the *World*'s executive offices.

Broun therefore agreed to write a weekly page of comment and opinion for *The Nation* at the urging of its libertarian editor, Oswald Garrison Villard, and despite the warning of Dorothy Parker that when he sat in on its editorial councils, "you won't be able to hear a thing for the clanking of Phi Beta Kappa keys."

He did find the atmosphere at *The Nation* a trifle stuffy, but Villard kept his promise that he could write on any subject he pleased to and without editorial interference. High-minded as he was, Villard must have been taken aback when Broun, in one of his early commentaries, advised *The Nation*'s editor to go slumming, take in a few nightclub "leg shows," and adopt a more relaxed attitude toward the follies of mankind. Some of Villard's more austere colleagues were similarly troubled by Broun's lack of dignity at editorial board meetings, at which national and international affairs were solemnly pondered. Broun would relieve the tedium of those lofty cerebrations by occasionally taking a swig from a battered gunmetal flask containing gin and bitters.

Broun wrote for *The Nation* for several years even while otherwise employed out of respect for its liberal principles and Villard's offering him shelter when he was cast out by the *World*. In one of his pieces he considered the *World*'s "group consciousness," its tenderness about offending various minorities, ethnic and religious. It was due, he believed, to sensitivity over its Jewish connections:

"When somebody gets angry and sends me a scurrilous postcard he almost always attacks the *World* on the ground that it is under Jewish influence and therefore Bolshevist. This, of course, is ridiculously wide of the mark. The *World* of today has few roots in the Jewish community. Very probably it does command a considerable circulation among the young intellectual group of the East Side, but the *Times* is very obviously the Bible of the arrived and successful Jewish citizen of New York. There is less standardization than in any other group. Save for downright abuse there is no resentment."

Broun had less kindly words for the sizable Irish-American minority and apparently saw nothing racist in being anti-Celtic, possibly because he was half (Scottish) Celt himself. "Admitting the danger of generalities I would contend that the Irish are the cry-babies of the Western world. Even the mildest quip will send them off into resolutions and protests. . . ."

He also used his page in *The Nation* as a platform from which to launch attacks against organized religion. Basically a moralist of almost Calvinist dimensions, he believed that the churches for the most part were doing more harm than good for the human condition. They were too concerned with ritual and empty forms and hierarchic pretensions; too many clerics were so conservative politically and socially that Jesus Christ would have renounced them, and their meddling in temporal affairs was unconscionable. He believed in God, but considered himself a freethinker. A dichotomy which would not endure because he was innately a man who sought institutional shelter, the warmth and comradeship of movements and causes. At the moment, however, he was most tolerant of those persuasions which did not attempt to apply a religious solution to areas outside their mandate. "Personally," he wrote, "I would prefer to have my favorite candidate Jewish,

Unitarian, or agnostic. These are denominations which meddle least."

During the period of his exile from Park Row, Harold Ross, who was editing *The New Yorker* and had once shared a house with Broun and Hale, also came to his rescue. *The New Yorker* had started its famous series of "Profiles," short and sharply written biographies of interesting people. That department hadn't ventured into autobiography, but Broun proposed and Ross accepted the idea of Broun summing up his life in a third-person accounting.

No doubt that brief autobiographical essay was inspired in part by the fact that he was little more than a year short of his fortieth birthday, and it seemed time, when he was partly unemployed and largely at loose ends, to do a little stocktaking. It should not have been a depressing inventory. In the past decade he had served as a war correspondent with the AEF, advanced from man of all work in the city room to widely read columnist, held a charter membership in the Algonquin group, had produced at least one fairly successful book (in collaboration), and indubitably was one of the town's characters, who was welcomed in any nightclub or speakeasy as a quasi-celebrity. And, not least, he had helped along the careers of many other people whose talents might otherwise have been wasted. One striking example of that was the joint effort of Broun and Woollcott in calling public attention to the magnificent voice of the black singer Paul Robeson, who had graduated from Rutgers with a Phi Beta Kappa key, had been an all-American end, and subsequently attended the Columbia Law School. Both Broun and Alexander Woollcott urged Robeson to forget about a legal career and cultivate his superb basso profundo. Along with Mrs. Robeson they persuaded Robeson to perform in a series of "concerts for unmusical people." New York was stunned by his rendition of "Old Man River," and his career took off like a rocket.

In his autobiographical essay titled "The Rabbit That Bit the Bulldog," Broun laid bare all his faults and eccentricities, yet left the impression with *The New Yorker*'s readers that, withal, he was a considerable fellow. The modesty and self-deprecation which allowed him to poke fun at his idiosyncrasies were not so overwhelming that he could forbear to picture himself as "a crusader riding out to do battle even though he dreads it." There was nothing paradoxical, in his view, of an overweight, slouching, and disheveled knight slaying dragons which came roaring out of the noisome caves of the American reactionary element. (He might have cited historical precedents; for instance, that blubbery but valiant Norman knight, Raymond the Fat, who conquered most of Ireland at the head of a few hundred men-at-arms, although it took four varlets to heave him into his saddle.)

But he set out by picturing himself as a timid soul. "Almost any mouse can frighten this elephant. A confirmed hypochondriac, he fears open places, closed places, high places, angina pectoris, cows, darkness and all loud noises. His collection of doctors is one of the finest ever acquired by a private connoisseur. When the mood is on him he has been known to visit as many as three specialists a day and he is completely cravenetted against reassurance."

Though he admitted in his third-person account that he was tempted to perform one rash act every seven years, he cited a number of incidents that supported his contention that he was not without physical courage. He recalled the dance-hall brawl in which he engaged when a member of the *Morning Telegraph* staff, a subway encounter with a couple of small but active ruffians who "with the aid of the ticket-chopper's chair and a subway lantern managed to give him quite a beating which sent him back into the ways of timidity for another seven years." During a tour of the front near Verdun as a war correspondent, he and his party had come under German artillery fire. "None of us ran," Broun says, "but we all walked briskly. And I didn't take the lead. I was merely a good strong third, but I never let them pocket me and I was always in a swell position to win that race if I had to." He also recalled an extremely rash intervention at an Irish rally. One of the speakers spoke ill of Michael Collins, formerly the hetman of the IRA but presently head of the Irish Free State, for having signed a treaty with Britain and having "sold out for British gold." Broun threw a handful of coins in the speaker's face, then attempted to stalk contemptuously away, but "four partisans collared him within fifty yards and he received one of the most extensive black eyes which have been known on Broadway."

He would never have backed himself into a position which cost him his column in the *World*, he maintained, if the management hadn't tried to shush him at a moment when his emotional tide was running high. When the *World* told him to shut up on that subject, he explained, it was something like shouting to a pole vaulter in mid-swing to come down and stop making a damn fool of himself.

He was cutting closer to the bone in dissecting his own character when he wrote, "In saying that Broun has small capacity for setting down indignation I do not mean to suggest that he feels none. Possibly the falsest item in the portrait of himself which he created was the expression of amiability. Heywood Broun is not in any fundamental sense a kindly person. He merely palms off timidity as something just as good as affability. Most of the people who read him had the feeling that he was Falstaffian. Hamletish would be closer, for his blood runs thinner than that of the fat knight and much more acid. Only by the grossest misapprehension could he be classified as belonging even to the lower orders of wits and humorists. To some extent he was engulfed in the generalization which the public made concerning what used to be known as 'the little Algonquin group.' . . .

"Although seldom identified by the public as one of the uplifters, this is the class in which Broun belongs by nature. If he ever grows more articulate in expression he will be readily identified as belonging to the reform group. To some he has seemed a somewhat pallid Mencken, but he is in fact a lesser Don Marquis [whose fables of archie the cockroach and mehitabel the cat were enlivening the pages of the New York *Sun*]. Like his more gifted model, his real interests lie in serious and even somber fantasy."

And he was jesting in tone but not in substance when he admitted that "Heywood Broun is an intensely ambitious man whose hopes of making a name for himself are seriously compromised by a monstrous inertia. Some years ago it was rather the thing to do to refer to him as a promising young man. He was no longer young, and he has not yet graduated out of the promising stage, so nothing may come of his aspirations." The time might yet come, however, when Broun would "swing a mace and crack a skull."

His brief self-analysis was determinedly facetious—it wasn't the contemporary style to take oneself too seriously in any public exhibition—but there were a number of small bitter truths concealed in that essay. Behind the façade of a man who, as he said, "regarded a typewriter as a sort of barricade," there was a yearning for recognition, provided it came without soiling himself too obviously in the marketplace. Inside the fat man larded with self-deprecation was a small, sinewy, and more aggressive fellow who silently clamored for attention. More and more, Broun had come to see himself as occupying an adversary position, one which said no, loudly and firmly, to the shibboleths of postwar America. Affluence had turned the country from the path of social progress charted by the prewar reformers who had nurtured Broun's idealism. H. L. Mencken would belabor the boobs, the smug citizenry of the Bible Belt, but there was something more fundamentally wrong with America than congenital stupidity, as Broun saw it. The national conscience was slumbering and would have to be awakened. That task was, of course, too much for one man, no matter how much his voice was amplified; the stock-market crash and consequent Depression would provide the seismic awakening.

Shortly before the end of 1927 conciliatory sounds were cooing forth from the old dovecote on Park Row. Swope felt the *World* needed Broun, the testimony coming from the circulation figures. (Something more seriously wrong than the disappearance of one of its more popular columnists was, however, responsible. The *World* was steadily losing ground to its rivals even though the Pulitzer-owned St. Louis *Post-Dispatch* was still making money. The trouble, according to Samuel Hopkins Adams, was that "Joseph Pulitzer had made a disastrous will, taking control of the paper from two sons who were able and devoted journalists, and vesting it in the cadet of the family, an amiable playboy.")

Just after New Year's, 1928, Broun's return to the *World*'s page opposite editorial was announced by Swope with the statement, "We have always been properly impressed with the value of Mr. Broun to the *World*. Mr. Broun has learned the value of the *World* to him. We are glad that he is returning."

Broun resumed his place in what he called "my old shop window" on January 2. Doubtless there was rejoicing all around. The *World* management was happy to have the prodigal back, presumably chastened by more than four months off the payroll. Certainly its readers welcomed his return. Broun was glad to recover his daily space, relieved to have that $500-a-week paycheck back again, and yet . . . things could never be the same. As Swope's biographer, E. J. Kahn, remarked a few years ago, the "shining integrity of the op ed page seemed to have been irreparably, if not fatally, tarnished" by the temporary silencing of Heywood Broun; the suspicion would linger that the columnists weren't absolutely free to speak their minds. And to Broun there was something both rankling and ominous in the second sentence of Swope's announcement that he, Broun, had learned how valuable the *World* was to him. Was his old friend and patron saying that without the *World* to display his talents Broun was merely another prophet crying in the wilderness?

Broun was also worried that by returning to the Pulitzer embrace like an erring husband, it would be taken as a sign that he had submitted to emasculation. He wondered just who had surrendered in the reconciliation. There was no controversy with the troublemaking potential of the Sacco-Vanzetti case on the horizon—the two anarchists had been duly electrocuted, upon which most people wrongly believed that they could be forgotten as a minor episode of postwar anarchy—but what would happen if he and the *World*'s editors again found themselves on opposite sides of the barricades? The *World* had not rescinded its ruling that it would not publish anything offensive to its policy.

Another possible flash point in his relations with the *World* management was his continued contribution to *The Nation*, where there were no invisible barriers to free expression. Doubtless the anti-Broun faction at the *World* was muttering the adage that a man couldn't serve two masters. He could only wonder what would happen if he wrote something for *The Nation* which the editors of the *World* found offensive. Would they again pull the blinds on his "old shop window" opposite the editorial page and its measured pronouncements?

It was an uneasy relationship, and it lasted just about four months. During that period Broun's columns lacked not only their zest for controversy and their enthusiasm for any issue which might outrage the sensibilities of the comfortable and established but the geniality and easy swing of his work before the possibility of censorship had arisen. Heywood Broun simply couldn't operate in a moral straitjacket.

Early in May, 1928, Broun of the *World* found himself in conflict with Broun of *The Nation*.

For the latter organ he had produced an article on the state of metropolitan journalism, in which he cited the need for a *courageous* liberal newspaper, one ideologically sited between the radical press and the *World*. He considered the *World* the closest approximation to the Manchester *Guardian*, which had long held an almost scriptural place in the affections of the world's liberals. To the argument that there might not be enough liberals of the sort he had in mind—that is, slightly to the left of Al Smith—he replied that liberals aren't necessarily born, "they can be trained by care and kindness."

The *World*, he explained, didn't fill the bill because "it switches front so often. New facts on any given situation may require a complete right-about-face . . . the *World* on numerous occasions has been able to take two, three, or even four different stands with precisely the same material. So constant were the shifts during the Sacco-Vanzetti case that the paper seemed like an old car going up hill. In regard to Nicaragua the *World* has thundered on Thursdays and whispered on Monday mornings." [American forces were bogged down in a long campaign against Sandino's forces in the Central American state, which ended only after a government satisfactory to the United States had been established].

What had particularly outraged Broun was the *World*'s stand on a recent controversy involving birth-control advocates. They had proposed to set up an exhibit, mostly charts and graphs showing the need for keeping the birth rate in check, at the Parents' Exposition in the Grand Central Palace. A number of groups had protested, and the Board of Education had rescinded its permission for the exhibit. The *World* had finally come down on the side of the anti-birth-control forces, stating, "Now it is quite obvious that a building swarming with children is no place for a birth-control exhibit."

To Broun it seemed that "in the mind of the *World* there is something dirty about birth control. In a quiet way the paper may even approve of the movement, but it is not the sort of thing one likes to talk about in print. Some of the readers would be shocked, and the *World* lives in deadly terror of shocking any reader."

Aside from congenital squeamishness, the *World* had backed away from supporting the birth-control exhibit because of the opposition of the Roman Catholic Church. In the minds of most liberals, at least non-Catholic ones, the Church was an omnipotent ally of the American reactionaries. The headquarters of the archdiocese had long been referred to as "the powerhouse" by liberals, in which nefarious schemes against any and all progressive movements were concocted by scarlet-robed clerics in constant consultation with the Vatican. In view of his future religious affiliation—Broun too was capable of startling right-about-faces—his denunciation of Catholic influence was especially ironic.

No newspaperman in New York City, he wrote, dared to criticize the Church. "There is not a single New York editor who does not live in mortal terror of the power of this group. It is not a case of numbers but of organization." The Church had bluffed its way into exercising a censorship over the press. And that was just one reason why New York needed a newspaper capable of defying such inimical forces.

Somebody saw to it that the publisher and editors of the *World* received copies of *The Nation* before it appeared on the news-stands.

On May 3, 1928, Broun's column was missing from the paper, and in its place was the curt announcement:

"The *World* has decided to dispense with the services of Heywood Broun. His disloyalty to this newspaper makes any further association impossible."

12. The New Shop Window

THIS time there was no hope of a reconciliation between Broun and the *World*'s management. Even executive editor Swope, so long his patron and protector, agreed that the rupture was permanent. To make it clear that Broun would never again be on its payroll, the *World* not only released him from all provisions of their contract but permitted him to take the "It Seems to Me" column heading wherever he chose to set up shop again.

Contractually a free agent, Broun immediately learned that other newspaper proprietors were not at all dismayed by the *World*'s "disloyalty" label. Newspapers all over the country urged him to open his new shop window in their space. For a time he was tempted by an offer from a former employer, the *Tribune*, now the *Herald Tribune*, but its editorial policy was conservative enough to appeal to its generally Republican readership and Broun couldn't see himself in such a contrasting setting.

A more attractive offer came from Scripps-Howard, a newspaper chain which had acquired the old pink-sheeted scandalmongering New York *Telegram* after it had passed through the hands of James Gordon Bennett and Frank Munsey. The mainspring of the Scripps-Howard organization was the small, eupeptic Roy Howard, chairman of the board, who had risen rapidly through the executive ranks and was possessed by towering ambitions. He needed a name like Broun to build the *Telegram*'s anemic circulation against vigorous competition from Hearst's *Journal*.

Elephantine Broun and toy-bulldoggish Roy Howard circled each other warily during the prolonged negotiations.

Howard cited the Scripps-Howard policy of "fighting for the underdog" and promised that he could say anything he liked in the *Telegram*. Furthermore, his column would run in other Scripps-Howard papers, and syndication, bringing a multiplication of readership, was attractive to any man who wanted to influence large numbers of his fellow citizens. And he would be given more space to express himself than he had in the *World*.

Broun, on his part, insisted that he must have complete freedom of expression. That, he maintained, was all that interested him.

When Howard tried to discuss his salary, however, Broun kept dodging away except to mumble that he expected more than the *World* had paid him. Howard couldn't pin him down; Broun flushed with embarrassment every time money was mentioned. The executive soon learned why. Morris Ernst, Broun's legal protector, then showed up to negotiate the salary issue. The figure settled on was $30,000 a year, later to be raised to $40,000. Only Walter Winchell and Dorothy Thompson, one a retailer of Broadway gossip, the other a weighty expounder of political affairs, were said to be fatter in purse.

He settled comfortably enough, at first, into his niche on the *Telegram*, but he would never find the atmosphere as congenial as he had on the *World* and eventually he would find that Scripps-Howard editors also were capable of wielding the blue pencil.

Other than professional bonds were snapping at that time for Broun. The old unbuttoned atmosphere of the Thanatopsis Literary and Inside Straight Poker Club was changing, and not for the better, in the opinion of its older members, as new and wealthier players were introduced to the group. The game moved from the Algonquin to a private room over the ritzy Colony Restaurant, a watering hole which catered to a Park Avenue clientele.

Through the years the Thanatopsis group had been so publicized by its members that it had acquired a social cachet not envisioned by the founding fathers when they first forgathered in a Mulberry Street tavern. Among those now taking a hand in the weekend games were a wealthy broker named Gerald Brooks, theatrical producer Alfred de Liagre, the publisher Haldeman-Julius, the composer Jerome Kern, the Rumanian prince Antoine Bibesco. All were better-heeled than the charter members, and most of them had been brought in by Herbert Bayard Swope, who was socially and financially on the rise.

In long-established poker games the stakes generally go up, rarely down. This became true of the Thanatopsis. Formerly it was possible for a player to drop a few hundred dollars, and that was serious enough for a man living on a newspaperman's salary or a free-lancer's income, but now you could hardly sit in on a game if you couldn't afford to lose thousands.

Swope was blamed for putting the game in the upper brackets and changing the atmosphere from that of the police headquarters pressroom to that of a Monte Carlo casino. It wasn't much fun to watch a multimillionaire walk off with your week's pay. One of the wealthier newcomers, who was rated as having $6,000,000 by Dun & Bradstreet, sat in on a game remarking that he didn't have a chance with such celebrated players. When he got up after a lengthy session, he was $410 heavier. One of the players went to the phone, called Dun & Bradstreet, and advised the rating service to list the man's net worth as $6,000,410.

"The Thanatopsis died of the dollar," Alexander Woollcott's biographer remarked. The higher the stakes went, the more explosive the tempers of the losers, especially those who couldn't afford their losses. A friendly game, as Woollcott complained, had been turned into a "financial enterprise." The fellowship begun over the scarred table at Monetta's Tavern became rancorous. Rumors about bad blood between the Thanatopsis members swirled around Broadway, which had always resented them as a clique of critics who could make or break a play. Heavy losses, like heavy winnings, were exaggerated in the gossip. Harpo Marx, for instance, was said to have won $30,000 one night after swooping in from Hollywood, but Harpo later reported that he never won more than a few thousand at one session of the Thanatopsis.

Not long before the economic collapse of 1929 Broun, along with Alexander Woollcott and Marc Connelly, dropped out of the Thanatopsis weekly sessions, all agreeing with Woollcott's statement that "poker is a preposterous waste of time."

By then, too, the matrimonial bond was also fraying. Even the premarital agreement that each party was to lead his/her own life couldn't prevent that. Nor the fact that, intellectually at least, they were soul mates.

Ruth Hale felt that, independent as she was in so many ways, her own career was being stifled by marriage. For a number of years she had worked off and on as a theatrical press agent, and she had not only been a semicollaborator with Broun on his column but had written book reviews and articles, mostly for the *World*. What bothered her was the nagging suspicion that she wouldn't have got those assignments if she hadn't been known as Heywood Broun's wife, despite her vociferous announcements that she was Ruth Hale, not Mrs. Heywood Broun.

The Brooklyn *Eagle*, under the editorship of Broun's Harvard classmate H. V. Kaltenborn had become a front-rank newspaper and was making its editorial influence felt outside that borough. To add to its appeal for readers throughout the metropolis, the *Eagle*'s editors suggested that Miss Hale might write a column of general interest for them. She was eager to accept. Then the *Eagle* let it be known that she would be expected to write as Mrs. Heywood Broun, to capitalize on her husband's name, and Ruth Hale called off the negotiations forthwith. Instead she free-lanced as an expert on marital problems.

She often expressed the belief that her own career would start an upward trajectory only after she emerged from Broun's bulky shadow. The possibility of divorce was frequently under discussion. Usually she was the proponent of the idea, and Broun exercised all his wiles and charms to talk her out of it. Their son, Woodie, was now ten years old and would be packed off to private schooling soon, and for various reasons Broun began arguing less passionately against the idea of a divorce. For years he had taken advantage of the "no strings attached" clause in their agreement and on his rounds of the speakeasies and nightclubs was often seen with young women on his arm. He found that the company of pretty girls immeasurably lightened the burdens of hypochondria, his other neuroses, his gloom over reaching his fortieth birthday, his ideological and professional concerns. Once or twice, it was said, he considered the possibility of opting out of the union with Ruth Hale and remarrying. It seemed likely to his friends that if he did remarry, his next wife would not be a member of the Lucy Stone League.

They decided finally to separate but not to divorce. Neither had any moral or religious antipathy for divorce, but it seemed, somehow, an unfriendly act. And dissimilar as they were in temperament, Broun the lackadaisical knight-errant, Ruth Hale always edgy and eager for battle on any of the many issues that concerned her, there was a strong emotional affinity between them.

The result was that they sold their brownstone house and moved into separate quarters. Even so they were separated only by seven or eight blocks that lay between her apartment on East Fifty-first Street and his penthouse, with a terrace which he sometimes used as an outdoor studio when he felt the urge to paint, on West Fifty-eighth Street.

Heywood Broun, champion of the underdog, lolling in a penthouse? Some of his admirers were shocked, but wouldn't have been if they could have seen his quarters. It was a small penthouse, for one thing, and it was soon overflowing with books and other debris. Except for the magnificent view from its terrace, it might have been the lodgings of any unsuccessful scribbler.

In any case, Broun could afford luxurious quarters, even though he had a habit of passing out five-dollar bills to panhandlers. The boom was still officially on, though there were signs late in 1928 and early in 1929 that prosperity was built on a shaky foundation indeed. Prices were high and inflation was, as the Democrats charged, rampant. But there was growing unemployment and something was jiggling the Dow-Jones index. In the late twenties, however, wages and prices weren't nearly so high as they would be in the early seventies. A hundred dollars a week was still a good middle-class income. And since Broun was drawing down six hundred, then eight hundred a week, as a syndicated columnist, he was firmly established in the upper brackets. He could afford his penthouse, prep school for Woodie, nights on the town (nightly), and socializing with the upper class.

Certainly he was overreacting when Deems Taylor and the Metropolitan dropped their plans for converting *Gandle Follows His Nose* into a more or less grand opera, and he wrote in his column, "Fame has jogged on by and left me jilted. A chance has gone to ride, even as far as posterity perhaps, by clinging to another's coattails."

He recalled that when he and Taylor had discussed the project, he had told the composer, with a lordly wave of his hand, "This is sheer luck for me, so don't let's mention money. I will be perfectly satisfied if I get a gold cigarette case out of this."

"A gold cigarette case!" Taylor had snorted. "I guess you have some misconception as to the rewards of music."

Broun could console himself instead with the rewards of journalism. The bosses at Scripps-Howard were allowing him to write without restrictions or, as yet, editing. He was allowed to keep up his drumfire on certain public figures he had long regarded with disaffection, such hallowed moral and civic leaders as Nicholas Murray Butler, the ultraconservative president of Columbia University; A. Lawrence Lowell of Harvard, John Roach Stratton, Canon William Sheafe Chase, and others who stood for political orthodoxy or Prohibition or literary/theatrical censorship.

He plunged into disputation every time one of his favorite opponents ventured a spoken or written opinion on matters he considered beyond their purview.

Canon Chase, a less picturesque successor to the late Anthony Comstock, frequently stood in need of correction and chastisement in Broun's view. Particularly when the cleric was outraged by Mary Ware Dennett's manual, *The Sex Side of Life*, for which Mrs. Dennett had been arrested, charged with producing pornographic literature, convicted, and sentenced to 300 days in jail.

Canon Chase had commented that Mrs. Dennett's pamphlet "does not correctly speak of sex desires as a longing for motherhood and fatherhood but as an opportunity for 'an unsurpassed joy' and 'the very greatest pleasure in all human experience.' Why did Mrs. Dennett misstate this to her children?"

Broun contended that Mrs. Dennett had been convicted "because she dared to say that love was beautiful. Some reformers hold that this is true but that the fact should be kept quiet in the presence of adolescents." With some exaggeration, he maintained that Mrs. Dennett's views placed her in the company of Shakespeare, Milton, Wagner, Shelley, and the author of the Song of Solomon.

Canon Chase had also urged that "the joy of winning an athletic contest" was greater than any dalliance with the other sex—muscular Christianity, with evangelist Billy Sunday as its spectacular exponent, then being very popular among the unenlightened.

Broun admitted that he had not distinguished himself as an athlete either on the playing fields or in the boudoir and, while disclaiming any expertise in those fields, decried the canon's tendency to equate romantic love with the hundred-yard dash. He averred that "I'd hate to hear that Antony actually asked for waivers on Cleopatra and finally traded her for a left-hand pitcher and a utility infielder from the Three-Eye League." If the canon was right, he added, "all lyric poetry had better be burned by the public hangman and there will hardly be an opera left fit for performance. . . ."

President Lowell of Harvard again tottered within Broun's range when his alma mater discharged twenty scrubwomen rather than raise their wages from 35 to 37 cents an hour in accordance with a new minimun-wage law passed by the Massachusetts legislature.

Broun was not impressed by the fact that Harvard was saving $600 a year by not granting the women a two-cents-an-hour wage increase, nor was his rage for social justice defused by the report that Mrs. Katherine Donahue, who had scrubbed floors in the Cambridge halls of learning for thirty-three years, had been discharged on the Saturday before Christmas. "In my opinion, Mrs. Donahue has done rather more to tidy up the place than even A. Lawrence Lowell himself. She has left no dark and clotted stains behind her."

He felt that Lowell, with all his white-bearded eminence as grand vizier of the Ivy League, had in fact been undereducated because he had never learned that there were some things men and colleges could not do without losing their honor.

Though not technically a member of the Harvard alumni, since he had not received his degree, Broun urged that Harvard men rise up and demand justice for the scrubwomen. Lowell's statement that "Some of them—I hope many of them—will be able to be employed at some other work in the university" wasn't a guarantee of anything satisfactory to Broun, merely "the pious hope of the president that possibly something will turn up."

He did not quite insist on Harvard alumni storming the campus in protest, but "unless Harvard takes immediate steps to fix a pension system for its veteran employees it will forfeit any right to stand as a leader in enlightenment. A university is a living organism and, when the heart has ceased to beat, death and corruption of the flesh set in."

The Scripps-Howard organization not only allowed him to zero in on targets long and lovingly favored, though its readership was not as sophisticated in liberal philosophy as the *World*'s, but did not object to his enthusiastic support of Alfred E. Smith for the Presidency against Herbert Hoover in the election of 1928, possibly because Governor Smith didn't stand much of a chance with Republicans still able to claim they were the godfather of prosperity.

Then came Wall Street's black-letter day, October 29, 1929, mass unemployment, breadlines, apple sellers on every street corner, and the corner that prosperity never turned even on command of President Hoover.

Broun's employers began to feel a lot less easy with their house maverick, their professional nay sayer, when he picked up a Socialist banner and proposed himself to the electorate as the Hon. Heywood Broun, with residence in Washington.

13. Broun for Congress

FOR a man acclaimed by his contemporaries for an almost legendary modesty, Heywood Broun seemed to have been thrust by invisible forces or was propelled by an inner voice into areas usually occupied by the preternaturally immodest: politics, the theater, labor agitation. Those forays from the traditional aloofness of the journalist made much of the last decade of his life hectic and full of angry passions, but seemingly he was not dismayed by having the spotlight focused on him.

The leftward turn in his political thinking was not as sudden as it might have appeared to his employers. That diluted brand of Marxism known as Christian Socialism in Europe, where it had given bith to political groups which differentiated themselves from the stringency of dialectical materialism, had long been attractive to him. Yet he was no closet Socialist, such as Mark Twain and William Dean Howells were revealed to have been in the latter's memoirs. He simply hadn't got around to embracing Socialism as a credo. At Harvard he had attended meetings of the Socialist Club organized by Walter Lippmann only in his fourth year at the university.

Early in his newspaper career he had become friendly with McAllister Coleman of the *Sun,* who was a member of the Socialist Party and tried to convert Broun. They had stayed friends through the years, but Broun always put off formally dedicating himself to the cause. He admitted to being strongly influenced by George Bernard Shaw, of the Fabian branch of Socialism, whose plays and pamphlets he constantly reread. He believed Socialism was the creed most likely to usher in the brotherhood of man, but like any civilized fellow, he was dismayed by the oppressions dictated by the Marxist-Leninist-Stalinist variation in Soviet Russia. He liked the idea of Christian Socialism, not because he was all that ardent a

Christian but because it seemed to promise a less fanatical and doctrinaire sort of governing power.

Those suspicious of Broun's conversion might have wondered whether, with the Depression demonstrating the failures of capitalism, he hadn't embraced Socialism as an idea whose time had come, hadn't come to see the light as a man of intellectual fashion. Such skeptics would point out that his liberalism before the Depression had similarly caught the tide of fashion. During the mid-twenties Carl Van Doren, in an article in *Century Magazine,* had placed Broun at the top of the list of popular commentators, ranking him above F.P.A., Christopher Morley, and Don Marquis in both wit and influence. The reason Van Doren gave was interesting. He believed that Broun had succeeded because of his liberal attitudes which were attuned to the current literary fashion; liberalism was holding sway over the educated people while conservatism was intellectually impoverished and unable to appeal to the popular imagination—a condition which, to a considerable degree, apart from such pyrotechnical performers as William F. Buckley, Jr., still prevails.

Since it was impossible to perform a trepanning on Broun's mind, even the skeptics could claim that he was merely latching onto Socialism as a fashionable doctrine. The evidence suggests that he had been long preparing to accept the milder prescriptions of Marxism by reading Debs' autobiography, Edward Bellamy's *Looking Backward,* Jack London's fulminations, and other prophets. He saw it as the most promising means of making humanity more humane, of preventing wars, of doing away with poverty and depressions. Even before the stock-market crash, he had taken note of the breadlines at the Little Church Around the Corner, interviewed the men waiting for a handout, and written about them in his column. Early in 1929, when the nabobs were still proclaiming an eternal prosperity, he was campaigning in print on the theme of "Give a Job Till June." It was up to the middle classes to bestir themselves and provide temporary employment for the millions who were out of work.

By the time the elections of 1930 were in prospect Broun had decided to run as a Socialist candidate for Congress against the Republican incumbent, Mrs. Ruth Pratt, and the Democratic candidate, Judge Louis B. Brodsky. Always lacking in generalship, he would fight in adverse terrain, for his home district, the

Seventeenth, was known with good reason as the Silk Stocking District and included the richest citizenry of Manhattan above Forty-second Street and east of Fifth Avenue.

There was a noticeable lack of enthusiasm for his candidacy except for one faction of the Socialist Party in which his old friend and preceptor McAllister Coleman was a leader. The old-line Socialists, whose leader was Morris Hillquit, were disinclined to fling their cloth caps in the air because Broun's conversion had come too late for their tastes; he had not served years of apprenticeship, passing out leaflets, demonstrating in Union Square, marching on picket lines, and many considered him a hobbledehoy because of his habit of swigging from a flask whenever he felt like it. And then there were all those rich friends of his. Nor did it seem quite fitting or sufficiently proletarian for Broun to open his campaign headquarters at the Algonquin Hotel, where Frank Case had provided space free of charge. So the old guard withheld their approval, and Broun was left with the support of Coleman's faction known as the Militants. Norman Thomas, the inveterate Socialist candidate for President, also supported the Militants as more likely to appeal to the younger recruits.

Even more dubious about the Broun-for-Congress movement were the brass hats of the Scripps-Howard organization. Broun told them he had decided to make a run for Congress as a Socialist before making the public announcement. The response of Roy Howard and the executive editor of the *Telegram,* Lee Wood, was loud and furious in opposition. But Broun would not be swayed.

Just after he announced his candidacy, Howard published a brief essay on why the *Telegram* believed its columnist should stay out of politics. Tactfully he refrained from mentioning the Socialist aspect of Broun's candidacy. No Scripps-Howard writer had ever gone to Congress or, he thoughtfully added, "to jail." Furthermore, Broun didn't stand a chance of being elected. Journalism was a more honorable profession than the political one. And since journalists were supposed by long and honorable tradition to be objective, they were ethically bound not to proclaim membership in any political party, else how could their readers trust them?

Broun replied to Howard immediately in his column. To Howard's view that he could be "more constructive in a column than in Congress," he retorted, "The two things are not mutually exclusive. During the campaign this column will appear as usual. I don't expect to see it get any better or any worse. . . ."

He suggested that the "real sticking point" was the fact that he was running on the Socialist ticket. Yet it should be "far more embarrassing for a liberal newspaper to have its columnist affiliated with the Tammany machine or the Republican organization . . . than to be serving under the leadership of Norman Thomas. . . . The Socialist Party offers the only existing machinery by which the Republican-Democratic alliance can be overthrown."

Howard's argument that he was taking on a losing cause wouldn't wash, in Broun's view, because the Scripps-Howard papers had always prided themselves on crusading no matter what their chances of winning the battle. "And yet he says that I should stay on the sidelines with him and the rest of the Scripps-Howard executives joining in the long-drawn independent-liberal cheer of 'Hold 'em, forces of reform and decency!' With all due respect for the cheering section the man who gets down onto the field and tries to spill a few of the trick plays is doing a great deal more."

He promised that he wouldn't use the column to promote his candidacy, his opponents being denied such display space for their views. "If I attacked Brodsky in this column he would have every right to demand an equal amount of space for reply. And as he is an amateur at the business maybe he wouldn't write a good column."

Somewhat craftily, he closed by remarking on how improper it would be to solicit campaign contributions in the column "to be sent to Morris L. Ernst, 285 Madison Avenue." (Attorney Ernst had been pressed into service as his campaign manager.) He was through with "weaving a daisy-chain of good intentions" and had "enlisted for the duration."

His campaign got off to a belated start because of the death of his father late in August. He finally decided to write a column about Heywood Cox Broun, he told his readers, because it seemed inadequate when the newspaper obituaries put their emphasis on a lifelong career as "the father of the newspaper columnist." That wasn't nearly good enough for his son; nor was the mere mention of the fact that he was the founder of a printing business and a member of the Racquet and Tennis

Club. He felt impelled to pay tribute to the elder Broun as a man of great charm, tolerance, and kindliness. "When I went to tell him that I was running for Congress on the Socialist ticket he was a little surprised and yet not displeased, though I was turning on a road which ran almost at right angles from his highway. We kept close through many episodes in which I followed philosophies quite foreign to his own. We kept close because of his wisdom. . . ."

Other members of the family circle had their reservations, too, about Broun's embracing Socialism. His mother's political beliefs were more in line with those of his conservative opponent, Congresswoman Ruth Pratt, but maternal loyalty prevailed and she announced her support of Heywood's candidacy. Although Ruth Hale had always prided herself on being much more of a fire-eater than her husband, she wasn't quite ready to throw in with people who more or less aimed at destroying the property rights of the individual. Socialism would have to stop at the boundaries of the Sabine Farm, she said. It could confiscate General Motors, but "this is mine," she maintained, indicating the freehold limits of her summer retreat. His son, Woodie, too, balked at linking himself with the proletariat, as he recalls, largely because he thought his father didn't stand a chance. Finally, like his mother, he threw himself into the Broun-for-Congress campaign and appeared on Manhattan streets caparisoned with a sandwich board urging his father's election.

To both his family and his friends, and to himself, Broun appeared to be a rather shy, pacific man who shrank from "loud noises," as he had put it, and enjoyed nothing more sanguinary than the clash of wits or a good-tempered debate on ideas. Once committed, however, he seemed to enjoy the blood-quickening of combat as much as any of his ancestors at Culloden.

In a sort of gypsy caravan of battered cars bearing oilcloth banners proclaiming the Broun crusade, he toured the streets of his district. The candidate himself was driven around, rather grandly, in a rented limousine. Whenever there was the possibility of a crowd gathering, he climbed to the top of the limousine on a stepladder, shouted his speech above the street noises, and occasionally paused to refresh himself from his flask of gin. Everyone agreed that he was a colorful campaigner, even if old-line Socialists objected to his drinking on the job.

"The Republican incumbent," he would tell a crowd, "is a reactionary. My Democratic opponent, Judge Brodsky, is an old-line Tammanyite. They tell me that the Democrats, especially Governor Franklin D. Roosevelt [then warming up for a Presidential candidacy in 1932], are endeavoring to steal my thunder. They may do that. They may steal our thunder. But they dare not steal our lightning!"

Meanwhile, Ernst and other advisers were organizing support for his candidacy and trying to widen his base from the Socialist Party to independents of all hues. An important part of the effort was organizing the literary, theatrical, and journalistic people to rally the citizenry on his behalf.

Alexander Woollcott, ordinarily apolitical, headed the Arts Committee and obtained, through various methods of pressure, endorsements from George Gershwin, David Belasco, Theodore Dreiser, Otto Kahn, Don Marquis, William A. Brady—none except Dreiser ever visible in any movements to the left of Al Smith. Dreiser, who was much more radical than Broun and sometimes considered himself a Communist, wrote in his endorsement of the Broun candidacy that he couldn't imagine why a decent fellow like Broun would want to "descend" to Congress, but "I do believe in Heywood Broun" and would support him even though "I do not believe in the basic principles of that [Socialist] party, however well-intentioned its purposes and however sympathetic and worthy some of its exponents. . . ."

Among those who announced that they would vote for Broun—many of whom had never considered voting for anyone on the Socialist ticket, and many therefore supporting him for sentimental rather than ideological reasons—were Minnie Maddern Fiske, Corey Ford, Deems Taylor, Walter Winchell, Floyd Gibbons, all of the Marx brothers, Eva Le Gallienne, DeWolf Hopper, Frank Crowninshield, George Jessel, Ed McNamara, James Weldon Johnson, Irving Berlin, Gilbert Gabriel, John Dewey, Brock Pemberton, George Soule, Clarence Darrow, Lynn Fontanne, Alfred Lunt, Frank Sullivan, Helen Morgan, Robert Benchley, Carl Van Doren, Edna Ferber, Ursula Parrott, Katharine Cornell, Fred Astaire, Stuart Chase, Floyd Dell, Elmer Rice, Ed Wynn, Charlie Butterworth, Irvin S. Cobb, Fannie Hurst, Ina Claire, Helen Hayes, Charlie MacArthur, and Grace George.

Few New York candidates, at least until Norman Mailer made

a run for the mayor's office, ever gathered so many gilded names in their support. The combined efforts of his glamorous endorsers, the organizational enthusiasm of his Non-Partisan Committee, the fact that late in 1930 the Depression was getting a lot worse and breadlines were lengthening (causing a natural swing to the left in the electorate), and perhaps to a lesser extent the activities of the candidate himself made it seem to his backers at least that he had a fair chance of winning the election.

In an excess of enthusiasm for identifying himself with the downtrodden, Broun even managed to get himself thrown into jail, probably not reckoning that in his Silk Stocking District a police record was not generally regarded as a qualification for political office.

The occasion he chose to symbolize his solidarity with the working class was a march along Fifth Avenue by 15,000 striking garment workers. The police objected to the lack of a parade permit. They halted the march and began ordering the marchers to clear off the avenue. Broun, declining to obey orders to disperse, insisted on being arrested.

Broun's arrest did not impress the old-guard Socialists who had suffered real punishment in the back rooms of police stations after being locked up for picketing or demonstrating in bygone struggles. There was a slightly facetious treatment of the whole affair, and besides Broun spent only two hours in jail. The newspapers sent a whole battalion of reporters and photographers, almost as though it were Jimmy Walker behind bars. His lawyer was Newman Levy, not ordinarily associated with police-court matters but a friend and neighboring cottager in Connecticut, and Mr. Levy managed to get his client sprung within minutes of arriving at the precinct station. Veteran Socialists were also affronted when Broun wrote a humorous column about being thrown in the slammer and ended with the wistful remark that he hadn't been given five dollars and a suit of clothes when he was released from jail.

Even getting arrested didn't help his cause enough to prevail over the two rival candidates. The Democrats had seized a majority in Congress, but Mrs. Ruth Pratt was sent back as the representative of the Silk Stocking District, most of whose voters felt President Hoover needed all the help he could get. It was a narrow margin of victory, however, Mrs. Pratt receiving 19,899 votes to Judge Brodsky's 19,248. Broun finished a poor third with

6,662 votes. He was however, uncrestfallen. Immediately after the results were tabulated, he announced that he was going to rebuild his organization for another try in 1932. Other matters, however, seized his attention, and it was his last time on the hustings.

14. Broun for Stardom

A FEW months after his rejection by the electorate Heywood Broun heard even sadder news than the message of the polls. The rumor in the newspaper business was that the Pulitzers, morose over the paper's balance sheets, had just about decided to merge the *World* with some other paper or, at worst, simply abandon the enterprise.

Broun took no visible joy in the fact that at least a minor factor in its decline—bad management was the prime one—was his disappearance from its pages. It was reckoned that Broun's by-line was worth about 50,000 in circulation, and there were intangibles connected with his presence on any newspaper's pages that contributed to the support of that portion of its readership which identified itself with the liberal establishment. The *World,* as F.P.A. testified, had never managed to replace Broun. "As late as 1930, three years after he had been discharged for alleged disloyalty, after dozens of pinch-hitters, substitutes, and more or less permanencies did their three-a-week best—Elsie McCormick, William Bolitho, Robert Littell—everybody, from the discharger down, generally referred to it as 'the Broun column.' I took a shot at getting people to write for it during the summer of 1930, and people on the staff always gave it to me for 'the Broun column.' I want it on the record that firing Broun, for anything, was a mistake."

Then the Park Row rumor suddenly became reality early in 1931 as the Pulitzers went to court for permission, under their father's will, to sell the *World* to the *Telegram.* Broun was greatly depressed, not only at the passing of what had been the nation's greatest newspaper, not only because he would always at heart be a *World* man, but because in the bitter late-winter months of 1931 so many of his former associates would be thrown out of work and many would never again obtain newspaper jobs.

The night the court announced its decision to allow the merger of the *World* and the *Telegram,* though the elder Pulitzer had forbidden any such transaction in his will, Broun was dining at the Herbert Bayard Swopes' apartment. Swope had left the *World* and become a very high-level public relations man, but another guest, F.P.A., was still a member of the *World* staff. A moment after someone called Swope with the bad news, F.P.A., gripped by an image of himself joining the hundreds of unemployed men selling apples on the Manhattan street corners, asked his former boss, "Mr. Swope, where have you been buying your apples?"

Down on Park Row a wake—traditional with the death of any newspaper, no matter how unworthy of continued survival—was surely in progress, and Broun felt that his presence as one of the mourners was required. He borrowed a bottle of scotch from Swope, called Ruth Hale to meet him downtown, and proceeded to the forlorn city room of the *World.*

By the time he and Miss Hale had arrived, the last edition of the *World,* dated February 27, 1931, had gone to press and the drinking men on the staff had repaired to a nearby speakeasy. Some of the mourners were bitter over what they regarded as the betrayal by the Pulitzers, since a last-minute offer by the editorial staff and its backers to take over the paper had been rejected. Some were despairing over the collapse of a great institution; others were worried by their grim prospects, knowing that few of them would be hired by Scripps-Howard in the merger. But all of them, regardless of their emotional bias, were fairly pickled in speakeasy whiskey. Alcohol had always been tolerantly regarded by the *World* management. Once Joseph Pulitzer, Sr., distressed because his staff at the moment couldn't boast a determined carouser, instructed his managing editor to scour Park Row and hire the most formidable boozer on the street. A really dedicated toper named Doc Cohen filled the bill.

Broun and his wife were not greeted with unqualified enthusiasm. Some of his ex-colleagues could remember when Broun and his fellow pundits under the golden dome were enviously referred to as "the dollar-a-word bunch." Others were bitterly conscious of the fact Broun had lucked out in being pushed over to the *Telegram* before the *World*'s collapse and was sitting pretty, in a penthouse, lunching at the Algonquin or 21 and knocking down $40,000 a year. Joseph Jefferson O'Neill, the wizard of the *World* rewrite desk, and several others who attended the wake said that they suspected, at first, Broun might have come down to do a little well-concealed gloating; after all, he had been fired by the *World* without a protest from the staff. It was also recalled that one of his former colleagues hissed that Broun was "a spy for Roy Howard."

Such ranklings were inevitable, but Broun soon won over his ex-comrades. No one suggested that he make a speech, but his recent Congressional campaign evidently had given him a taste for speechifying. Not everyone was pleased by what he said. The *World,* he told them, had "died of a final lack of courage." And it was just as well Scripps-Howard had acquired the *World* because the *Telegram* in recent years had been even more liberal and courageous than the *World.* He went on to say that the *World* wouldn't have been able to disperse them with a final paycheck if they had followed his advice and unionized themselves. The trouble was, he continued, despite glowering disapproval from some of his audience, that newspapermen wouldn't join in collective action because "every reporter believes he carries the baton of a managing editor in his knapsack or thinks he can get to be the dramatic critic." The newspapermen of his generation had, of course, always prided themselves on an individualism J. P. Morgan would have respected if J. P. hadn't detested newspapermen. His auditors were not greatly pleased at being told they were not only jobless but had long persisted in error.

Broun finally wound down, amid a discomfiting silence.

He and Ruth Hale stayed on until dawn, matching his newspaper colleagues drink for drink, joining them in threnodic song, and finally convincing them that, down deep, he was still one of the boys and ached for them. Ruth Hale was so overcome by the lachrymose sentiment of the occasion that she failed to rebuke someone who called her Mrs. Broun.

In his column the next day Broun took a soberer and more measured view of what had happened to the *World*, which had now been metamorphosed into the *World-Telegram*. He must have pleased the Scripps-Howard management by proclaiming that the chain was "qualified by its record and its potentialities to carry on the Pulitzer tradition." So far as courageous journalism was concerned, he indicated, it may even have been a good thing the faltering *World* had been merged with the *Telegram*; he forebore, however, to state that the old scandal sheet had acquired a new respectability.

The attempt by the *World* staff to take over the newspaper before it disappeared into the maw of the Scripps-Howard chain, he averred, gave him new hope for his profession, because "for almost the first time in my life I watched reporters animated by a group consciousness. Newspapermen are bland and, I think, blandly individualistic." For the first time a newspaper's staff had experienced the "excitement of mob movement . . . of people rubbing shoulders and saying, 'We are in this boat together.' " (That sentiment, however, disappeared overnight as the *World*'s staff dispersed far and wide and concentrated on finding new jobs instead of worrying about solidarity.)

Broun took cheer also in the fact that during the negotiations by which Scripps-Howard acquired the *World* the physical property of the latter, including its gold-leafed dome, was not part of the considerations. "I am glad that for once the emphasis was taken away from mere machinery. The fact of presses and linotype equipment was never stressed in the proceedings. This didn't count. The intangibles of a newspaper are the men and women who make it." The sale of the *World* to the *Telegram* was "a deal for a name and for some of the people who contributed to the making of the same."

Certainly Broun did not suffer from the merger. At a time when many newspapermen were being severed from the payroll or taking successive ten-percent pay cuts, he was sitting on top of the world, or at least on top of the *World-Telegram*'s split page, with the management promoting him under the slogan, "He Writes and Does as He Pleases." No widely read newspaper writer was more finely tuned to the troubled times than Broun. The work still came easily to him; it rarely took him more than an hour, usually only half that much, to write his column. He also found time to collaborate with George Britt on a book to be titled *Christians Only*, which was both an exploration of and a jeremiad against anti-Semitism in the United States.

The Hitlerite menace in Germany was only a smudge on the horizon when the book was started, but he was sensitive enough to the contemporary spirit to be alarmed by the dire possibilities of racial, national, or religious prejudice. It had been a considerable factor in the execution of Sacco and Vanzetti. The anti-Jewish prejudice was even more serious, and he was determined to scotch it before it became critical. He had been struck by Professor Albert Einstein's apothegm uttered in an address at the Sorbonne: "If my theory of relativity is proven successful, Germany will claim me as a German and France will declare that I am a citizen of the world. Should my theory prove untrue, France will say that I am a German and Germany will declare that I am a Jew."

In *Christians Only* many of the observations were shrewd and prescient. Jews, he noted, were taking on part of the ill will, the jealousy, and suspicion with which the rest of the country viewed cosmopolitan New York and explained, "New York has the largest Jewish population, and Jewish names are associated with the theater, the motion picture industry, and the entertainment world in general. And so, Puritan prejudice will vent itself upon all and any who have a particular part in catering to the pleasure principle. In fact, this point was made in the now thoroughly discredited Protocols of Zion. These fake documents were used to foment the theory that Jewish theatrical managers and motion picture producers were consciously trying to impair the morals of the American people in order to make them weak and ripe for conquest." On the other hand, he seriously underestimated the potential force of the Zionist movement and the determination to reclaim Israel as the homeland of the Jewish people. "Curiously enough, this movement should be enthusiastically accepted by prejudiced Gentiles. After all, it is an effort to preserve a Jewish Homeland, to give a national reputation to the Jew. But I don't assume that even the most ardent Zionist has ever thought it possible, or desirable, to make Palestine the literal home of all the Jews of the world. Its position in Jewish thought is rather more romantic than anything else."

Christians Only concentrated its fire on the social prohibitions against Jewishness and the application of a quota system in many universities to keep the number of Jewish students down. The authors discovered that "prejudice against Jews in colleges generally may be said to correspond to the area of density of Jewish population. It is strong in the big Eastern colleges—Columbia, Yale, Harvard, Pennsylvania, the New England schools as a whole. . . . The sporting principle that the race is to the swift applies only with reservations. The practical attitude in many cases seems to be that preferably the Jew ought not to run at all, but, running, if he happens to prove the most swift he should not get the blue ribbon." Broun and Britt also discovered that many fraternities made it a policy to exclude Jewish students.

Country clubs, resort hotels, and real estate developments were found to be practicing a policy of exclusion. During the supposedly enlightened twenties there had been a long sequence of ugly incidents, recited in detail by the authors, resulting from the "Gentiles Only" restrictions throughout the United States. And even in New York City there were office buildings on Wall Street and Broadway which excluded Jewish tenants without being punished for their abrogation of civil rights.

For all its eloquence, *Christians Only* created only the slightest stir among the readership at which it was directed, even though with tragic irony it was published just as the Nazis were moving toward a seizure of power in Germany and the resultant holocaust which all but consumed European Jewry.

During the spring of 1931 Broun's attention was drawn to the fact that the theater, like most other sectors of the economy, was suffering severely from the Depression and that many actors and other theatrical employees hadn't a hope of getting a part in a new show. Through his newspaper column Broun had already made one fairly successful attempt to stimulate employment. In the previous spring he had noticed the crowds of jobless hanging around the entrances to the employment agencies on Sixth Avenue as unemployment soared after the stock-market crash. The Hoover Administration was proceeding on the theory that public confidence would be restored if a cheerful front was maintained, but Broun believed the "trouble went deeper than a state of mind. . . . I couldn't help being stirred by the hardships of those who were physically cold and physically hungry even if the depression did happen to be psychological."

So he urged those readers who needed a job and those capable of creating one to join in his "Give a Job Till June" campaign. The resultant mail indicated just how serious the problem was. Within a few days he had received more than five thousand letters appealing for any kind of work and only twenty from persons able to provide a job. He promoted his job-finding campaign not only in his column but in a series of talks over the radio and speeches before various clubs and organizations. The result was that approximately a thousand of the unemployed were placed in more or less artificially created jobs.

Something like that might work for the unemployed in the theatrical industry, it seemed to him. He had presided over a few benefits for unemployed actors but they had resulted in only stopgap assistance for their beneficiaries. One night he was discussing the growing distress in the Broadway sector as he sat in a speakeasy with the singers Helen Morgan and Helen Kane, and Milton Raison, a Broadway press agent. Out of their talk grew the idea of producing a revue more or less on the cuff, which would provide work for actors, singers, musicians, and others. It would be a cooperative venture, the Socialistic aspect of which naturally appealed to Broun. Well-known writers and composers would contribute the words and music. Broun would appear as *conférencier*, as he had in *No Sirree!*, and besides acting as Greek chorus would, more or less, dance and sing.

The result of those deliberations was a revue titled *Shoot the Works*, from which some hitherto unknown talent emerged and eventually flowered, including Imogene Coca and George Murphy, the latter then a song-and-dance man, later a film star, and still later a conservative Republican Senator from California.

Broun exerted his influence on prominent writers and composers to provide material out of the goodness of their hearts. Dorothy Parker was now on the MGM payroll as a screenwriter but took the time to write a skit based on her short story "You Were Perfectly Fine." Other sketches were provided by E. B. White, Peter Arno, Dorothy Fields, Harry Hershfield, Sid Herzig, and Nunnally Johnson, then a newspaperman, who went on to a notable career as writer and producer in Hollywood. Broun persuaded Irving Berlin, Ira Gershwin, and E. Y. Harburg to write the music and lyrics. And from a number of people who hadn't been cleaned out in the Wall Street crash he raised enough money to rent a theater and put the show on its feet.

Broun acted as coproducer with director Johnny Boyle and flung himself into the casting calls and subsequent rehearsals with the brio of a Belasco. He had always been stagestruck, but it took a little time, as he wrote, to accustom oneself to the convolutions of the theatrical temperament.

Watching the rehearsal of a revue provided one with "some idea of what the word chaos means. The nature of man is stripped bare. Intellect is banished as emotion clashes with emotion and passions bump against passion. In my unsophistication I foresaw a hundred bloody brawls. During a rehearsal, it seems, it is customary for the actor every little while to toss away his part and then catch it again on the first bound. Even a Republican Cabinet could hardly offer the spectacle of so many resignations flung out in fury. After a bit I got the hang of it. I found that when one of my fellow actors said, 'All right, I'll quit,' he merely meant to say no more than a simple 'Is that so!' "

A streak of ham had long been developing in him, and he confessed, "I remembered that David Garrick had been an actor, and Shakespeare and Molière, and this seemed just the place a person ought to be at four o'clock in the morning. . . . And I realized that I too belonged among the troupers and I knew that the life had got me."

Putting on a cooperative revue was a lengthy process, and during it Broun kept producing his column on a regular schedule. He was one of the few New Yorkers who weren't bedazzled by the playboy Mayor Jimmy Walker, whose career at City Hall was striking proof that the New York electorate was as gullible as any other. Mayor Walker had just admitted that he was "more or less shocked" by reports that a number of women had been framed by the police on charges of prostitution. He then departed for a few restorative weeks at Palm Springs, California.

Broun was willing to grant that Walker might require a vacation in the sun to recover from a winter's nightclubbing, but he doubted that the mayor's health was as precarious as the city's. "It is a pity the mayor cannot take the metropolis with him on the trip. New York stands in need of scathing sunlight, fresh air and a fine rousing wind to clear its lungs and vitals." Furthermore, he understood that out in the California oasis "the palms will be straighter and itch less than those of Tammany." Broun's suspicions of Mayor Walker's probity were confirmed shortly by the Seabury investigation, at the end of which Walker's career lay in ruins.

A short time later he was defending the growing number of activists charged with increasing unrest in a nation over which Herbert Hoover still presided from the White House. Agitators were promoting strikes in mills and factories where wages had been drastically cut and workers were being laid off. Violence on the picket lines had resulted. But Broun refused to be shocked by the term "agitator," declaring that George Washington, Thomas Jefferson, Patrick Henry, William Lloyd Garrison, and many other honorable men had been charged with troublemaking. Men's dreams of freedom from social or economic oppression, Broun maintained, often had to be brought to fruition by outsiders, agitators. "The agitator in all fields of human endeavor is the person who insists, sometimes with violence, that the world as it stands is not good enough. This insistence partakes of a very necessary quality of life. Contented organisms have already felt the touch of degeneration." Broun, like most Socialists, considered himself a pacifist but was prepared to be uncritical of violence committed in a cause of which he approved.

Thanks to Broun's newspaper connections, *Shoot the Works* opened at the George M. Cohan Theater in a fanfare of publicity. The opening night was July 21, 1931, not an auspicious date because even in the best of times the New York theatrical business is in the doldrums until cooler weather in September. If it could last through the rest of the summer, Broun and his confreres believed, it might stand a chance for a profitable run that autumn and winter. It was ardently hoped that the economic aspects of the enterprise—the angels taking out nothing but their original investment, chorus girls paid off the top of the gross at above-Equity scale because Broun felt they'd been victimized since the days of the Floradora Sextette—would encourage large numbers of theatergoers to attend no matter what the critics might say.

Opening night attracted a larger collection of celebrities than might have been expected of a show which, according to Broadway rumor, lacked the expensive finish and panache of a Ziegfeld production. Mayor Walker, unoffended by Broun's criticism of his frivolity and Tammany Hall loyalty, trotted in under a silk hat. Nonprofessional critics who attended *Shoot the Works* recall it as something of a mishmash with only a few memorable moments. Few of those who witnessed Broun's theatrical comeback believed that he should invest too much of his time in the theater, except as a member of the audience. Elephantine was the word for his style, bumbling for his manner. He came out in front of the curtain to cajole the audience and several times during the show essayed a song or dance, which displays were not likely to arouse the envy of a Ray Bolger or George M. Cohan, though nobody faulted his courage in pitting his talents against those of the professionals onstage.

The show-business weeklies, *Variety* and *Billboard*, being required to take a hard-nosed attitude toward any performer no matter how admirable his intentions, advised Broun to stick to his typewriter. They predicted a quick closing for *Shoot the Works.* The critics for the dailies, however, were conscious of the fact that Broun had once practiced their craft and evidently felt constrained to be gentle. The *News* and *World-Telegram* didn't go overboard but took a tolerant view of Broun's antics and the show, which they felt should be allowed to survive on philanthropic grounds. The most ferocious of all the critics was Percy Hammond of the *Herald Tribune*, whose shafts still protruded from a whole generation of actors, directors, producers, and playwrights like the survivors of an Indian uprising. He and Broun had never been on friendly terms, and perhaps because he was conscious of that long-standing hostility, Hammond did his best to be kind. Broun, he noted, was the "most versatile and brilliant of our public men." On being charged with avoiding the issue of whether Broun should be allowed to display himself behind the proscenium, Hammond admitted in elliptical fashion that he did not consider Broun to be an ornament of the musical stage. "When I see a Titan slowly stirring from his comfortable perch in order to ameliorate the distress of others, I am overcome by a desire to applaud," he explained. "Also I take a pigmy's enjoyment in the discomfiture of a colossus trying to be a clown."

Shoot the Works continued running through the summer and into the fall, its survival largely due to the presence of "guest stars" who donated their services. People bought tickets knowing the Marx Brothers might show up in full force and turn the show into a shambles, that Helen Morgan or Helen Kane might appear for a song or two. Other big names who came on for a turn included the great tap dancer Bill "Bojangles" Robinson, Harry Richman, George Jessel, Al Jolson, Texas Guinan, Eddie Cantor, Sophie Tucker, and Morton Downey.

Thus the revue survived for a respectable 89 performances. It closed finally when Broun became exhausted from writing his column daily and appearing onstage nightly. The cast decided the show wouldn't hang together without Broun's presence and it was time to ring down the final curtain.

An extra added attraction of *Shoot the Works* so far as Broun was concerned was meeting a pretty black-haired girl named Connie Madison, who kicked up her heels in the chorus line. She was the physical type that attracted him, small, dark, lively; his older friends noted a resemblance to Lydia Lopokova. He began squiring her around town after the nightly performances, an odd pairing even on the Manhattan speakeasy circuit, given their disparity in age, experience, and backgrounds.

The girl, Connie Madison, was the widow of Johnny Dooley, who had been featured in the Ziegfeld shows until his death several years before. Madison was a stage name. Born Maria Incoronata Fruscello, she was the daughter of Italian immigrants from the Abruzzi region and lived with them and her young daughter, Patricia, out in Yonkers. Obviously she wasn't the stereotyped, dizzy-blonde "pony" of the chorus lines pursued by stockbrokers and playboys, or Broun wouldn't have felt a strong, continuing attraction. "She was unusually intelligent," her daughter remembers her, "with a brilliant sense of humor. She never grew old and was always sparkling and gay. She was a brave, funny, honest, generous, independent woman, with plenty of Italian temperament, and I think she made Heywood happy."

Connie called Broun "Commander" for some reason unfathomed by their friends—he wasn't exactly the commanding type—and bullied him into following his doctor's orders during the illness that closed the show. Not having a taste for New York night life, she still was willing to accompany him and his "entourage"—a dozen or so hangers-on, not his old friends dating back to the Algonquin Round Table, whose constant presence certified his importance as a public figure—as they made the rounds of the speakeasies and nightclubs. Because of Broun's capacity for alcohol, which was considered unique even in a profession which prided itself on absorbing more than its share of the bootleg distilleries' output, being Broun's No. 1 drinking companion, even though she didn't drink much herself, was a demanding avocation for Connie Madison. There weren't too many people, of the kind that had to show up for work in the morning, who could stand the pace.

His hypochondria, his constant pulse taking, and his dramatic announcements almost hourly that he wasn't long for this world also made a relationship with him, whatever its degree of intimacy, a continuing ordeal. Those who knew him best, of course, simply laughed off his woeful complaints. A short time before he met Connie Madison, it was recalled, he passed through a medical crisis every weekend at the Sabine Farm. One weekend, with a fluttering of eyelids, he announced that he was having a major heart attack. "Hit him over the head with a cocktail shaker," suggested his son, Woodie, who was then about twelve years old, "and he'll come to." Broun laughed so hard that he could no longer pretend to be dying.

Not all his friends were pleased with the news that Broun was getting serious about a chorus girl or the possibility that he might divorce Ruth Hale to marry her. They regarded it as a middle-aged man's fling, undignified and unseemly.

One night Broun brought her to a session of the Thanatopsis Poker Club, now meeting irregularly and without any interlopers from Wall Street or Park Avenue. The game had already started, and before sitting down at the table, Broun introduced her to George S. Kaufman.

Kaufman didn't even look up when Connie said, "Pleased to meet you, Mr. Kaufman."

"Oh," he said, keeping his gaze fixed on his poker hand. "A dancer."

Despite the inimical attitude of some of his friends, Broun continued to spend as much time as possible with Connie Madison.

15. The Perils and Pleasures of Union Leadership

DURING the early thirties Broun was increasingly absorbed by the ideological passions, the threatened outbreak of warfare between the social and economic classes, which characterized the period. Herbert Hoover, now sardonically referred to as the Great Engineer, had failed to get the economic machinery turning over again, but was willing to try for a second term. His opponent in 1928, former Governor Al Smith, felt that he was entitled to renomination by the Democrats, but that sentiment was not shared by the governor of New York, Franklin D. Roosevelt.

Meanwhile the breadlines were lengthening and the millions of unemployed—unemployment insurance being four years in the future—had nowhere to turn in their privations. Wall Street was a disaster area. Homes and farms were being foreclosed all over the country, and banks were barring their doors against depositors raging to withdraw their savings before it was too late. Yet there was amazingly little civil disorder; apathy rather than rage was the prevailing mood. The last real depression had been in 1907, and no one quite knew how to behave after the "eternal prosperity" promised by various political and economic prophets turned out to be as much of a mirage as the Republican campaign pledge of a chicken in every pot and a car in every garage.

Broun continued to believe that only a more radical formula than those offered by the Republicans and Democrats would rescue the foundering nation. But his Marxism was the milder form, which would have preserved most democratic institutions. The Communist newspaper, the *Daily Worker*, regarded him as much of a class enemy as any plutocrat and asked in regard to him, "Shooting may be deserved—and we do not exclude that from possibilities—but how about taking his gin away from him and putting him to work as a stoker in a steamer carrying workers to the Bermudas [*sic*] for their vacations?"

As a private citizen Broun attended the Socialists' national convention of 1932 in Milwaukee and flung himself into the struggle between the old guard and the Militants, whose candidate he had been for Congress. He was disillusioned to some extent by the parliamentary quibbling on the convention floor, which seemed to make the Socialists the mirror image of the two capitalist parties, and by a ridiculously verbose platform, which he and Oscar Ameringer, the editor of the *American Guardian*, revised to a cogent 287 words. Before the convention was over, he confided to some of his comrades that the Socialists simply weren't in touch with reality. They were fighting the battles of the 1890's against a background of smokeless factory chimneys and streets lined with idle men.

As a journalist he attended first the Republican convention and watched the listless renomination of Herbert Hoover, then the much livelier convocation of the Democrats in Chicago, at which Governor Roosevelt would be wafted to the nomination while the bands endlessly blared, and not quite accurately predicted, that "Happy Days Are Here Again."

Rooseveltian partisan though he became, Broun was not then impressed by the governor of New York, whom he referred to in his columns as "Fearless Frank." His man was Al Smith. Forgetting that he was committed to the Socialist candidacy of Norman Thomas, casting aside the generally sacred principle of journalistic objectivity and nonpartisanship, he jumped out of the press section at the convention when Smith's name was placed before the delegates and joined the parade through the aisles. A lost cause, for which he had a lifelong predilection. His Socialist comrades, on hearing that he had illicitly demonstrated on behalf of a capitalist candidate, prepared to read him out of the party, by which time, of course, Broun had forsaken the party anyway.

There was to be one more passionate commitment to activism in Broun's career. The cause, which would leave the aloes of regret in his system, mostly for personal reasons, was the unionization of the journalistic profession or craft; no one was quite sure whether newspapermen were working at a trade or were members of a low-grade profession, somewhere between chiropractors and horse doctors, though in a lower economic grouping.

A decade earlier Broun had been involved in an attempt to organize the working newspapermen with Lewis Gannett, then a member of *The Nation* staff, and his old Socialist friend McAllister Coleman of the *Sun*. The idea was Gannett's, but when reporters working on the daily newspapers proved reluctant to join with the staffs of liberal magazines in the Journalists' Union, Gannett decided that a presence like Broun was needed to rally the men on the dailies. Broun consented to be president of the union. His own efforts were desultory, however, and the effort soon petered out.

He had brought up the subject of unionizing the editorial staffs again when the *World* folded, but nobody had responded. For the past several years, however, the newspaper business had come to seem a lot less glamorous to its practitioners, with newspapers collapsing and salary cuts ordained for employees of the survivors. Reporters, as Broun and others saw it, had been sold a bill of goods by the publishers. They had been propagandized into accepting low salaries in return for the excitement and romance of a reporter's career. Then, too, many newspapermen (remembering the examples of Mark Twain, Jack London, Ernest Hemingway, Richard Harding Davis, and so many other literary stars who had once worked for newspapers) regarded it as a training ground for writing novels or swanking around foreign capitals as correspondents.

By the summer of 1933, with Roosevelt in the White House for less than six months, Broun had come to see that the New Deal might benefit his profession. The New Deal, he wrote, was "an opening wedge into the creation of an entirely new state of society." Utopia, if not prosperity, might be just around the corner. Among the bureaucracies fabricated at assembly-line speed by the Roosevelt Administration was the National Recovery Act, which would codify and regulate every industry, including newspapers, to provide shorter hours of work and thus more jobs. With the Blue Eagle of the NRA watching benignly and the Wagner Act soon to provide legal protection for the organization of unions, the editorial employees of newspapers would be enabled to band together, receive a decent minimum wage, and no longer be summoned from their beds to cover a fire or an ax murder at the whim of the city desk but with no extra pay.

Newspaper publishers, of course, were resisting to the best of their ability. At hearings on the Publishers Code section of the NRA they urged that reporters be classified as professional men and women and thus excluded from the five-day week. A professional, in the publishers' view, was anyone making more than $35 a week. That still covered most New York newspapermen, though they had taken two ten-percent salary cuts involuntarily, but many reporters out in the hinterlands were working for less.

Broun believed that given their strong individualistic bent, newspapermen would continue to work long hours for low pay, unprotected by provisions of the NRA and other New Deal institutions, if they weren't roused to collective action.

Early in August, 1933, Broun unfurled his banner proclaiming the brotherhood of the working press. It was hardly the most strident of battle cries. Most of the more calefactory statements in the column were attributed to a letter which, he said, he had received from a fellow signing himself "Reporter Unemployed." The anonymous correspondent quoted by Broun deplored the fact that reporters liked to refer to themselves as "the gentlemen of the press" and were too dignified, too snobbish, to organize themselves like the printers and other blue-collar craftsmen. Yet the men in the composing room, for all their lack of social status, were getting paychecks thirty percent higher than those received by the men in the city room. It was time, "Reporter Unemployed" declared, for newspapermen to take a more practical view of their working conditions and organize against the rapacity of the publishers.

Speaking for himself, Broun wrote, he had always felt kindly toward his editors and publishers. Instead of brutalizing him, they had given him promotions, had provided him with the cushiness of a columnist's ivory tower. It was hard for him to think of his employer as a Simon Legree and himself as a field hand on the Scripps-Howard plantation. "But the fact that newspaper editors and owners are genial folk should hardly stand in the way of the organization of a newspaper writers' union. There should be one. Beginning at nine o'clock on the morning of October 1 I am going to do the best I can to help in getting one up. I think I could die happy on the opening day of the general strike if I had the privilege of watching Walter Lippmann heave half a brick through a *Tribune* window at a non-union operative who had been called in to write the current Today and Tomorrow column on the gold standard." A half brick came readily to Broun's hand whenever he thought of Lippmann, whose Brahmin-intellectual manner he still furiously resented, who had moved to the conservative *Herald Tribune* after the *World* collapsed.

Not altogether unwittingly, it would seem, Broun had cast himself in the leading role of the organization of what became the American Newspaper Guild. The private vision of himself had always been, ridiculous as it would seem to others, a gallant and heroic one. He could easily conceive of himself center stage with the spotlight focused on him. He affected an aw-shucks modesty which wore well in the abrasive democracy of the newspaper office, but privately considered that the Leader of Men role was not beyond him.

It would take a little redesigning, however, to shape him into the role of labor leader. His consciousness of labor solidarity occasionally blurred. Back in 1931 he had raged at certain friends who crossed the picket line of waiters at the Algonquin. Just about the time he was helping organize the Newspaper Guild, he joined Dorothy Parker and Alexander Woollcott in participating in a demonstration on behalf of hotel employees on strike against the Waldorf Astoria—the favored radical-chic gesture of the well-heeled in the thirties. After the demonstration Broun and Miss Parker walked over to Jack and Charlie's 21 for a restorative drink, ignoring the picket line of 21 waiters on strike. When Robert Benchley strolled into the room, they scrunched together in a corner, Miss Parker hiding her face under the brim of her floppy black hat. Benchley, however, spotted them and headed for their corner. Outraged, he berated Broun, as a nascent labor leader, for having committed the cardinal sin of crossing a picket line. "And," Benchley added, turning to Miss Parker, "don't blink those ingenue eyes at me."

Many times Broun would have to remind himself that, though he lived in a penthouse and was making a corporation president's salary, he was the leader of the proletarians of his profession.

His penthouse may have symbolized the epitome of luxurious living, but it also served as the headquarters of those planning the organization of the Newspaper Guild—their underground cellar. There the plans were formulated for organizing other branches of the Guild throughout the country, for publishing the *Guild Reporter*, for demanding a five-day, forty-hour week, a minimum-wage scale, the right to collective bargaining. Broun and his junta met for a number of evenings in his Fifty-eighth Street penthouse before the formation of the Guild was formally announced. A dozen or so persons participated in the meetings, including Doris Fleeson (a future Washington columnist), Lewis Gannett, George Britt, Allen Raymond, Ed Angly, Frederick Woltman, and other top-flight practitioners of their craft. Also present was Broun's old schoolmate, Morris L. Ernst, to whom he invariably turned in times of stress, whether of the legal or emotional variety.

Ernst recalls that one of the problems of enticing other newspaper people into their union was the silent but implacable opposition of the publishers to unionization of their editorial departments, which they feared partly because it would increase salaries but also because, as they put it, union members would not be as objective as journalists were traditionally supposed to be. Ernst recalled a *Times* reporter whom he named Bill who appeared at the meetings in a highly furtive manner. Bill also brought his wife along so that if word of his presence at the Broun penthouse reached his bosses, he could claim he had gone there for a social evening.

To Ernst the alarming aspect of Bill's fearful attitude lay in the fact that "dozens of other Bills lived in similar fear . . . fear of loss of employment if it were known that they desired to create an organization which might someday have sufficient bargaining power to trade with the publishers. If men working for the *Times*—in most ways the best employer in the field—lived in such fear, imagine the state of mind of reporters working for less objective and socially minded papers. . . ."

On September 17, through arrangements made by Ernst, a meeting of those interested in organizing the New York newspapers was held at the City Club. Several hundred attended, and it was obvious that the Guild was an idea whose time had come. The main argument was centered on the question of whether they would organize a professional guild or a trade union. Most favored the guild idea, perhaps because it had a more distinguished tone.

In practically all newspaper publishers' offices, including the *World-Telegram* and other Scripps-Howard papers (which were officially tolerant of unionism, but during the early thirties paid many reporters only $15 a week), the news of Broun's union activity resounded like a thunderclap. Roy Howard was bitterly opposed to the unionization of his editorial employees, and from then on Broun would not be one of his favorite people.

Broun soon came to the realization that even a fairly innocuous-sounding "professional guild" wasn't going to be accorded much tolerance by the publishers, even those who had supported the union movement in other industries. He also recognized that the opposition would be covert, in some cases, as well as openly reactionary. He appeared as chief representative of the newspaper employees at an NRA hearing on the formation of the Newspaper Code. "Quite inadvertently, I am sure, some of the publishers have allowed the feeling to grow and spread that newspapermen and women who join organizations of their own creation will be subject to penalties," he noted. "The penalty may not be dismissal. All newspapermen know of an institution known as the Chinese torture room. A reporter who incurs the displeasure of the boss by organizing activity may find himself writing obits for the rest of his life. . . . You can't call it a free press that rests upon the fears and apprehensions of reporters who are frightened and who feel that they have good reason to be frightened."

Broun and his fellow organizers rapidly enlisted members of the New York Guild even as newspapers in other cities were being similarly organized.

Most of the New York publishers made it plain that they would fight the Guild and everything it stood for. Roy Howard summoned the editorial employees of the *World-Telegram* to a meeting at which he warned them that "Broun never finished anything he starts." Tolerance of the Guild came from the most curious sources. The publisher of the New York *Daily News*, Captain Joseph M. Patterson, was politically the crustiest of conservatives, yet, unlike many publishers whose papers laid claim to liberal attitudes and a fondness for the working class, he felt that reporters needed some protection from their employers. "I'll tell my reporters only this," he informed Ernst, "that 'If I were working for Patterson or any other publisher, I'd join the Guild.'" David Stern, the publisher of the *Post*, was also sympathetic. The rest of the city's publishers, Ernst recalled, were "scared stupid. They thought they could smash a society of journalists. They resisted, they sniffed, they jeered, they bribed by giving better wages and shorter hours. They would do anything but recognize a guild of their favorite and most important workers."

During the latter months of 1933, therefore, the Guild continued to be a sort of underground movement, with its partisans huddling conspiratorially in such newspaper hangouts as Jake Bleeck's Artists and Writers Club, a former speakeasy a few doors down from the *Herald Tribune*, and the Pen and Pencil Club, where *Mirror* reporters congregated. Every newspaper had its watering hole, usually just across the alley, and Broun made the rounds almost daily, his capacity for gin now serving in a just cause.

Often he would encounter the cynicism which most reporters wore with the same devilish panache—*Front Page* style—as they generally affected snap-brim hats, unpolished shoes, stained neckties at half mast, cigarettes dribbling smoke out of the corners of their mouths. What, they demanded, was all this organizing activity going to do for Heywood Broun? A good question. Usually he answered it by saying it was his "contribution" to the profession he had practiced for almost a quarter of a century. Or that his son, Woodie, soon to join the staff of *PM*, would benefit from being protected by the Guild.

But there was more to it than that. A certain amount of ego was involved. If there hadn't been, Broun, as a highly paid columnist, working under contract rather than at the pleasure of a city editor, would have stepped back once the organization of the Guild was well under way and let those directly concerned take over its direction.

Instead he was sorely disappointed when the New York chapter of the Guild elected him to the vice-presidency rather than the presidency, which it bestowed on a less celebrated member. The growth of the Guild movement throughout the country eventually provided him with the more glorified office of national president. Whoever the New York Guild made its president, it was identified with Broun, who gloried in the role of its disheveled totem. He fought with Major General Hugh S. "Iron Pants" Johnson, the NRA administrator and a man who not only loved an argument but liked it fully detailed in the press. The issue between Broun and General Johnson was Lindsay Rogers, who had been appointed to oversee the Newspaper Code section of NRA and was loath to saddle publishers with the necessity of paying reporters overtime if they worked more than 40 hours a week. Broun and Johnson exchanged compliments for several weeks after Broun learned of a memo from Rogers to Johnson said to favor someone else for the national Guild presidency. Broun, however, won the office and served as La Pasionara of the cause closest to his heart.

It was not long before he discovered that the growingly active American Communist Party, making the most of its opportunities in troubled times, was burrowing into the Guild's structure. By using tactics out of the agitprop handbook, they managed to take control of many chapters and part of the national leadership. The takeover was accomplished through small factions extending Guild meetings hour after hour, until most of the members left in boredom or disgust, then ramming through measures they advocated.

Broun and the Guild's unpaid legal advocate, Morris Ernst, did their utmost to combat the Communist inroads. Before Ernst withdrew in disgust at the Communist tactics, he assumed the burden of testing the constitutionality of the Wagner Act, which provided legal protection for those active in union organization, in the case of Morris Watson, an Associated Press reporter who had been fired for Guild activity. The issue was fought up to the United States Supreme Court and resulted in a decision which practically guaranteed the Guild's survival. The high court held that the Associated Press' "freedom of the press" defense, which was also generally used by the publishers, was not sustained by the law and could not be used as an excuse for resisting the unionization of its reporters and editors.

Many newspapers, less openly now, continued to oppose the formation of Guild units in their city rooms. Conscious of the Communist faction's claims that it could gain more for the Guild through direct action, Broun demonstrated his own brand of militancy wherever the Guild was struggling against the newspaper managements. In Toledo he marched in the picket line with Guild members on strike. The state police decided to break up the demonstration and hurled tear-gas grenades at the strikers and then, wearing gas masks, charged the picket line. Broun led the retreat, but ripped his trousers in hurdling the nearby fence.

A short time later he was arrested on a downtown street corner and taken to the local jail, where he was identified by one of the arresting officers as a "rich New York Communist." "Uh-uh," Broun corrected him, "rich New York *columnist*." He was released a few hours later.

During that period of the Guild's development he traveled around the country addressing mass meetings and urging the whole newspaper profession to unionize itself. He had become a stirring orator, though emotion outbalanced logic in most of his speeches. Admittedly he was enjoying himself and neglected few opportunities for self-dramatization. "I am, of course, subconsciously an exhibitionist," he confessed. "And not so very subconsciously at that."

Pitting his personal appeal, his ability to charm and influence people singly or en masse, and making the most of the fact that he was the most admired journalist in the country, he labored endlessly to keep the Guild from splitting along ideological lines. Communists and anti-Communists were struggling for control, with Broun as arbiter.

A few publishers understood that he represented the best of the alternatives, but most stubbornly refused to deal with the Guild on any basis, and as Ernst noted, they "drove the Guild to the left." Continued rejection of the Guild by the publishers simply turned the movement from Broun and the moderates toward those who proposed radical remedies. "For a time," Ernst recalled, "the Communist faction took over the national organization. It is the usual pattern of American trade-union development. Union leadership, responsible and honest, holds power only if the bosses deal with labor on decent bargaining levels. . . . Rejection of labor organizations invites crooks or Communists or demagogues to take over the power. Moderates, like Broun, can't hold power if the bosses will not even confer with them."

Broun attempted to conciliate the Communist faction, perhaps to a greater extent than Ernst recalled. Like most liberals of that "popular front" period, when Stalinism was presenting itself as an ally of the democracies against the threat of Hitlerism, he accepted the Communist Party as a legal, unsubversive political movement rather than the arm of a foreign power. He joined what were later revealed as Communist-front organizations, addressed a Communist rally for the Scottsboro Boys, and suggested in one column that no one could be really well informed unless he read the *Daily Worker* as well as other newspapers.

Just how much his association with Communist activities was rooted in the current liberal tendency toward an "opening to the left," as it later became known, and how much in tactical maneuvers to co-opt the Communist influence in the Guild, it is impossible to say. But he did work hard to ameliorate the Communist influence—perhaps too hard at times. Once he brought Harry Raymond of the *Daily Worker* to a forum conducted by a Rand School committee and humorously introduced the inoffensive Raymond as "Exhibit A of the red menace in the labor movement." When his auditors failed to respond favorably, he told them bluntly, "If you belong to a union without any reds in it, for God's sake go out and recruit a few!"

Ernst recalls that Broun was worried about the Communist infiltration almost from the beginning of his campaign to organize the Newspaper Guild. He believed that one of the paid Guild officers was also receiving a secret subsidy from the American Communist Party and was suspicious of the fact that Earl Browder, the Communists' chief commissar in the United States, and one of his collaborators were occupying a suite at the hotel where a national Guild convention was being held. Anyone attending Guild meetings during the formative years will remember how cohesive little cabals of that persuasion bulldozed their way to seizing control of the various locals. They persisted in maintaining control for more than a decade in many places, not only during but after World War II. The Los Angeles unit of the Guild, as its survivors will remember, was particularly dominated by a vociferous minority of the comrades and their camp followers. It finally came to grief in a long and futile strike against Hearst's Los Angeles *Herald-Examiner*, the other surviving Los Angeles paper, the *Times*, having succeeded in keeping the Guild out of its editorial departments. That, too, pointed to the failure of Heywood Broun's highest hopes for the Guild movement: that it would provide more employment. Instead in New York and other cities ultramilitancy not only caused strikes but, when impossible demands could not be met, the publishers simply closed down their operations. For many a Guild member, his last membership card from the organization signifies joblessness; he will never again work in the profession or craft for which he was trained.

The Guild had been Broun's baby, though some share of paternity could be claimed by Lewis Gannett, McAllister Coleman, and others, and he remained loyal, in much the same fashion as a father whose son has turned out to be the most wayward delinquent on the block. He saw no alternative but to play ball with the left-wing faction if the circumstances seemed to warrant it and found himself practicing a pragmatism his younger self might have found repellent.

One instance of that pragmatism was his role in engineering a pay cut for Guild members, if the city-room rumors were correct. The New York *Post*, published by J. David Stern, the first publisher in New York to extend recognition to the Guild, was suffering financial reverses. "Presuming on his status as a pro-labor employer," as one former *Post* reporter has related, Stern "told a meeting of his editorial employees that he would sell the paper unless they immediately accepted a pay cut, to be repaid out of revenues—when there were revenues. The resourceful publisher took other steps to bolster his position. . . . Stern went to the White House to inform President Roosevelt that the only New Deal paper in New York would founder unless it got help. Roosevelt talked to CIO President John L. Lewis, Lewis called Heywood Broun, president of the Newspaper Guild, and Broun spoke to a Communist functionary in the New York local who then rammed the pay cut down the throats of the reluctant Guild members at the *Post*."

Such actions no doubt were distasteful, but Broun had wholly committed himself to making the Guild a success, whatever obstacles thrust themselves in his way, and permanently establishing it as the economic shield of a notoriously insecure occupation. He made no secret of the fact that he regarded the Guild as the capstone of his career, the one thing for which he would deserve to be remembered. In that determination he never spared himself. He not only flung himself into the violent strike against the Newark *Ledger*, published by a man who descended on the city room in red pajamas and ordered wholesale firings at midnight, but brought along his son, Woodie, to march with him in the picket line.

For all his efforts, however, Broun was maintained in the

national presidency of the Guild only (as Ernst noted) "as a symbol." He would serve as a totem figure while the Guild's left wing and the larger number of moderates fought it out. One of the bitterest moments of his life would come when he was rejected, rather openly, and just when his journalistic career was touching bottom, by the men he had crusaded for without any hope of material gain for himself.

16. "My Best Friend Died"

THE reality of Heywood Broun evaded everyone, most of all himself. None of his friends claimed to know the inmost recesses of his character. His son, Heywood Hale Broun, remembers him, thirty-five years after his death, as an often silent and always reticent man. Trooping through speakeasies with a dozen companions, apparently friendly and gregarious, confiding his hopes and fears to the newest of acquaintances, he appeared to be jovial and Falstaffian, outgoing, a fellow of immense cheer. Yet those who knew him best were the ones who admitted they knew him least.

Behind the large, untidy, hail-fellow façade, behind the physical bulk which people generally associate with an easygoing disposition, there existed the real and anxiety-ridden, death-fearing, and monumentally insecure Heywood Broun, whose character could be glimpsed only in fragments, in prismatic flashes of self-revelation. Something like the elephant in Aesop's fable as described by six blind men, each of them having thoroughly explored one part of the beast. You could detail his richly eccentric habits, you could describe him in action as a partisan of various causes, you could evaluate him through his friends' praise of a generous and often self-sacrificial personality, you could assess his frequent examination of himself (or a part thereof) in his writings, but somehow a three-dimensional portrait of Heywood Broun escapes the observer.

The man who knew him longest and perhaps best was Morris Ernst, a shrewd and perceptive man, but he confessed that "no one, least of all I," could honestly claim intimate knowledge of Broun; yet Ernst had known him from school days to his death and for fifteen years had spent two or three evenings a week in his company.

Ernst recalls he understood him only a little better after one night-long discussion of what was wrong with Broun's life. It was almost as though the two men were trying to put together a psychic jigsaw puzzle, that night about a year and a half before Broun's death. Broun was puzzled by himself, he admitted, even after spending $70,000 over the years in consultations with psychiatrists and psychoanalysts, long before such séances became the standard procedure for anyone who made good in Manhattan.

They discussed, as Ernst remembers, Broun's "pathetic sexual insecurity stemming from bits of still prevalent gutter folklore which circulated, at least in New York, at the turn of the century." They also searched for meaning in his "desire for certainty . . . his search for authority in the Socialist Party," which he found less than overwhelming, "his long life with Ruth Hale," which they apparently equated with his yearning for a polar absolute on which to peg his life. "Violent, strong, mathematical" Ruth Hale, as Ernst described her. They also delved for significance in his neurotic fear of crowds and of riding on trains (in the latter respect, at least, he was exceeded by a poet of some regional renown, Professor William Ellery Leonard of the University of Wisconsin, who stayed within the city limits of Madison for decades out of fear of what he called "the locomotive god"), his hypochondria (or, as Ernst put it, "his one-man art show of cardiograms"), and his constant fear of death. Only a friend of the longest duration would have endured such a session or be subjected to it. But for all their mulling and pondering, they came to no conclusions. One thought which might have occurred to them was that a large number of other middle-aged American males in Broun's approximate circumstances, if they weren't more concerned where the rent money was coming from, could have filled almost as lengthy bills of particulars. Broun was in plentiful if not good company.

The most unique feature of Broun's life undoubtedly was his tortured relationship with Ruth Hale, whose inner torments evidently were of a more painful order, though not as frequently exhibited, as her husband's.

Early in 1933 they had resumed living together in Manhattan. One couldn't call it a reconciliation, because there had never been a breakup except in the sense that they occupied separate apartments; but even then they continued to spend the warmer months together at the Sabine Farm. Broun gave up his penthouse, Ruth her apartment a few blocks away, and they moved into a suite at the Hotel Des Artistes at West Sixty-seventh Street and Central Park West. No one could say exactly why, unless it was for their son's sake. They continued to live separate lives under the same roof. Heywood still saw Connie Madison and believed himself to be in love with her.

A few months after they moved into Des Artistes, however, Ruth Hale decided that she wanted to break all legal ties with Broun. What she yearned for, what she had wanted for many years, she told Broun, was "freedom." She had always hated the technical designation "Mrs. Heywood Broun," as though marriage leached away all her individuality. Somehow, she felt, Broun had engorged her. If she hadn't been a woman, born in the nineteenth century, she would have been able to achieve something on her own. As it was, her career had been bound up in his, with all the credit going to him.

She could not or would not comprehend that for all her intensity, her knowledge (superior in some respects to Broun's), her drive and courage and flaming spirit, she could not achieve what Broun offhandedly, almost effortlessly had achieved. The difference was talent. It must have galled her to watch Broun toss off a column or an article in less than an hour while she sweated for days over a similar composition. And then to hear people say, with poisonous indifference, "Ruth Hale? Oh, yes, you're Heywood Broun's wife."

Broun may have opposed a divorce because he sensed that she might need him, if only she didn't resent the situation so much, because she was burning herself out with frustration, with the conviction that her life was worthless, particularly after her dramatization of *The Venetian Glass Nephew* folded after a few nights on Broadway. Their mutual friend Deems Taylor put it rather well when he told her, "Ruth, you have more capacity for emotion than anybody I ever knew. I wish I had it, because if I did I wouldn't waste it in such narrow channels."

But she could not rid herself of the conviction that somehow, as long as she was married to Broun, she was deprived of her individuality, even her identity. Nor of the bitterness she felt regarding that deprivation, which was not lessened by Broun's concessions to her ego or his sympathy for her predicament.

Broun finally agreed to a divorce, which she obtained in Mexico on November 17, 1933.

It was too late, however, for Ruth Hale to win the struggle, the arena of which existed in her own mind, for an unfettered life. She was forty-eight years old and often had said that "a woman is through after forty." She feared old age as much or more than Broun feared death.

She also found that divorce had not broken all ties with Broun. They continued to see each other frequently, and she remained his adviser; it seemed to some that she now believed she should have worked harder at the marriage and resented it less. In the summer of 1934, less than a year after the divorce, she fell seriously ill and stayed at the Sabine Farm, which Broun continued to share. Divorce, like marriage, was merely a formality in their relationship; whatever bound them was stronger than any legal rituals.

Her condition worsened, but she refused to allow a doctor to be called into consultation. She had, it seemed, turned her face to the wall. One day in mid-September she sank into a coma and was removed to a New York hospital. On September 18, 1934, she died without regaining consciousness.

Broun was badly shaken. It was literally true that part of himself died with her, because as he wrote in his column the next day, "for seventeen years practically every word I wrote was set down with the feeling that Ruth Hale was looking over my shoulder." In his moving tribute beginning, "My best friend died yesterday"—possibly the most accurate description of their relationship—he acknowledged her role as his moral and literary conscience, as virtually his collaborator. "It was a curious collaboration," he told his readers, "because Ruth Hale gave me out of the very best she had to equip me for the understanding of human problems. She gave this under protest, with many reservations, and a vast rancor. But she gave.

"I understood then and will always understand the inevitable bitterness of the person who projects herself through another, even if that one is close. . . . Since it is true that very many of the ideas for which I seem to be sponsor are really hers, in the last analysis I am the utterly dependent person. . . .

"It would be a desperately lonely world if I did not feel that personality is of such tough fiber that in some manner it must survive and does survive. I still feel that she is looking over my shoulder."

Great though his sense of deprivation at Ruth Hale's death, he soldiered on, busying himself with the Guild's struggle against the publishers, with his column, and with Connie Madison Dooley, whom he planned to marry. He had hesitated over remarriage while Ruth Hale was still alive, and even now he and Connie agreed to the old-fashioned belief that it was only decent to wait a year after his first wife's death before remarrying. It was only several months later, however, that Broun and Connie Madison were married. The civil ceremony was performed at City Hall on January 5, 1935. As a devout Italian Catholic Connie felt the marriage wasn't sanctified without a religious ceremony, which was performed several weeks later at the Actors Church.

Subsequently Connie's nine-year-old daughter, Patricia, joined the household and was delighted with her stepfather and her new life. A short time later Broun adopted her. Patricia was overjoyed to escape from the stern, knuckle-rapping nuns at St. Denis Parochial School in Yonkers. "It was like getting out of jail," she recently recalled. "Heywood, who had escaped from a Victorian upbringing, and I, who had escaped from the nuns, had something in common. Although he was impressive because of his size and aura of greatness, Heywood seemed shy and I took to him right away. He asked if I would like to change my name to Broun and I said yes and that was that. . . . I was happy to have a father and, after being an only child, happy to have a brother. My admiration for Woodie Broun was overwhelming and I find it hard to say that he is my 'step' brother or that Heywood was my 'step' father."

Patricia Broun remembers one of the rare occasions when the serenity of Broun's new household was ruffled, if only for the moment. "I was listening to the radio with Mother on a visit to my grandparents and heard that Heywood was in jail for leading a picket line. Mother was upset, thinking of handcuffs and windows with bars, but I said, 'Don't worry, Mom,' he's enjoying himself.' And so he was. He told us that he enjoyed singing with the other men in jail and Mother, who was still annoyed, said: 'You can sing at home!' "

The Brouns gave up his apartment at the Des Artistes and made their home at the Sabine Farm, which was renovated and made habitable for winter as well as summer. An effort at interior decoration was made under the new Mrs. Broun's direction; the swamp was drained and replaced by a pond, which was stocked with pickerel and bass. The second Mrs. Broun was more feminine and less feminist than her predecessor and briskly set about remodeling Broun's habits as well as his habitat. Drinking was reduced to less gargantuan proportions and feeding was regularized, and even his style of dress was altered along more conventional lines, though no one would ever mistake him for Adolphe Menjou or Jimmy Walker. Broun liked it, even took to swaggering around in a double-breasted camel's-hair overcoat, which was then the height of masculine fashion.

He had come to enjoy the rural life, and now he and Connie went into town only when there was some compelling reason. Then, too, Fairfield County was beginning to fill up with others newly elevated to the squirearchy, and there was enough social life to satisfy him in the rolling country around the Sabine Farm.

He would never be the compleat squire himself, being too sedentary, for one thing, and having no taste for the huntin', shootin', ridin' pleasures of the conventional country gentleman. He particularly abhorred hunting, dreaded the autumn afternoons when the urban sportsmen invaded the woods and fields and unlimbered with their artillery. He could see little sportsmanship in a man with a shotgun blasting away at an unarmed rabbit. In the past several years the wooded hills north of Stamford had been denuded of partridge and pheasants. The deer were also getting scarce.

He realized, he wrote in an article, that sports provided a tremendous booster shot for the masculine ego. The greatest bore in the world was the golfer who had just broken a hundred and could not restrain himself from replaying the game hole by hole, but "I would rather listen to him than hear the hunter's story. Colonel Bogey is a foeman worthy of any man's mettle. Rabbits and squirrels are slight creatures." During the deer-hunting season, he related, he had to dress up like a masquerader in a red shirt and other colorful bits of costuming to keep from being slaughtered as a deer; the eagerness of the hunters to shoot and kill anything that moved was appalling, so "let's be done with musketry. Cease firing. None of us is here forever and the span of the little animals is even less. . . ."

Even from the rural perspective he kept a sharp eye on the political scene, particularly the events leading up to the reelection of President Roosevelt. Broun had found an ideological

home in the New Deal. Necessarily he had to forsake his old
sentimental feelings about Al Smith, who had taken a sharp turn
to the right in reaction to Roosevelt's social and economic
programs. Smith, he wrote, had "come out for Grover Cleve-
land" as Walter Lippmann had "come out for both Hamilton
and Jefferson" (he still couldn't resist taking a potshot at
Lippmann whenever the opportunity was offered). He had
always felt a deep devotion to Al Smith, but the ex-governor had
betrayed his former progressive self.

The man he had formerly scoffed at as "Fearless Frank" was
now his idol. In the 1936 campaign President Roosevelt had
easily turned aside Smith's bid for the nomination under the
banners of the conservative Liberty League, and Broun accurately predicted that he would win the election by a wider
margin over Alfred M. Landon of Kansas than he had four years
earlier over ex-President Hoover. Broun did not deny that he was
a "Roosevelt enthusiast" and deplored comparisons of Franklin
Roosevelt and his fifth cousin Theodore Roosevelt, who "never
had one-tenth the force and driving power of Franklin."

Broun's militant liberalism was becoming as irksome to the
Scripps-Howard management as it had been occasionally distressing to the Pulitzers. The chain was not nearly so enamored
of the New Deal as its star columnist was. It was also true that
Broun's reactions to any issue were utterly predictable. In a
columnist, part of whose function is to entertain, to surprise, and
occasionally startle the reader, predictability is not an unalloyed
virtue. You aren't going to turn to him with mild excitement,
wondering what he'll say next, if his attitudes are utterly
consistent and he never shakes you up by departing from them.

For the sake of "balance," the *World-Telegram* therefore
decided to offset Broun's liberal humanitarianism with the
corrosive offerings of his opposite in ideology and temperament.
Westbrook Pegler, ex-columnist for the Chicago *Tribune*, then the
organ of the right wing, was the man. Pegler, Roy Howard
proclaimed, would offer "the drollery of Ring Lardner, the
iconoclasm of H. L. Mencken, the homely insight of Will
Rogers"—quite a package, never quite delivered.

In one of his first columns for the *World-Telegram* and the
Scripps-Howard syndicate Pegler showed that he would provide
an antidote for Broun's humanism. His eruption was occasioned
by news dispatches from San Jose, California, describing how a

mob had broken into the local jail and lynched two men charged with having kidnapped and murdered a Santa Clara University student. Forty years ago lynching was still regarded in some areas of public opinion as a worthy survival from the frontier days, an economical and timesaving form of rough justice, and not only in the South, as some Northern liberals learned to their astonishment. The governor of California, James Rolph, Jr., considered the lynching "a fine lesson for the whole nation." And three New York City newspapers agreed with him, praising the revival of the "pioneer spirit" and enthusing over the efficacy of vigilante action at a time when bank-robbing gangs were beginning to cause concern.

Pegler in his column breezily agreed with Governor Rolph about the salubrious effects of administering justice with a lynch rope. Broun predictably reacted in opposite fashion. He rarely resorted in his column to savage phraseology, but this time he gave full vent to his outrage. "If it were possible to carry on a case history of every person in the mob who beat and kicked and hanged and burned two human beings I will make the prophecy that out of this heritage will come crimes and cruelties which are unnumbered. . . . To your knees, Governor, and pray that you and your commonwealth may be washed clean of this bath of bestiality into which a whole community has plunged. You, James Rolph, Jr., stand naked in the eyes of the world. . . . I don't believe you can get away with it. There must be somewhere some power which just won't stand for it."

Despite the bristling confrontation in their respective columns, Broun and Pegler were on friendly terms. They had met as war correspondents in France, which formed something of a bond, and Broun realized that Pegler in print wasn't Pegler in person. As a columnist Pegler assailed everything Broun valued (with Roy Howard silently cheering him on), especially the New Deal and President and Mrs. Roosevelt. Verbal violence aside, and taking into account a dog-in-the-mangerish disposition, Pegler seemed to Broun a rather shy and gentle fellow who needed, but didn't quite know how to reach out for friendship. Pegler, Broun believed for a time, was reclaimable. So he was encouraged to journey from his home at Pound Ridge to join the sportive Connecticut literary set that included in addition to Broun, Harold Ross, John Erskine, Hendrik Willem van Loon (an immensely popular historian), Ursula Parrott, and the literary agent George T. Bye. Pegler was also invited to sit in on the neighborhood poker game, doubly welcome because he was an inveterate loser. Even after it became obvious that Pegler had maneuvered himself into a more favored position with the Scripps-Howard management, if only because his political views were in line with Roy Howard's, Broun continued to defend their friendship. He smiled bravely when Pegler sneered at his liberal attitudes and referred to him as "Old Bleeding Heart" in his column, perhaps because that placed him in what he considered honorable company.

Determinedly tolerant of his Scripps-Howard stable mate, Broun often told fellow liberals who wondered how he could value personal friendship with a reactionary like Pegler that "Peg" turned rabid only when he sat down at his typewriter.

He even invited Pegler to attend a picnic given at the Sabine Farm in honor of Eleanor Roosevelt, who would shortly join Scripps-Howard as a fellow columnist. If he hoped that personal contact with the Roosevelt charm would soften Pegler, he was proved overoptimistic. During Mrs. Roosevelt's visit Pegler was introduced to her and exchanged a few polite words when she left, but in between, glowering into his highball, he stayed at the bar while the other guests clustered around her. Subsequently she invited Pegler to a picnic at Hyde Park and again to a White House occasion, but after each invitation he wrote angrily anti-Roosevelt columns, leading the First Lady to conclude that the friend of her friend (Broun) would never be a friend of hers. She wrote Pegler off as a congenital misanthrope, explaining, "If you believed him, you would be depressed about human nature, not only in the individuals whom he mentions, but in the feeling you get of general cynicism about people." To Broun and his friends, that was putting it rather gently.

Several disillusioned years later Broun wrote a definitive analysis of the Pegler character in which he maintained that the latter wasn't the blackhearted wretch he pretended to be but was a fictional character, a persona created for public view, while inside was a gentle and decent man struggling to get out. Pegler was "shy, sensitive and sentimental" until the moment he sat down to bang out his column, upon which he became a "Damon Runyon version of Peter Pan."

Pegler's tragedy, he insisted, was that he was perverting his natural instincts to pose as a hard-boiled assailant of the

humanist, or liberal, attitudes. "His native sympathies are wide
and deep. When he is aroused about some ancient wrong he can
be more eloquent than any newspaperman I know. The most
understanding and sensitive column I can remember was written
by Peg in Germany about the peculiar persecution visited upon
Jewish children. And recently he broke through a long string of
his regular higher-bracket moans to cry out passionately against
the fearful housing visited upon one-third of the nation. And yet
upon all too frequent occasions he writes as if he has taken over
the role of light heavyweight champion of the upperdog and
game warden for the preserves of the overprivileged. Some day
somebody should take the hide off Peg because the stuff inside is
so much better than the varnished surface which blinks in the
sunlight of popular approval." Pegler was suitably outraged by
the Broun commentary because, with some accuracy, and despite
its forbearing Christian tone, it exposed him as a kindly fellow
who posed as a villain for the sake of professional advancement
just at a time when he was a hero to the considerable minority,
not all "upperdogs" by any means, which believed the New Deal
was wrecking the country.

Another addition to the Broun circle at the Sabine Farm was a
burly red-haired Irishman named Quentin Reynolds, a sportswriter on the *World-Telegram* whose dispatches from the Brooklyn
Dodgers' training camp had attracted Broun's favorable attention. In the several years before Reynolds switched to magazine
writing as a member of the *Collier's* staff and became one of the
outstanding correspondents of World War II, Broun practically
adopted him and made him a favorite drinking companion.
Reynolds, according to one Broun intimate, patterned himself in
the Broun mold, not only in his casual attitude toward the gents'
tailoring industry but in his manner and political stance; he also
adopted the seemingly artless and simplistic Broun literary style,
which wasn't as easy to imitate as many would-be imitators
hoped.

What Broun wanted from Reynolds, at first, was a reintroduc-
tion to the baseball world, with which Broun had lost contact.
The latter was thinking of writing a sequel to his baseball novel,
The Sun Field. Reynolds, in effect, was bringing the research to
Broun's penthouse when he appeared with ballplayers Lefty
O'Doul and Johnny Frederick in tow. No sequel resulted from
the sessions, but Broun was pleased by listening, after all those

years' absence from the press box, to professionals talk about their game. "When Johnny Frederick called Dazzy Vance the fastest right-hand pitcher he had ever seen, and added, 'Dazzy could throw a cream puff through a battleship,' Heywood glanced at me and nodded. This was the kind of talk he wanted to hear.

"For every story Frederick or O'Doul told, Heywood came up with something from the days when he traveled with the Giants, being paid forty dollars a week and piecing it out by playing bridge on the long train rides. His partner had usually been Christy Mathewson, whom Heywood considered the greatest pitcher he ever saw. It was out of these experiences that Heywood's novel *The Sun Field* had come. At one point O'Doul recalled the lead of the story Heywood had written the day Babe Ruth, in a World Series game, had beaten the Chicago Cubs with two home runs. 'The Ruth is mighty and must prevail,' O'Doul quoted. Heywood was touched to find that a player had remembered his line."

Reynolds also recalled Broun's fear of airplane travel, exhibited when he and Reynolds and other newspapermen flew out to Indianapolis with Captain Eddie Rickenbacker for the 500-mile auto race. "Although the weather was perfect, it was soon apparent that Heywood thought he was living his last hour. 'There are twelve of us on this damn thing,' he grumbled at one point. 'Suppose we crash and we're all killed. You know how the story will read in tomorrow's papers? "War Hero Eddie Rickenbacker Killed in Plane Crash." Way down at the end of the story it will say, "Among the other victims was Heywood Broun, a newspaperman." And ten to one they'll spell it "Brown." ' " The anecdote, an echo of the time Broun was an also-ran in the newspaper account of the automobile accident in which he and Herbert Bayard Swope were involved, also illuminated his anxiety about how he would be regarded by posterity, which undoubtedly was greater than his fear of flying.

Reynolds was fascinated by his senior's contradictions. "Tough-minded about social justice and conditions for the working man, for example, he was indifferent to his own wages and hours and was even a markedly easy touch. A slashing writer in his columns, he appeared to many of his readers an agnostic; yet during the years I knew him he was groping toward his belief in God."

Between Broun's newfound friends and additions to the Sabine Farm drinking, debating, and poker-playing society, Pegler and Reynolds, there were few intimations of the palship which bound them to Broun. Both were of Irish ancestry, but Reynolds was the bluff outgoing type while Pegler was the angry repressed man staring into the turf fire in a country pub. Eventually mutual distaste would develop into an enmity and a ruinously debilitating libel suit, which sprayed vitriol over the Fairfield literary colony and constituted the epitaph, many years later, for the long summer afternoons on which Broun and his friends disported themselves in rural Connecticut.

Broun's position at the *World-Telegram* was seriously eroding not only because of his adoration of President Roosevelt but because of his continued militancy on behalf of the Newspaper Guild. Roy Howard was following Guild developments with what one observer called an "agonized intensity" stemming from fears that his editorial department would soon be ruled by commissars rather than the front office. When a Guild strike was threatened—it didn't come off—Broun made it plain that he would walk out with the other editorial workers. That, to Howard and the other brass hats, reeked of disloyalty.

Nor were the Scripps-Howard bosses hugely delighted when Broun's career was encapsulated among the "dangerous" subversives listed by Elizabeth Dilling in her best-selling anti-Communist book, *The Red Network*. In her potted biography of Broun, Mrs. Dilling made him appear to be a clear and present danger to the republic. To his campaign for Sacco-Vanzetti, she linked other dubious accusations: "once engaged by the radical *Nation*" . . . principal speaker in 1928 before a group "barred by D.A.R. as subversives" . . . served on reception committee for Soviet aviators in 1933 . . . joined the National Committee to Aid the Victims of German Fascism. Broun discussed his immortalization in an article for the "radical" *Nation*. He believed that she had given him too much credit as a menace to democratic institutions. Her "all-too-brief biography of Broun, Heywood," represented a failure for both his mini-biographer and himself. "She has not made out her case and I do not deserve the accolade she has offered. As I read the account of this '*World-Telegram* newspaperman' I find, not the solid outline of a red, but merely the portrait of a joiner. Better luck next time, Mrs. D."

There were rumors, which naturally came to Broun's attention, that Scripps-Howard might not renew his contract. Yet his mildly leftish opinions did not dismay the rival Hearst chain, which had veered even farther to the right than Scripps-Howard after William Randolph Hearst helped to engineer President Roosevelt's first nomination (more out of hatred for Al Smith than love for Roosevelt) and had become disillusioned when Roosevelt did not accept his advice on how to put the country back together again.

Despite his detestation of the Guild, despite his personal disagreement with Broun's opinions and outlook, the Lord of San Simeon, recognizing Broun's ability to pull in circulation, was determined to make Broun a Hearstling. He assigned his two top executives, Arthur Brisbane, his editor in chief, and the genial Joe Connally, the head of King Features, the Hearst syndicate, to cajole Broun into donning the Hearst livery.

Much as he had always deplored the Hearst policies, Broun was tempted by the offer of $1,000 a week, plus syndication fees, which would have topped what he was getting from Scripps-Howard. He was also offered a $25,000 bonus for signing a Hearst contract. And he would be given the freedom to write as he pleased—a pledge that didn't mean so much in consideration of his treatment by Pulitzer and Scripps-Howard. It would have pleased him, too, to bid good-bye to Roy Howard and his predilection for Westbrook Pegler's cannonading.

Only one thing stopped him from signing the Hearst contract, as he told his son, Woodie, and that was the mental picture he had of the press lord whose employees were required to call the Chief, "that old man sitting in his palace out in California," Citizen Hearst.

A short time later, with that same image of the Lord of San Simeon in the front of his mind, he journeyed out to Milwaukee to aid the Guild strike against the Wisconsin *News*, a Hearst newspaper which was paying its reporters $15 a week, hardly enough for the feed bill of one of the lions in the San Simeon zoo.

The police ordered him not to address the strikers outside the picketed *News* building on the grounds that it might cause a riot. Broun, nevertheless, spoke. He was immediately arrested, briefly jailed, and fined for disturbing the peace.

Broun continued to preside over the embattled affairs of the Newspaper Guild, though at least one comrade objected to his influence as "a lively controversialist . . . notoriously prone to shock the bourgeosie" which caused many newspapermen "who should be Guild supporters but are not" to shy away from involvement with the union. Unperturbed by such criticism, Broun led the fight against being engorged by the American Federation of Labor, whose president, William Green, threatened to organize a rival union, and for joining the CIO, the Congress of Industrial Organizations. The CIO promptly organized noneditorial employees and brought them into the Guild; a typist and a star reporter were thus equal in union brotherhood. Walter Lippmann turned in his Guild card rather than accept such a decline in status, or at least that was the reason Broun ascribed to Lippmann's defection.

17. Half-Century Mark

ON December 7, 1938, Heywood Broun would celebrate his fiftieth birthday, and for several months leading up to that event he brooded over its significance. Outwardly he gave the impression that it was an occasion for ribaldry and gallant comments to the effect that he was "practically halfway home." Privately, with his fear of death, it did not appear a happy prospect. It was a time of assessment, of measuring growth or at least movement, and yet he could claim only to have held the same sort of job for about fifteen years. There are no rank badges for columnists, only salary increases and an increment of readership, and who could say that he was a better columnist now than he had been ten years earlier? He hadn't produced a book for years. He hadn't done anything but turn out his daily stint and a few magazine articles.

For the past several years he had been happily rusticating in Connecticut with his second wife and stepdaughter. Connie supplied the wifely touch lacking in his first marriage, and no one doubted that Broun valued it. Nor that if he had married Connie first, instead of Ruth Hale with her fever of ambition, he might still be a boozy, amiable baseball writer in eternal orbit around the National League.

In ruminating on the approach of his fiftieth birthday, he pondered the significance of his friends' always referring to him as "good old Broun." He had to admit that he deserved his reputation for amiability. "Save for deficiencies in prose style and intellectual capacity I was a sort of road-company Chesterton in my early youth. If I had been able to do jingles I might almost have been a bush-league Eddie Guest.* Good old Broun—the fat

* Edgar Guest was a syndicated poet of great popularity among the untutored.

friend of all the world!"

As with so many inveterately amiable people, he admitted, his sunny disposition partook largely of timidity. With some regret he recalled that he had never been able to rev up his ego by bawling out copyboys and waiters, that "of all the early worms in the newspaper craft" he was the most "abject." He was frequently "forced to blush when ex-office boys of the *Morning World* happen to alight from their limousines at the precise corner where I am walking. Most of them are high-powered scenario writers, although a few have gone into banking and the arts. But each and every one of them greets me with well-simulated enthusiasm. . . ."

Whenever he allowed a tincture of asperity to seep into his column writing, he complained, his followers would advise him, "Broun, don't you think that you are making a mistake in raising controversial issues? Better stick to your old charm and let it go at that."

The mood of self-deprecation was largely uncalled-for, however. The popularity of his column was attested by the Hearst offer; it was attuned to the mood of the great majority of the electorate, which, like Broun, descried a halo over the White House and regarded the Roosevelts as a later generation would the Kennedys, as patrician saviors of the lower orders.

He was knocking down well over $1,000 a week at a time when other men were supporting families on $25-a-week salaries or slightly less on government make-work projects. He had also been tapped for the lucrative but undemanding post of one of the judges of the Book-of-the-Month Club. Indubitably, along with Dorothy Thompson and Walter Winchell and Louella Parsons, he was a leading figure in popular journalism, an opinion molder, a genuine celebrity, at a time when the newspaper column was reaching the apex of its influence, only to yield it to well-tailored and beautifully coiffed young men "commenting" before television cameras. The polar attraction of such journalistic performers for the White House was attested when Broun and his wife were invited for dinners at 1600 Pennsylvania Avenue and luncheons on the lawn of the Roosevelt residence at Hyde Park.

In the spring of his fiftieth year, too, he acquired a new and momentarily fascinating hobby as one of the editor-founders of a very sophisticated country newspaper. A number of the Fairfield

County gentry got together and started up the Connecticut *Nutmeg*. In addition to Broun they included Ursula Parrott, Deems Taylor, Gene Tunney (long retired, undefeated, from the heavyweight championship), George T. Bye, Quentin Reynolds, Jack Pegler (brother of Westbrook and an advertising executive), Stanley High, Colvin Brown, and John Erskine. The *Nutmeg* was an eight-page tabloid, a sort of gentleman farmer's essay in journalism, in which playfulness of the Algonquin Round Table variety was the guiding spirit. A sustained facetiousness, a nudging of the reader's ribs over all that high-priced talent fooling around with rural journalism, a bantering among the founding fathers and much retailing of private jokes was the established tone of the *Nutmeg*. The idea of Heywood Broun as "nature editor" was very humorous to the participants, as were their scurrilous remarks about each other in print. The *Nutmeg*, however, was more fun for them than for the readers. Its files encapsulate a journalistic curiosity, some of its contributions of passing brilliance, but it was the sort of venture most of its participants would lose interest in as soon as it failed to accomplish a wider purpose. The *Nutmeg* did circulate throughout the country and was widely quoted in newspaper columns, but the most that could be said for it was that it was fun while it lasted. The only diehard among its founders was Broun himself.

Inevitably, too, there were disagreements among the board of editors when the columns of the *Nutmeg* began to reflect more serious events taking place far from, yet pertaining to, Fairfield County. One such clash of opinion occurred when Prime Minister Neville Chamberlain signed the "peace in our time" agreement in Munich with German Chancellor Adolf Hitler.

Editor Tunney delivered the opinion that Chamberlain had taken the only feasible course because Britain in its present state of unpreparedness would simply be overrun by the Nazi war machine—a respectable enough opinion at the time, fashionable though it was to disavow it several years later.

Editor Broun took the view that the now-evident evils of German Fascism must be opposed with whatever resources were available, no matter what the consequences. Once strongly inclined toward pacifism, remembering the glimpses of trench warfare he had witnessed during World War I, Broun now took a strong line toward the potential aggressors. "The Gargantuas of the world," he wrote in answer to Tunney in the *Nutmeg*, "make a most fierce appearance and when they thump their chests the forest echoes to the sound as if great drums were beating. And yet it is a hollow sound although in sheer volume it may almost deafen those who stand by the good word. And Tunney should not forget the lesson which he himself expounded. [Broun was referring to Tunney's prediction that Joe Louis would win his second bout with Max Schmeling, a heavyweight title fight in which good liberals took a personal interest because it pitted the Aryan champion against the black contender.] Remember well, Gene, before you surrender the world over to the fury of the Fascists that there is such a thing as 'the imponderability of spiritual fortification.' "

The Connecticut *Nutmeg* in its original form lasted less than a year, Broun's comrades having lost their zest for country journalism. On April 15, 1939, it became *Broun's Nutmeg* and for its sole proprietor a satisfying venture in personal journalism.

He labored to keep it afloat without letting it absorb most of his income. Yet on September 30, after five months as the personal mouthpiece of Heywood Broun, it came close to foundering on a reef of unpaid printers' bills. Editor Broun was forced to inform his slender readership that there were problems in the countinghouse and "the little publication is reeling around the ring." Financially, he admitted, it was undernourished. "Among all our advisers there is general agreement that what *Nutmeg* needs is more working capital. Or at any rate more capital. But upon close question it turns out that not one of the suggesters is himself a capitalist. Indeed I have yet to find that any one of them has got a friend." Subscribers were assured, however, that the *Nutmeg* would continue publication. "Sicker enterprises than *Nutmeg* have eventually recovered and lived to blossom and burgeon. Several such cases can be found in the *Lives of the Saints*." It was obvious that proprietor Broun's concepts of financial management were a bit unconventional. He proposed to refinance the *Nutmeg* by speeding off to the track and picking a few winners. "My left is shattered. My right is crumpled. My center is disorganized. I shall attack at two-thirty this afternoon at the Aqueduct race track." He must have been lucky at the track, for the *Nutmeg* continued to make its weekly appearance.

On December 7, 1938, Broun reached his fiftieth birthday and found that, contrary to his expectations, he was in a cheerful mood. Physically, he noted, he may have declined somewhat, but he was conscious of having more faith in humanity than in his younger years and that "people are better than I thought they were going to be." He was also consoled by the belief that he was a more skillful fighter for the causes he deemed just. "I'm more radical and things which once were just a sort of sentimental solace are now realities. Brotherhood is not just a Bible word. Out of comradeship can come and will come the happy life for all. The underdog can and will lick his weight in the wildcats of the world."

A few weeks later his fiftieth milestone was inscribed with whatever immortality a Presidential radio broadcast could confer. For his Christmastime "fireside chat"—one of the frequent homilies delivered into a microphone over a national hookup from the White House, the Squire of Hyde Park speaking cozily to-a tenantry of millions—the President was going to read a column of Broun's titled "Even to Judas."

The parable, one of those Broun published from time to time when the freethinker was overwhelmed by a religious spirit lurking beneath layers of doubt, told of Broun's visit to a dominie in his room above a chapel. The dominie was struggling to find a theme for his Christmas sermon. Broun helped him pick a text at random from the Bible: the twenty-sixth chapter of St. Matthew. It was the verse relating to Christ's forgiveness of Judas Iscariot's betrayal. As Broun quoted his imaginary dominie: " 'Mark that,' cried the old man exultantly. 'Not even to Judas, the betrayer, was the wine of life denied. I can preach my Christmas sermon now, and my text will be 'Drink ye all of it.' Good-will toward men means good-will to every last son of God. Peace on earth means peace to Pilate, peace to the thieves on the cross, and peace to poor Iscariot.' "

Broun got advance notice of the President's intentions, and at 5:30 P.M. on the appointed afternoon he and Connie, with his son and her daughter, gathered around the radio. He calmed his nerves with several stiff drinks because (as he revealed for readers of the *Nutmeg*) "it so happens that I have a sort of phobia which makes me hideously unhappy if I have to sit and watch somebody read something of my own, aloud or to himself, when I am present."

A moment after the President's Ivy League-accented voice filled the room with the words Broun had written, he rushed out into the hallway and wept. Later in the evening he sent the President's press secretary a telegram asking him to tell Roosevelt that "he did it even better than I could have done it myself." Since both men had their actorish moments, the compliment no doubt was appreciated, as from one trouper to another.

During the following month, January of 1939, an incredible rumor began circulating around New York among the newspaper people and literati and theatrical folk he had known for two decades. The old scoffer, the veteran critic of the cloth, the proclaimed freethinker—yes, Heywood Broun—was considering a conversion to the Roman Catholic faith. He had never taken a kindly view of Catholicism, had regarded the hierarchy as reactionary, had professed the opinion common to many Manhattan liberals that the Archdiocese of New York was wielding too much temporal power through its influence on Catholic politicians. Yet he had not been entirely consistent in the past and had changed his political stance more than once. Furthermore, as some of his older friends would point out, the incense, the votive candles, the priestly ritual at the altar, the bells, the robes and miters, the sonorous Latin would appeal to his theatrical sense. Too, his second wife was Catholic. And there was that Christmas parable which President Roosevelt had read over the air, which suggested that indeed Broun was "getting religion." For a die-cut liberal, of course, immersion in one of the less fundamental faiths was not unthinkable. Unitarianism was well thought of, its creed being liberalism incarnate. But for a man with Broun's credentials to plunge into the sacerdotal mysteries of Catholicism, the religion of the superstitious peasantry, the faith of Irish ward heelers and Italian bootleggers, that was downright traumatic. The most generous interpretation of his reported intention was that he had, during a bout with delirium tremens, suffered some St. Paul-like delusions and been frightened into the nearest rectory.

The rumor, though not its embellishments, was founded in fact. Without undue pressure from Connie, he later affirmed, he had decided to become a Catholic. It was as much an ideological as an emotional or a spiritual prompting that had overtaken him. Something was missing from his life, otherwise satisfying in the material rewards of his career, the recognition he had received, the journalistic heights he had attained. It may have been the lodestar of absolute authority, which could be offered only by the Church of Rome or the Communist Party. The reason Broun later gave, however, was that Catholicism would provide him with spiritual security. He had always been obsessed by the pursuit of the brotherhood of man, which he now believed could reach "full fruition" only "under the fatherhood of God."

For several months he discussed the possibility of conversion with various priests. In early February, 1939, he and Connie journeyed to the Southwest to investigate reports of desperate housing conditions. In a tour of the San Antonio barrios, "the most fearful slum in all America," his guide was Father Tranchese, the pastor of the Church of Guadalupe, who was a prototype of the worker priests who decades hence would lead the Church toward social revolution. Broun's doubts about whether a man could be both a Catholic and a militant liberal were disarmed by Father Tranchese, who told them as they started their tour of the tin-roofed shacks of his parish, "It may be dangerous if you go with me, for there are many who have made threats because I am in favor of the federal housing project." His talks with Father Tranchese convinced him that there was room in the Church for other than well-heeled papal knights and old women in black shawls.

Further proof was supplied when he and Connie, on their way back to New York, stopped off in St. Louis to visit with the Reverend Edward Dowling, who was editor of the local Catholic weekly and an ardent member of the Newspaper Guild. Father Dowling had been a ballplayer and newspaperman before ordination. He told Broun that "the doctrines of the Church are far more radical," in essence, than anything Broun had campaigned for.

By early spring Broun had just about made up his mind to apply for admittance to the Catholic fold. But he continued to seek advice among his Catholic friends and, finally, with Morris Ernst, whose counsel he had always relied on in both legal and extralegal matters. The fact that Ernst was Jewish was utterly beside the point.

One night when Broun and Ernst were dining at 21 with their wives and several other persons, Broun slipped his friend a note under the table. It read, "I need you—for no less than two hours and no more than twenty." They met after taking their wives home and talked for hours about Broun's plan to join the Catholic Church.

What seemed to worry Broun the most, Ernst recalls, was in a sense the public relations aspect of his conversion. His first question was, "Will people think that Connie made me do it?" Broun also fretted over the possibility that people would think he joined the Church to "scare" Roy Howard into not curbing his freedom of expression or into renewing his contract. He was also concerned that it might be said he "got religion" out of fear of death—and, conversely, that he had been secretly religious all along and concealed it to make himself more credible as a crusader for liberal or radical causes. None of those motives, he said, was correct. He planned to become a Catholic simply because he felt a strong pull toward the first of the Christian faiths.

Broun was so uncharacteristically solemn about it all, so desperately serious, that Ernst tried to lighten his mood. Why not join the Jewish faith? Ernst playfully inquired. "We were being beaten all over the world, and Heywood was a star masochist."

In the end, though, Ernst advised him to join the Church and stop fretting about it. Years later he would rejoice in his advice because "Broun got much out of it. Connie with her native humor and her foot clamped on all the little checks (Broun grabbed the big ones and spent them gathering up tabs at saloons for twenty years) gave him a background of comfort and ease. The Church gave him the kind of discipline he wanted, even though during his instruction and later he jested about how he had comprehended the concept of the Virgin Birth along the scientific lines of high-church Romanes but could not quite understand the Immaculate Conception."

A few weeks later Broun took the plunge. The most famous modern proselytizer was Monsignor Fulton Sheen, whose radio pastorals, his burning eyes and magnetic presence, his erudition as a Church philosopher had made him a famous figure among Broun's contemporaries. Monsignor Sheen had the reputation of converting or bringing back to the altar rail "hard cases," doubting intellectuals, Manhattan sophisticates. Among his more famous converts was Clare Boothe Luce. Monsignor Sheen's celebrity as a missionary to the elect naturally attracted Broun, who liked to go first class when it came to important things. He invited the priest out to the Sabine Farm for the weekend, and after hours of discussion Broun agreed to begin taking instruction in the catechism.

Evidently a quick study, Broun was ready for baptism and confirmation by the middle of May. His entrance into the Church was kept secret from all but his family and a few close friends, and he was baptized on May 23, was confirmed by Archbishop Francis Spellman (again making Broun feel that he was being accorded the red-carpet treatment), and took his first Communion on Pentecostal Sunday at the altar rail of the Lady Chapel in St. Patrick's Cathedral.

Broun had all the typical devotion of the convert, and it bolstered him against the open and covert criticism—some of it rather harsh—with which word of his conversion was received. Broun was aware that some of his oldest comrades-in-arms were saying that he had forsaken liberalism and become a religious fanatic reactionary, damn near a Fascist, that no man could serve both a secular master and an authoritarian religious one. They called on him for an explanation, if not an apology.

From now on, however, Broun would make his explanations to God through His servants. He made that clear in an article for a liberal magazine in which he refused to make any alibis for having become a Catholic and noted, "It is a little illogical for the same correspondent to complain that all newspaper columnists are too ready to be dogmatic on the international situation and at the same time demand that one of the most slapdash commentators of the crowd should forthwith put in type his own most intimate feelings about Catholicism and the cosmos."

Many letter writers insisted that they deserved an explanation because Broun was a public figure and his readers had a right to pry into his psyche, much as tourists gaped at the homes of Hollywood film stars, but he pointed out that "under the obligation of a daily or weekly deadline it is not always easy to put down with simple dignity your feelings about something which is dear to you." He further explained:

"In part it is my feeling that no man should discuss those things which are closest to him without taking great care to express himself as well as his best potentialities permit. And again I bridle, for the moment at least, because most of the missives appear to come from those who seem quite ready to condemn with an answer or without. Indeed they seem to ask not so much a statement of belief as an immediate apology.

"Very many begin, 'Of course a man's religion is his own business, but—' And the conjunction is used as a dull blunt instrument with which to club me on the head."

Heywood Broun had always been and would always be his own man. He had created a persona in print, had made of himself a public figure in many guises (ranging from musical-comedy performer to pop intellectual), but his private self remained inviolate.

18. A Time of Endings

THE summer of 1939. A time of endings. Many then alive would never watch the trees turn green, then autumnal red and gold. The tank engines of the Nazi panzer corps already were warming up. Many would never see the New Year in or find out whether President Roosevelt achieved his unprecedented third term in office. The Nazis and their supposedly sworn enemies, the Soviets, made a deal and thereby guaranteed a continental and then another world war. Many would not have time to wonder why the summers just before a major war are invariably a golden perfection—it had been true in 1914 and it was true in the summer of 1939. Long golden days. A last blessing.

For Heywood Broun, as for so many of his contemporaries, it was also a time for endings—his last summer, last autumn, last early winter, last newspaper job, last breath.

It was not to be a quiet ending or a long descent into invalidism. On the surface he appeared as lethargic as ever, but many other men would have foundered under the pace of his activities. Besides turning out his newspaper column and occasional magazine pieces, he kept his personal organ, *Broun's Nutmeg*, appearing weekly. He was writing most of its issues under various pseudonymous by-lines, and either to fill space or trot it out for another round of applause, he serialized *The Sun Field*.

That summer, just after his own conversion, he was preoccupied too with rescuing a few brands from the burning for the church to which he had committed his own immortal soul. It seemed to him that he ought to snatch at least one soul, among his worldly friends, for the Church. His first choice was Alexander Woollcott. Back when the Algonquin Round Table was still in session, he recalled, there was talk that Woollcott rather fancied the role of being an American G. K. Chesterton and had spoken favorably of Catholicism—if only because, as a dramatic critic, he approved of the superior staging the Church provided for its rituals, its sense of drama, its splendid costuming.

Broun decided to broach the matter over lunch at 21 and ordered all of Woollcott's favorite wines and food, knowing that the evangelical mission could not be accomplished with anything so primitive as loaves and fishes.

But the moment Woollcott became aware of Broun's purpose, he began glowering across the luncheon debris. Broun had hardly launched his appeal when Woollcott raised a pudgy hand and growled, "Not me, my dear old friend. One literary fat ass is enough for the Roman Catholic Church."

There was little time to enjoy the perfection of that last summer. Even those who believed that Hitler might be satisfied with having engorged the Rhineland, Austria, and Czechoslovakia could see that the civilized order was breaking up, that the Nazis and their allies were writing a new book of rules. It could be sensed in the tragic voyage of the *St. Louis,* a salt-rimed and wallowing old steamer bearing 900 Jewish refugees from the Nazi oppression. No nation cared to allow the ship into one of its harbors, not even the United States with that glowing inscription on the Statue of Liberty which had welcomed so many desperate migrants in the past century. The wanderings of the *St. Louis* inspired Broun to write a column which won the Headliners Club award that year. He pointed out that if the *St. Louis* flashed an SOS signal, the ships of every nation were honor bound to rush to its rescue without inquiring as to the nationality, religion, or economic status of its passengers; "there would not be the slightest hesitation in a movement of all the allied fleets to save these members of the human race in deep and immediate distress."

The hypocrisy of the democratic nations professing to believe in the Christian message of almost two thousand years before and yet declining to give refuge to the *St. Louis'* passengers disgusted Broun immeasurably. "At any luncheon, banquet or public meeting the orator of the occasion can draw cheers if he raises his right hand in the air and pledges himself, his heart and soul to the declaration that he is for peace and amity and all men are brothers. He means it, generally, and so do the diners who pound the table until the coffee cups and the cream dishes rattle into a symphony of good feeling and international sympathy."

From the coldly logical viewpoint, he wrote, it would be better if the *St. Louis* sank in forty fathoms. Then its passengers wouldn't face the possibility of being returned to the port of embarkation, Hamburg, and thrown into concentration camps. Those nations which could still claim to be civilized were being put to the test. "What price civilization? There is a ship. Who will take up an oar to save 900 men, women and children?"

Later that summer he journeyed out to San Francisco to observe the latest religious movement, Moral Re-Armament, a catchy slogan in itself. Dr. Frank Buchman and his disciples had created it out of the Oxford Movement, a high-toned revivalist operation which had its beginnings among the gilded British youth, and were holding a rally in San Francisco in the canny belief that Californians would be especially susceptible to their credo. Broun, in fact, came across a film producer who testified that after weeks of haggling over her contract with one of his actresses he had persuaded her to join Moral Re-Armament and she had been so spiritually transformed that she immediately signed the contract.

Broun was not impressed by the Buchmanites' spiritual values, was repelled by their materialism, and as was usually the case when his feelings were aroused (for or against), he produced one of his better columns on the subject. It seemed to him that they were using a jerry-built pseudoreligious creed as the springboard to increasing their earthly possessions. They were the "smuggest aggregation" he had ever seen; it was a "little tough to take morals from men who wear them across their stomachs like gold watch chains."

He told of watching a young man approach the MRA display table in its hotel headquarters and inform the sleek fellow on duty, "I have a wife and two children. I get eighteen dollars a week. We can hardly survive on this. Is there anything in Moral Re-Armament which would help me?"

"If you join MRA you will be much better off," the supplicant was told, "because you will cease to worry."

It seemed to Broun that the core of Dr. Buchman's message to the world was that "the poor should give their goods to the rich and let them be administered by the benevolent." He was repelled by the "house-party" confessionals which Dr. Buchman's followers employed as a supposed spiritual cleansing. Although he had a certain amount of respect for other "aberrant" forms of religion, he preferred to "take my Holy Rollers straight rather than in the streamline form which had been set off by the Oxford Movement." Quite predictably that column brought him and his increasingly disenchanted publishers a flood of mail charging Broun with religious intolerance.

Summer waned, the German panzers roared across the Polish border, and Germany and Russia stunned the Western world by coming to terms over a new partition of Poland.

To Broun and most liberals the Nazi-Soviet pact was a shattering event. They had been convinced, until Hitler's and Stalin's representatives rushed into their disastrous embrace, that Soviet Russia was faithfully serving as the Eastern bulwark against Fascism. If worst came to worst and the German armies could not be contained, Russia would constitute one flange of a pincer, Britain and France the other, which would pluck the evil flowering of Fascism out of the Eurasian body politic. Now "the masquerade is over," Broun conceded, and it was possible to examine objectively the "faces of the various ones who pretend to be devoted to the maintenance of democracy."

Broun's attack on the Hitler-Stalin agreement was in accord with the feelings of most Americans, but according to Morris Ernst, the "Communist-line Newspaper Guild boys," some of them executives of the union, as well as other Communist sympathizers who refused to be disillusioned by the latest switchback in the party line, turned on him as a traitor to their cause. Broun, of course, had never conformed to any party line, and it was incomprehensible that they could have considered him a comrade at a time when he was considering his candidacy on the Democratic ticket for Congressman in Connecticut. Feelings were running high, however, with so many formerly fervent supporters of Soviet Russia, particularly in the literary and theatrical worlds, unable to stomach Stalin's temporary friendship with the Nazis. A schism never to be quite mended had developed in the "popular front" of the radicals and liberals, and even many Communist Party members tore up their cards in revulsion over the sudden affection between two dictatorships whose ideologies were supposed to be diametrically opposed.

Several weeks after the Hitler-Stalin agreement was announced, while the German armies were overwhelming Poland and meeting up with Russian divisions advancing from the East, Broun wrote a reasoned consideration of the pact's effects for a liberal magazine. He warned that it was "unwise to be too cocksure about the result of Stalin's strategy," and he was worried over the backlash which had resulted in American reactionaries (Pegler among the noisiest) rejoicing in the disillusionment of those who had hoped that Stalin's Russia would serve the cause of peace and humanity. And he was particularly distressed by those who, taking advantage of that backlash, "insist that now is the time to smash labor unions in America."

Certainly Broun was certifying his liberal credentials when he urged that "those who feel that Fascism has been strengthened by Soviet action should fight all the harder for the maintenance and extension of democracy in America. Surely no logical answer will be made to the Russian action by those who insist that there should now be a non-aggression pact, if not a military alliance, between liberals and Herbert Hoover. . . . It will be even sillier now than it was before to shout that Roosevelt is the conscious or unconscious agent of Communism."

Liberals, he wrote, shouldn't feel ashamed because they had linked arms with the Communists in just causes in the past (among which he cited the fight to free the imprisoned anarchist Tom Mooney and the campaign for the Scottsboro Boys, the left's *cause célèbre* in the thirties). It was absurd to claim that henceforth a true liberal would have to take an opposite position to that advocated by the Communists regardless of the merits of the controversy. "Such a procedure," he held, "would reduce the progressive to the estate of the fanatic who insisted that he wished to contract a venereal disease because he understood it was being fought editorially by the Chicago *Tribune*."

Broun would not join in the *mea culpas* being uttered by other liberals who had been disillusioned by the pragmatism freshly exhibited by the Kremlin. In his opinion the fact that Hitler and Stalin were now bedfellows didn't excuse the parallel fact that "many of the Red-baiters have the same spiritual dandruff as afflicted them before. Not all the leopards have changed their spots."

Three weeks later, however, he was outraged when *Izvestia*, furthering the German-Russian détente, said in an editorial that Hitlerism could be liked or disliked just like any other political system. Broun wondered whether Stalin and his henchmen had forgotten how many German Marxists had been beaten and tortured by storm troopers. Or the recent times when "Communist leaders expressed horror at the treatment of Jews in Germany." He found it indefensible that the Kremlin believed that "things which are the essence of existence" weren't worth arguing about.

After washing his hands of the Soviets, he meditated on his own experiences at the front in World War I and how they might differ from what had now become World War II. Organized slaughter, however, must be pretty much the same. It was the time of the *sitzkrieg,* when the giddier optimists suggested that Hitler might not attack in the West after having got what he wanted in the East, but there was still sporadic fighting on the Franco-German frontier. Recalling his brief time as a war correspondent, he brooded over the fact that "the fairest days are the foulest along the front," that now a full moon was only a "lamp to light the way of the bombers." Now a dedicated countryman, he was saddened by what war did to nature, the "skeletonized" trees against the skyline, the scarred earth turning a dirty chalk white from high explosives, the way "the very gifts of nature are turned into a curse."

The news became more melancholy as winter approached, nor did his personal situation improve. Intimations had come from the executive suite at the *World-Telegram* that his contract would not be renewed early in December when it expired. There was little doubt that he was in disfavor with Scripps-Howard. His column had been cut to 600 words and was given less prominent display on the split page. It was obvious that Westbrook Pegler's star was rising as his was falling; at times it hardly seemed paranoia to suspect that one of Pegler's chief services to Scripps-Howard was not only to "balance" Broun's liberalism but to bedevil him with personal attacks. Broun was particularly wounded by a Pegler column which alleged that Broun, as publisher of *Broun's Nutmeg,* kept the Newspaper Guild out of his own shop. It was true that the *Nutmeg* wasn't unionized, but only because its staff was so small it didn't qualify as a Guild shop. Another ominous sign was the way Lee Wood, executive editor of the *World-Telegram,* the flagship of the Scripps-Howard fleet, heavily edited his columns.

The emanations of displeasure from Roy Howard and his editors only increased as contract-renewal time approached.

Just before his fifty-first birthday he was summoned to the presidential headquarters to hear the bad news. Scripps-Howard was paying him $49,000 a year and felt it couldn't afford his salary any longer, though Pegler's larger paycheck was presenting no financial problems.

"I've talked it over with my associates," Howard told Broun, "and we've decided not to make you an offer. It would be just too much grief. The price of newsprint is going up and we think that the place to cut expenses is among the high-priced specialists in order to protect the run-of-the-mine reporter."

"Roy," Broun replied with a stiff upper lip, knowing the "grief" aspect of their relations, not the price of pulp, was the real reason he was being fired, "I can't possibly make any squawk about that because I've made the same speech myself at dozens of Guild meetings."

They shook hands, had a drink from Howard's office bar, and parted on friendly terms.

There was no great joy connected with the celebration of his fifty-first birthday. He brooded over the fact that he had been fired for the third time in his career and wondered where he could find another berth for his column. Morris Ernst, as usual, was serving as his unpaid agent and canvassing the New York dailies. He spent his birthday in bed, he reported to *Nutmeg* readers, taking stock of himself. Self-examination in middle age, he decided, was more sedative than tonic. One of the great weaknesses of the aging, he wrote, was that "we wander about with arched backs hoping for a friendly pat from someone who will say, 'Don't let them kid you. I've known worse jerks than you are.' "

Ernst's hurried scouting of newspaper offices had turned up an offer from the New York *Post*, which Dorothy (Schiff) and George Backer had recently acquired. The *Post* was liberal enough to accommodate Broun's views, and once again he was promised full control over what he wanted to write about and how he would do it. The salary would be only one-fourth what Scripps-Howard had paid him, but would be augmented by fees from syndication.

Broun could endure a salary cut, but what really hurt was the attitude of his fellow Guildsmen. One thing he wanted more than anything else was some sort of reassurance from his comrades, for whom he had sacrificed much in time and money, not to mention his job security with Scripps-Howard. It would be excessive perhaps to claim that he lost his job because of his Guild activities, but certainly it was a contributing factor. Furthermore, he had labored for the Guild without any hope that his own salary would be increased. The Guild had won minimum-wage scales from the publishers, but the Guild minimum became the publishers' maximum and the result was that newspaper people of talent and ambition were impelled sooner or later to leave journalism.

He went downtown for a farewell tour of the *World-Telegram* city room expecting that the reporters and rewrite men would gather around him, slap him on the back, and express sorrow and/or indignation at the termination of his contract.

Instead he was virtually ignored, or as Morris Ernst recalls, "the pro-Communist Guild leaders down there shunned him."

The only person who came up to him as he ambled around the desks was a young copyboy who shook Broun's hand and told him, "Too bad, Mr. Broun, but thanks to you I'm getting two dollars a week more and a vacation with pay."

Broun retreated to Ernst's office uptown in a near-tearful condition, and Ernst would remember how "it hurt to see his beautiful face on the verge of weeping."

To raise his friend's spirits, Ernst immediately set about planning a party for Broun at Sardi's at which his real friends could express their feelings. He rented the top floor of Sardi's for midnight, January 8, 1940. It would be informal, no banquet or speeches, with an admission price of fifty cents (the cost of a drink then). Ernst sent out invitations to Secretary of the Interior Harold L. Ickes, Jack Dempsey, Helen Hayes, John L. Lewis, Walter White (then president of the NAACP), and less celebrated but equally valued friends among the horde of cab drivers, waiters, and bartenders Broun had known for years.

Broun would probably have loved that party more than any ever given for him, but he was unable to appear because of a prior, involuntary but ultimate commitment.

Death, like Sandburg's fog, often comes on cat's feet. Broun always had his dire premonitions, but they did not seem to be shadowing him immediately after Scripps-Howard fired him. He was full of enthusiasm for his new place on the *Post* and planning to write a number of columns from the spring-training camps of the ball clubs in Florida. He was heartened by the *Post*'s agreement to handle the Manhattan newsstand distribution of

Broun's Nutmeg. Even more pleasing was a joint exhibition of his and John Groth's paintings (Groth did the illustrations for the *Nutmeg*) at a hotel in Stamford, for which a throng of his friends appeared.

The day after his birthday he came down with a cold. At first the medication he prescribed for himself came out of a whiskey bottle. He refused to stay in bed. It hardly lifted his spirits when Harold Yudain, the managing editor of the *Nutmeg*, brought over a copy of the *World-Telegram* and informed him that Pegler's column that day consisted of a brutal personal attack on him. Broun refused to believe, at first, that "Peg would hit me when I was down." But a reading of Pegler's column showed that Peg the unchivalrous wouldn't wait until an unhorsed fellow knight got to his feet before smiting him.

With little or no basis for the charge, Pegler accused Broun of supporting the Soviet press censorship, which was then beclouding the Russian occupation of eastern Poland. He was also magisterially dissatisfied with the disavowals of faith in Russian purposes which Broun had made following the Nazi-Soviet agreement. "I have seen recent superficial expressions of disappointment in Moscow, but never an outright incantation, and even if I saw one I would have to treat it the same as I treat changes of front by Stalin, Hitler and Earl Browder." The rabidity of Pegler's attitude toward his former friend could be judged by his placing Broun in the same category as Stalin and Hitler. Yet fate, often excessively ironic, stores comeuppances for those inclined to overkill. It was to be yet another column, in which Broun figured in the postmortem sense, which resulted in the lawsuit that all but ruined Pegler.

The heavy cold persisted, and Broun's system seemed unable to throw it off. But he turned out the last columns due under the Scripps-Howard contract and went ahead with plans to visit the Harry Guggenheim plantation in South Carolina with Connie and then proceed to the Florida spring-training camps. Against his doctor's advice he left the Sabine Farm for the Hotel Chatham in New York to write his first column for the *Post* and prepare for the journey south.

His first—and last, as it turned out—column for the *Post* considered the matter of the controversial third term for President Roosevelt. Despite the strong opposition to breaking a precedent established with the first President, Broun believed

Roosevelt should run again, that the issue would be decided not by politicians and public opinion but by "the President, his better nature, and his devotion to his country." Even so he was unable to understand how any man would want to hold the office when it would be a "constant grim-lipped enterprise of keeping our own barbed wire up when it is smashed by passing shell raids. Who wants such a third term in his right senses? Nobody. But to hold the office marks the man in history."

Had antibiotics been developed a few years earlier, Broun would easily have won his struggle against the congestion in his chest. Instead his condition steadily worsened. On December 15, the day that last Heywood Broun by-line appeared, it developed into pneumonia. He was removed to the Harkness Pavilion at the Columbia Presbyterian Medical Center.

His temperature soared and for the next two days he was unconscious most of the time, with Connie and his son at his bedside and his friends gathered in the corridor outside or in the waiting room. He was placed under an oxygen tent to aid his labored and rachitic breathing.

On the morning of December 17 he was given the Last Sacrament by Monsignor Sheen, but later in the day he rallied and regained consciousness.

"How am I?" he asked the doctor in a whispery voice.

"Getting along."

"Have you sent for the priest?"

"Yes, but you are somewhat better now."

"If I pull through," Broun said, "I'll remember that Ring Lardner would have lived longer if he had only written what he really wanted to write. And I will write only about horse racing, night clubs, gambling, and life."

That last promise to himself would never be kept. Within a few hours his temperature began to rise again, this time more alarmingly, until it seemed that he was being consumed by internal fires. It reached 107.2, and life stopped, Sunday, December 18, at 9:50 A.M. All night an assemblage of his friends had waited for the outcome of his struggle, the sort of deathbed gathering accorded either a man who was much loved or whose passing would leave a large vacant space in the life of his time. His contemporaries believed he was both.

Epilogue

IT was a great man's funeral, held amid the vaulting splendors of St. Patrick's Cathedral. The cathedral was thronged by a diversity of mourners which attested the wide-ranging quality of his friendship—Cabinet members rubbing shoulders with cab drivers, ballplayers, actors, newspapermen, labor leaders, waiters, writers, doormen, ex-convicts. Even, to the disgust of many who attended the funeral, Westbrook Pegler was there. The eulogy was delivered by Monsignor Fulton Sheen.

Connie Broun almost collapsed when the requiem mass ended, and she was supported on the long walk up the aisle by Mayor Fiorello La Guardia on one side and Quentin Reynolds on the other. Connie rode out to the cemetery with her stepson, Heywood Hale Broun, Reynolds, and Monsignor Sheen. Reynolds tried to comfort the sobbing widow by recalling what Broun had told him, some months before, when Reynolds' mother died: "You can't live with a ghost—even with the ghost of someone you loved."

Several weeks later there was a memorial service of a less religious nature held at the Manhattan Center. Again Westbrook Pegler, in the apparent belief that his differences with Broun were more professional than personal, attended, although according to his biographer, he had been "appalled by the rudeness of the reception he got from friends of Broun at the cemetery." One fellow journalist, commenting on Pegler's insistence on paying his respects to his late opponent, wrote that "Pegler saw nothing inconsistent in attending the funeral of the late Heywood Broun within a few days of his most disgraceful diatribe against that great American while Broun lay on his deathbed." That wasn't quite the way it happened, but the rancorous observation expressed the feeling that Broun's end was hastened by Pegler's enmity.

For years the memory of how he had been treated at the two services rankled and festered in Pegler, who like many people who specialize in wounding the sensibilities of others was quite thin-skinned, an injustice collector who brooded when the slings and arrows were coming the other way.

Almost exactly a decade passed before the ulceration of Pegler's psyche reached its painful climax and resulted in one of the most celebrated libel suits in American legal history.

The traumatic event was a book review written by Quentin Reynolds. Its subject was a biography of Heywood Broun written by Dale Kramer and published in 1949. In the review published in the Sunday book section of the New York *Herald Tribune*, as Reynolds remarked in his own account of the affair, "I made the mistake of quoting some passages in which Kramer discussed Westbrook Pegler's dim views of Heywood's liberalism, in particular his part in the founding of the Newspaper Guild. While it was Kramer, not I, who was taking Pegler to task for his unfairness to Heywood, it was I, for some inexplicable reason, who became the fresh object of Pegler's wrath. . . ."

Actually Reynolds had written something more offensive to Pegler than that. His review's concluding paragraph read, "Broun could talk of nothing but Pegler's attack on him. He returned to his hotel, but not to sleep. It seemed incredible that he was allowing Pegler's absurd charge of dishonesty to hurt him so. But not even Connie could make him dismiss it from his mind. The doctor told him to relax; he'd be all right if he got some sleep. But he couldn't relax. He couldn't sleep. And he died."

To Pegler that read as though he were being accused of homicide. He sat down in a flaming rage and wrote in his column, now distributed by the Hearst newspapers, that Reynolds was a "Ferdinand the Bull" among war correspondents, a war profiteer, a social climber, and a man who bent to tie his shoelace when the check was presented in a nightclub or restaurant; that he was a member of the "parasitic, licentious" group that surrounded Broun. He further charged that Reynolds was a nudist, that he was present at a frolic at the Sabine Farm during which "a conspicuous Negro Communist seduced a susceptible young white girl." The charge that most deeply wounded Reynolds, however, was Pegler's claim that Reynolds, then unmarried, had proposed to Connie Broun on the trip to the cemetery from St. Patrick's Cathedral.

Reynolds promptly engaged the celebrated trial lawyer Louis Nizer and filed a $50,000 libel suit.

There is no present need to rake over the ashes of that case, which has become a legal landmark, except as it affected Broun's memory and involved both his friend and his enemy, not to mention the other members of the Sabine Farm group accused of participating in "interracial orgies." The eight-week trial in 1954 caused a rattling of many old skeletons and briefly revived old ideological feuds which most people believed had been decently interred with the thirties.

On the witness stand Pegler did not hesitate to disclose a strong revulsion, if not hatred, for Heywood Broun. Under the goading cross-examination of Louis Nizer, Pegler described the Sabine Farm as a "low dirty place" which he shunned as much as possible; Broun himself "filthy, uncombed and unpressed, with his fly open, looking like a Skid Row bum." Reynolds, he added, emulated Broun except that Reynolds "wore laces in his shoes." He testified that he had learned of Reynolds' nude bathing from Connie Broun. Broun's widow, however, took the witness stand to deny ever telling Pegler anything like that. A number of notable witnesses testified to Reynolds' courage under fire as a war correspondent in Europe. In his own testimony Reynolds answered Pegler's charge that he had proposed to Connie Broun immediately after her husband's funeral by pointing out that she was under sedation on the trip to the cemetery and that they were accompanied by Broun's son and Monsignor Sheen. And the jury returned a verdict, not for the $50,000 Reynolds had sued for, but a total of $175,001 in punitive and compensatory damages. For his pains in defaming Reynolds and through him Heywood Broun, Pegler was rewarded by the steady decline of his credibility and the disfavor of his employers. His contract was eventually terminated by the Hearst Corporation, and he wound up writing a monthly column for the organ of the John Birch Society.

The important side effect of the Reynolds-Pegler trial was to wipe away the mud flung at Heywood Broun's memory. Not that much of it stuck as far as those who really knew him were concerned.

His journalistic achievements, though most such are as fragile as the yellowing newsprint on which they appear, would be remembered. He had made himself one of the most eloquent and revered totems of the liberalism of his time, perhaps because he typified its yearnings and unrealized hopes. He had many of the virtues of the modern liberal, chiefly the shared conviction that mankind is good and inherently perfectible, and some of the flaws, chiefly an excessive optimism and an intolerance for anyone professing a grubbier sense of reality.

Aside from being circumscribed by ideology at a time when anyone to the right of Franklin D. Roosevelt was regarded as a near Fascist, Heywood Broun was his own man, with a striking ability to hold himself aloof from surrounding influences. An original. No one observing him in the press box at the Polo Grounds would have guessed that he spent four years at Harvard; no one coming across him on Forty-fourth Street outside the Algonquin would have taken him for one of the glittering personalities of the Round Table. Nor would anyone meeting him in a speakeasy or watching him swig from his flask at some public occasion have pegged him as a social and political crusader. Nor would the corpulent figure lolling in a hammock at the Sabine Farm have been readily identified as the man who provided much of the propulsive force of liberalism during the twenties and thirties. Nothing could persuade him to dress the part, modify his manner, or act any role but the one he had chosen for himself at the age of fourteen, for he would always regard himself as one of that careless, hard-living, but in retrospect quixotically gallant brotherhood that once inhabited Park Row.

Notes on Sources

THE complete listing of most of the sources indicated below under the authors' surnames may be found in the Bibliography, which follows.

1. The Atypical Harvard Man

The atmosphere of Harvard during Broun's years there can be recaptured in Kaltenborn, *Fifty Fabulous Years, passim.*

John Reed's views on his "gold coast" classmates and their exclusive attitudes, Walker and O'Connor, *The Lost Revolutionary*, a biography of Reed, p. 28.

Something of Broun's boyhood can be gleaned from his autobiographical novel, *The Boy Grew Older.* His recollection of the racial prejudice of his boyhood, *Christians Only: A Study in Prejudice*, on which Broun collaborated with George Britt, pp. 3–4.

His memories of the West Side of Manhattan during his early years, Connecticut *Nutmeg*, December 1, 1938.

His decision to make a career in journalism, New York *World-Telegram* column, June 26, 1937. His early gift for self-expression was recalled by Ernst, *The Best Is Yet*, p. 78.

Broun's description of Professor Kittredge was contained in his column, *World-Telegram*, May 5, 1936, on the occasion of Kittredge's retirement.

His recollection of Professor Carver's lectures, "Carver to Speaker to Broun," *New Republic*, November 17, 1937.

2. The Car-Barn School of Journalism

The ambience of the New York *Morning Telegraph* during the years he was employed there was suggested in his article, "The Old, Old Telegraph," *The Nation*, September 5, 1936.

The anecdote concerning sports editor Bat Masterson is contained in O'Connor, *Bat Masterson*, p. 241.

Broun's aborted interview with Valeska Suratt, "The Old, Old *Telegraph*," *op. cit.*

The long-running poker game at the *Telegraph, ibid.*

Broun's views on the attributes of the "perfect reporter," which he admittedly did not possess, *World-Telegram* column, June 26, 1937.

Broun recalled the details of his trip to China in his *World-Telegram* column, December 6, 1937.

Gene Fowler's description of Broun's inferior style of dress, *Skyline*, p. 120.

Broun confessed to his unprofessional lack of objectivity in the press box in his *World-Telegram* column, April 10, 1936.

His admiration for John J. McGraw's showmanship was expressed in his column in *Broun's Nutmeg*, May 6, 1939.

Broun's imbroglio with an actor over his denigratory views of the latter's performance, Churchill, *The Great White Way*, p. 226.

His praise of George M. Cohan's professionalism, *ibid.*, p. 226.

Ethel Barrymore's resentment of Broun's criticism, Kramer, *Heywood Broun: A Biographical Portrait*, p. 68.

The feud with Eva Tanguay was recorded by Churchill, *op. cit.*, pp. 208–209.

Broun's review of "The Antick," in which Lydia Lopokova appeared, New York *Tribune*, October 6, 1915.

3. Then and Always, Miss Ruth Hale

Broun recalled the "curious collaboration" with Ruth Hale in his *World-Telegram* column, September 19, 1934.

The anecdote concerning her correction of his supposed errors as an official scorer, *ibid.*

Broun's views on the commemoration of heroism in war, "The Unknown Soldier," which may be found in *Pieces of Hate*, one of the earlier collections of his writings.

George Oppenheimer's opinion on Ruth Hale's influence on Broun was delivered in his autobiography, *The View from the Sixties*, pp. 70–71.

The adventures of the press contingent traveling to France with the first echelon of the AEF, Crozier, *American Reporters on the Western Front*, pp. 133–134.

Broun's first dispatch from French soil, in which he described the attempted torpedoing of his transport, was published by the New York *Tribune*, July 7, 1917.

4. At War with the Army

Broun described his outfitting as a war correspondent in his *World-Telegram* column, October 13, 1939.

His initial confrontation with the AEF censorship, Crozier, *op. cit.,* 134.

Broun explored French attitudes toward the first American soldiers to arrive in France in the "Franco-American Honeymoon" chapter of his book *The AEF: With General Pershing and the American Forces.*

His description of the Indiana soldier complaining of the French girls' familiarity, *ibid.*

Broun recalled his tour of the British sector of the western front in his *World-Telegram* column, October 13, 1939.

His difficulties with his army guardians over "going AWOL" from AEF headquarters were described by Crozier, *op. cit.,* pp. 162–165.

William Slavens McNutt's recollection of Woollcott's military style at the front, Adams, *A. Woollcott: His Life and Times*, pp. 88–89.

Broun's methods of evading the AEF censorship were described by Crozier, *op. cit.,* pp. 178–179.

The AEF's consideration of lifting Broun's credentials, *ibid.,* pp. 191–192.

Broun's story of a large batch of major generals sailing to France on one vulnerable transport was published by the New York *Tribune*, March 16, 1918.

5. The Self-Discovery of a Columnist

The upheaval on Park Row just after World War I is described by Churchill, *Park Row, passim.*

Broun's minor feud with Scott Fitzgerald, Turnbull, *Scott Fitzgerald*, pp. 110, 346.

Broun's letter to the suitor of an unliterary girl, "The Library of a Lover" chapter, *Seeing Things at Night*, a collection of Broun columns.

Broun on Prohibition and its effects, quoted, Sinclair, *Prohibition: The Era of Excess*, pp. 197, 234.

George Oppenheimer's recollection of the Broun Sunday-night parties was contained in *View from the Sixties*, pp. 70–71.

Lucy Stone's background and achievements are limned by Holbrook, *Dreamers of the American Dream*, pp. 175–193.

The quotation on Lucy Stone's "engaging" survival in the feminist movement, *ibid.,* p. 175.

Broun's views on caring for an infant were contained in the "Holding a Baby" chapter, *Seeing Things at Night.*

6. Under the Golden Dome

The *World* admirer was Denning Miller, Alice Duer Miller's son, quoted in Kahn, *The World of Swope*, p. 235.

Swope's editorial method of operation quoted, *ibid.*, p. 235.

Stanley Walker's awe at Swope's "gift of gab" was recorded in his article "Symphony in Brass," *Saturday Evening Post*, June 4, 1938.

Swope described his creation of the op ed page in a letter to Gene Fowler, quoted by Kahn, *op. cit.*, p. 260.

Swope on Broun's sartorial deficiencies, and Broun on Swope's volubility, *ibid.*, pp. 19–20, 80–81.

F.P.A. on the atmosphere under the *World*'s golden dome, Barrett, *The End of the World*, pp. 21–22.

Samuel Chotzinoff on the same subject, *ibid.*, pp. 190–192.

Frank Sullivan's description of his interview with Swope, *ibid.*, pp. 199–200.

Adams' meditations on Broun's character and personality were included in his *Nods and Becks*, pp. 202–204.

Arthur Krock recalled his days as part of the "gifted company" under the golden dome in his *Memoirs*, pp. 64–65.

E. J. Kahn's observations on the "logrolling" tendency among the *World*'s special writers, *The World of Swope*, p. 268.

The front-office opposition to "ideas of liberalism" on the op ed page, *ibid.*, p. 274.

Broun's comments on the Rocky Kansas–Benny Leonard fight, "The Orthodox Champion" chapter, *Pieces of Hate.*

His report on his son's reaction to *A Doll's House*, the "Chivalry Is Born" chapter, *ibid.*

7. Poker Among the Olympians

The formation of the Thanatopsis Poker Club and its early membership were described by Teichmann, *George S. Kaufman: An Intimate Portrait*, p. 176–177.

The early sessions of the poker club were recalled by Krock, *op. cit.*, p. 68.

Broun's punning at the poker table, *ibid.*, p. 69.

The quality of play among the Thanatopsis members was analyzed by Teichmann, *op. cit.*, p. 176.

Broun's loss of money put aside for a country house was recounted by Teichmann, *op. cit.*, p. 177.

The psychoanalyst's reasons for Broun's obsession with poker playing were quoted by Kramer, *op. cit.*, p. 133.

8. We Charming Few

Marc Connelly's query on letting the *Follies* run was quoted by Teichmann, *op. cit.*, p. 70.

How the Algonquin Round Table came into existence was engagingly recorded by Margaret Case in her history of the group, *The Vicious Circle*, p. 21.

Edna Ferber recalled the "merciless disapproval" registered by Round Table members if one of their number failed to live up to its high standards, *A Peculiar Treasury*, pp. 292–293.

Samuel Hopkins Adams' observations on the rivalry of the wits gathered at the Round Table were included in *A. Woollcott*, pp. 120–121.

Broun recanted his initial disapproval of *Abie's Irish Rose* in *Christians Only*, p. 331.

The production of *No Sirree!* was described by Case, *op. cit.*, pp. 89–101.

Laurette Taylor's review of *No Sirree!* appeared in the New York *Times*, May 1, 1922; Wilton Lackaye's in the *World*, same date.

Dorothy Parker's biographer was John Keats; his comments on the Round Table's influence were included in *You Might As Well Live*, p. 84.

The contradictions of the Broun personality were recorded by Case, *op. cit.*, p. 68.

Broun's limerick on his hernia operation was quoted by Adams, *op. cit.*, p. 122.

E. B. White recalled Broun's constant pulse taking in letter, May 3, 1974.

The incident backstage at a performance of the Marx Brothers' *The Cocoanuts*, Teichmann, *op. cit.*, p. 93.

Broun related his reactions to the fiery cross burning on his lawn in "The Rabbit That Bit the Bulldog," an autobiographical essay published by *The New Yorker*, October 1, 1927.

Edna Ferber on the "melting away" of the Round Table membership, quoted by Case, *op. cit.*, 288.

Margaret Case's own reflections on the reasons for disbandment, *op. cit.*, pp. 295, 297.

Donald Ogden Stewart on the same subject, quoted by Keats, *op. cit.*, pp. 119–120.

Broun's denunciation of his friends for "strike breaking" at the Algonquin was related by Case, *op. cit.*, p. 291.

9. A Few Flings at Literature

Margaret Case described the Broun households in Manhattan and at the Sabine Farm, *op. cit.*, pp. 69, 129.

Ed McNamara's presence in the households as a long-staying guest, Oppenheimer, *op. cit.*, p. 70; Case, *op. cit.*, p. 231.

Broun as a country-house guest and croquet player, Case, *op. cit.*, p. 69; Krock, *op. cit.*, p. 70.

John Baragwanath ruminated on the ruthless style of the Round Table membership's croquet playing in his memoir, *A Good Time Was Had*, p. 109.

How Broun "lost" the Comstock documents and how they were recovered were recalled by Oppenheimer, *op. cit.*, p. 70.

Broun's long-term contract with cab-driver Charlie Horowitz, Case, *op. cit.*, p. 68.

The circumstances surrounding the Swope-Broun automobile accident and the resultant headlines were recorded by Kahn, *op. cit.*, pp. 269–270.

10. Exile from the Golden Dome

F.P.A.'s opinion of Broun as "one of the great journalists of all time" was included by Barrett, *End of the World*, p. 22. The book, edited by the *World*'s city editor, was a collective obituary of that newspaper.

Broun reflected on Debs' death in his column in the *World*, October 23, 1926.

Robert Benchley's involvement in the Sacco-Vanzetti case is recorded by his son, Nathaniel, in *Robert Benchley: A Biography*, pp. 175–177.

Ralph Pulitzer's warning to Broun on pursuing the Sacco-Vanzetti matter, quoted by Kramer, *op. cit.*, p. 175.

Dwight Taylor's recollection of Broun waiting to plead his case with Swope was included in *Joy Ride*, pp. 127–131.

Broun's attack on Judge Thayer, *World* column, August 6, 1927.

That Swope went off to attend the Saratoga races as usual was recounted by Kahn, *op. cit.*, p. 221.

Pulitzer's statement on why he refused to publish further Sacco-Vanzetti columns is quoted in *The Collected Edition of Heywood Broun*, edited by Heywood Hale Broun, pp. 204–205.

Broun's reply to Pulitzer quoted, *ibid.*, pp. 205–206.

Broun's "farewell" column explaining his obdurate defense of Sacco and Vanzetti was published by the *World*, August 17, 1927.

11. Back on Top of the World

Broun's views on the "group consciousness" of the *World* were contained in an article in *The Nation*, May 4, 1928.

The joint effort of Broun and Woollcott in furthering the singing career of Paul Robeson was detailed by S. H. Adams, *op. cit.,* pp. 137-138.

Broun's autobiographical essay, "The Rabbit That Bit the Bulldog," was published by *The New Yorker*, October 1, 1927.

Samuel Hopkins Adams' analysis of the *World*'s management problems was included in his Woollcott biography, *op. cit.,* p. 180.

E. J. Kahn on damage to the "shining integrity" of the op ed page done by Broun's suspension, *op. cit.,* p. 222.

The Nation article that resulted in Broun's final departure from the *World* was published May 4, 1928.

12. The New Shop Window

After Roy Howard signed Broun to a Scripps-Howard contract, he wrote the paragraph himself which was to precede Broun's column on the split page of the *Telegram*. It read: "Ideas and opinions expressed in this column are those of one of America's most interesting writers, and are presented without regard to their agreement or disagreement with the editorial attitude of this paper."

The decline of the Thanatopsis Poker Club, from the viewpoint of its founding members, was detailed by S. H. Adams, *op. cit.,* pp. 125-127; Teichmann, *op. cit.,* pp. 176-177.

Broun's mourning that "fame has jogged on by," *Telegram* column, February 19, 1929.

His animus toward Canon Chase's moralizing was expressed in his *Telegram* column, May 8, 1929.

His demand for justice for the Harvard scrubwomen fired in an economy wave, *Telegram* column, January 27, 1930.

13. Broun for Congress

Broun's long-standing friendship with McAllister Coleman was recorded by Kramer, *op. cit.,* pp. 53-54.

Roy Howard expressed his opposition to Broun's running for Congress as the Socialist candidate in the *Telegram*, August 17, 1930.

Broun's reply was contained in his "It Seems to Me" column in the *Telegram*, August 19, 1930.

His meditations on the relationship with his father, *Telegram* column, August 30, 1930.

His standard speech to the electorate, quoted, Kramer, *op. cit.*, p. 207.

Some of the events of the Broun campaign were abstracted from the New York *Times* and New York *World* files of September and October, 1930.

Broun told his readers all about his arrest for disobeying police orders in his *Telegram* column, October 10, 1930.

14. Broun for Stardom

That Broun left a considerable vacuum with his departure from the *World* was attested by F.P.A. in Barrett, *End of the World*, pp. 21–22.

The obsequies attending the death of the *World* were related by the participants, *ibid., passim.*

Broun's reflections on that event appeared in his *Telegram* column, February 28, 1931.

Quotations from *Christians Only* appear on pp. 15, 79–80, 83–84, 316.

The results of his "Give a Job Till June" campaign, *ibid.*, pp. 188–190.

Milton "Mike" Raison recalled for the author how the idea for *Shoot the Works* was conceived years later in Hollywood, where Raison was functioning as a screenwriter and mystery novelist.

Dorothy Parker's contribution to *Shoot the Works*, Keats, *op. cit.*, pp. 161–162.

Broun's observations on the "chaos" of rehearsing a musical revue were made in the "In Which He Rehearses" chapter, *Sitting on the World.*

His views on Jimmy Walker's performance as mayor, *World-Telegram* column, March 6, 1931.

The reviews of *Shoot the Works* appeared in the *Daily News, Herald Tribune* and *World-Telegram*, July 22, 1931.

Heywood Hale Broun's suggestion for reviving his father during an imagined heart attack was overheard by Oppenheimer, *op. cit.*, p. 71.

George S. Kaufman's initial snubbing of Connie Madison, Teichmann, *op. cit.*, p. 177.

15. The Perils and Pleasures of Union Leadership

The *Daily Worker* assault on Broun as a "class enemy" quoted, Kramer, *op. cit.*, p. 240.

Morris Ernst supplied many details of the first organizational steps in unionizing the newspaper business, *The Best Is Yet*, pp. 83–85.

Broun's column on the necessity for a journalists' union appeared in the *World-Telegram*, August 7, 1933.

Broun and Dorothy Parker crossing the picket line, Keats, *op. cit.*, p. 191.

Ernst's recollections of organization meeting, *op. cit.*, pp. 82–83.

Broun's remarks on the way publishers might punish reporters who joined a union, quoted by Kramer, *op. cit.*, p. 246.

Captain Joseph M. Patterson on the need for a union, quoted by Ernst, *op. cit.*, p. 85.

Broun's introduction of Harry Raymond to a Rand School forum, Pilat, *Pegler: Angry Man of the Press*, pp. 137–138.

Broun's suspicion of Communist influence on the Newspaper Guild leadership were detailed by Ernst, *op. cit.*, pp. 88–89.

Heywood Broun's reported role in engineering the New York *Post* pay cut, Pilat, *op. cit.*, p. 158. Broun always claimed his actions in that regard were misunderstood. In the long run, of course, they may have saved the *Post* from going under and its employees from being thrown out of work. Stern soon was forced to sell the paper, though he continued to publish the Philadelphia *Record*.

16. "My Best Friend Died"

Broun's night-long brooding over his life and his insecurities were recalled by Ernst, *op. cit.*, p. 79.

Deems Taylor's remark about Ruth Hale's emotional drive was quoted by Broun in his *World-Telegram* column, September 19, 1934. This was the column Broun wrote immediately after her death.

His diatribe against hunting appeared in the Connecticut *Nutmeg*, November 10, 1938.

Broun's reflections on the latest turn in Al Smith's career appeared in his *World-Telegram* column, November 27, 1933. Those on President Roosevelt and the San Jose lynching, *ibid.*, October 28, 1936, and November 28, 1933.

Pegler at Broun's picnic for Eleanor Roosevelt, Pilat, *op. cit.*, pp. 150–151.

Broun undertook his analysis of the Pegler character in an article in the *Nutmeg*, June 10, 1939.

That Quentin Reynolds consciously patterned himself after Broun was noted by Ernst, *op. cit.*, p. 77.

Reynolds' recollection of his friendship with Broun was contained in his autobiography, *By Quentin Reynolds*, pp. 84–86.

Hearst's offer to Broun was detailed by Kramer, *op. cit.*, p. 260.

The criticism of Broun as a "lively controversialist" was made in a letter from Allen Raymond, then president of the New York Newspaper Guild.

17. Half-Century Mark

Broun ruminated on the approach of his fiftieth birthday in an article, "Columnist's Progress," *New Republic*, May 4, 1938.

Broun's letter to the subscribers to his Connecticut journal was published in the *Nutmeg*, September 30, 1939.

Broun recorded his reactions to listening to President Roosevelt read his Christmas parable, *Nutmeg*, December 22, 1938.

He discussed the attraction of the Catholic faith in the *Nutmeg*, June 10, 1939.

Broun's account of his tour of the San Antonio barrios and his meeting with Father Tranchese appeared in his *World-Telegram* column, February 6, 1939.

His long talk with his friend and lawyer about his intentions of converting to Catholicism was recorded by Ernst, *op. cit.*, pp. 78–79.

His refusal to make any apologies for his conversion to liberal friends troubled by his act, "Not in This Issue," *New Republic*, July 26, 1939.

18. A Time of Endings

Broun's attempt to win over Woollcott to Catholicism, Kramer, *op. cit.*, p. 296.

His column on the refugee ship *St. Louis* appeared in the *World-Telegram*, June 9, 1939.

His reflections on the Moral Re-Armament rally in San Francisco, *World-Telegram*, August 9, 1939.

Communists in Newspaper Guild leadership turn on Broun for his denunciation of the Hitler-Stalin agreement, Ernst, *op. cit.*, pp. 80–81.

Broun delivered his judgment on the agreement in "Not All the Leopards," *New Republic*, September 20, 1939; on the *Izvestia* editorial in his *World-Telegram* column, October 11, 1939.

His sorrow over war's disastrous effects on nature was expressed in his *World-Telegram* column, October 18, 1939.

Broun related the circumstances of his firing by Scripps-Howard and his stocktaking on his fifty-first birthday in the *Nutmeg*, December 9, 1939.

Ernst recalled Broun's distress at the way he was shunned by his *World-Telegram* colleagues and his hiring by the *Post*, *op. cit.*, p. 81.

Pegler's attack on Broun just after he had been fired appeared in the *World-Telegram*, December 10, 1939.

Broun's first and last column for the New York *Post* appeared December 15, 1939.

His last words were reported by Ernst, *op. cit.*, pp. 81–82.

Epilogue

Pegler's appearance at the Broun funeral, Pilat, *op. cit.*, p. 165.

The funeral was described by Reynolds, *op. cit.*, p. 154.

Rudeness of Pegler's reception, Pilat, *op. cit.*, p. 165.

Reynolds recalled how he became embroiled with Pegler over a book review that led to the libel suit, *op. cit.*, p. 320.

Selected Bibliography

Adams, Franklin P. *Nods and Becks*. New York, 1944.

Adams, Samuel Hopkins. *A. Woollcott: His Life and Times*. New York, 1945.

Baragwanath, John. *A Good Time Was Had*. New York, 1962.

Barrett, James W., ed. *The End of the World*. New York, 1931.

Benchley, Nathaniel. *Robert Benchley: A Biography*. New York, 1955.

Broun, Heywood. *The AEF: With General Pershing and the American Forces*. New York, 1918.

———. *The Boy Grew Older*. New York, 1922.

———. *The Collected Edition of Heywood Broun*, ed. Heywood Hale Broun. New York, 1941.

———. *Gandle Follows His Nose*. New York, 1926.

———. *It Seems to Me*. New York, 1935.

———. *Pieces of Hate and Other Enthusiasms*. New York, 1922.

———. *Seeing Things at Night*. New York, 1921.

———. *Sitting on the World*. New York, 1924.

——— and George Britt. *Christians Only: A Study in Prejudice*. New York, 1931.

——— and Margaret Leech. *Anthony Comstock: Roundsman of the Lord*. New York, 1927.

Case, Margaret. *The Vicious Circle*. New York, 1951.

Churchill, Allen. *The Great White Way*. New York, 1962.

———. *Park Row*. New York, 1958.

Crozier, Emmett. *American Reporters on the Western Front*. New York, 1959.

Ernst, Morris. *The Best Is Yet*. New York, 1945.

Ferber, Edna. *A Peculiar Treasure*. New York, 1939.

Fowler, Gene. *Skyline*. New York, 1961.

Holbrook, Stewart H. *Dreamers of the American Dream*. New York, 1957.

Kahn, E. J. *The World of Swope*. New York, 1965.

Kaltenborn, H. V. *Fifty Fabulous Years*. New York, 1950.

Keats, John. *You Might As Well Live*. New York, 1970.

Kramer, Dale. *Heywood Broun: A Biographical Portrait*. New York, 1949.

Krock, Arthur. *Memoirs: Sixty Years on the Firing Line*. New York, 1968.

Loos, Anita. *But Gentlemen Marry Brunettes*. New York, 1928.

O'Connor, Richard. *Bat Masterson*. New York, 1957.